The Science of Personal Dress
Complete Study

Written and Illustrated by

Irenee Riter

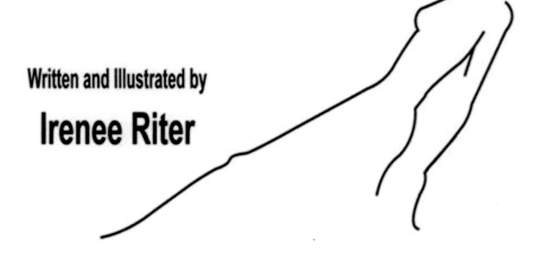

Edited by Marian Chapman and Marilyn Sandon

Updated Fourth Edition

"You may not know what is wrong. You may not even know there could be something better. But you always know when something is really right…you can feel it.   Now why is that? There must be a reason when our intuition feels it so clearly and immediately. There is, and herein lie the answers that that will validate your knowing and count you among aware elite designers."   ~ Irenee

TABLE OF CONTENTS

PREFACE

"I didn't invent a color system, so much as discover an order to human colors and body lines which already exist, and then organized them into harmonics based on art principles exhibited by Nature. Just as sound exists within a certain range of human perception, so does color and line; just as music creates mood, has a theme and evokes emotion, so does color and line. I have orchestrated, if you will, colors and lines just as musical notes of the scale are organized so that one can deliberately create with color and line."

Because of this Order, we now have a system which can be quickly learned so that a person can compose with not only color, but visible texture and shape which portrays each color. All this profoundly applies to how we dress and gives us better tools to express who we are through our individual taste and self image.

In the early days of color analysis, just to determine if you had Winter, Summer, Autumn or Spring coloring was life changing for many people. Totally clueless before my color analysis experience, I tested as a Winter, was given a packet of fabric swatches, and was particularly pleased to discover hunter green, *my green*. I bought all four season color packets to study and the adventure began.

My life was transformed from that very first day—to know there was order and meaning to my coloring and body was thrilling. I gathered every color of fabric that would simulate the colors which were tested on me and started working with my family and other people. Right away I could see that any color put up to a skintone would draw that color forward and become more accentuated. It became obvious that *The Law of Attraction* was the basis for these changes—like attracts like.

I must state here before going further that the reason this work has been so successful is because early on recognizing the skin and hair undertones were opposite and complementary—not the same. We had it right and proved it through testing everyday. Then when I arranged the colors in harmonic sequence, that cinched it for good and we did not pay attention to other analysis methods wrongly teaching that skin and hair undertones were the same which has caused so much confusion. A gold-tester flatters cool skintones and a silver-tester flatters warm skintones—proving providentially each skintone is brought into balance by its opposite hair color, just as nature designed it.

Intrigued to see the changes colors brought, I began doing color analysis for clients in a progressive clothing boutique. This is when I discovered that many people needed colors from two seasons and began rearranging the color packets—mixing together the less extreme colors from each season into Inter-season color groups. This evolved into a quickly expanding business training colorists all over the country and providing them with necessary materials and tools for color analysis work.

Then a very astute woman showed me how certain colors had tones of the same "quality" as she draped them together on her arm; the display included a color from each family (red, orange, yellow, green, blue and purple) but the chosen colors all had the same tone, a quality of energy that I could feel as well as see. This insight was an important step—colors had vibrational frequencies! I began the process of sorting all colors according to energy and vibration, disregarding other 4-season methods in favor of harmonic sequences of color in vibrational families. This catapulted me into the study of color theory, color relationships and color phenomena.

After years of testing skintones and tracking patterns of trait associations, *The Science of Personal Dress* evolved with clear-set proven concepts offered in this study. Anything true is ultimately simple. In the beginning it was difficult to see into the different layers of skin pigments, so a comprehensive Color Tester was developed with 60 ink-dye colors representing all 10 color families. Arranged in harmonic sequence, this tool demonstrated the dramatic changes color can make interacting with a person's coloring. The testers were placed under the face and designed to flip down so that the eye had the chance to see differences through quick color changes. This gave a basis for comparison—proved easily and seen with verifiable results.

So early on we had a very sophisticated Inter-season color program, but one day a woman I had analyzed came to me with a problem and asked, "Why is it I love this dress so much? You said it is the wrong color for me but I like it." I looked at her and said, "I don't know. I like it too…let's find out." Somehow this particular dress was so perfect for her body it went beyond colors so we began to focus on the lines of clothing.

Synchronically, I had previously studied face structure in Personology classes. Because of this knowledge it didn't take long to see the correlation between the lines of faces, the lines of body shapes and the lines of clothing—lines perform similar functions whether expressing a particular personality trait or expressing a particular function on a garment. Straight lines are masculine and circle lines are feminine. Furthermore, the 4 geometric forms (oval, circle, square, triangle) correlate precisely to the lines and patterns of the 4 seasons (winter, summer, autumn and spring.) An archetype language of line and color is creatively operating throughout all of creation and we became conscious that these relationships were significant, consistent, orderly and harmoniously related to a person's body and form of dress. This connection truly made all the difference in the success of effective color and body analysis.

Another dimension of analysis work came into focus from an experience I had tying a bow on the neck of a satin blouse to wear under a suit. I tied a nice big bow and tried to adjust it but knew something was not quite right. Suddenly it occurred to me to pull the ends and make the bow smaller. As I gradually changed the size of the bow, my features came into focus with the blouse and the whole outfit worked. Thus came about the development and design of a tester based on "the bow" experience, and colorists all over the country used it to determine this aspect of personal dress. Using the right size shapes, patterns and lines is key to flattering inside detail lines of clothing.

The Academy of Art in San Francisco offered me a teaching position for their required foundation classes. Because of my background, through these classes art students received the advantage of understanding not only how to consciously create with colors and lines, but the deep-rooted psychological and metaphysical aspects of the Universal Archetype Language of Colors and Lines.

"It's like breaking a secret code or learning a foreign language!"

This is the consensus of thousands of students and colorists who have learned that colors and lines express a language of their own. Through this work, men and women are coming to know there are consistent laws of order, harmony and beauty which apply to all art forms. This also extends to their body shape, features, coloring and clothing; they understand they are not a hap-hazard mix of genes or DNA, but have been orchestrated to perfection down to the tiniest fleck of color in the eye or turn of the nose. Because of this, personal dress becomes an <u>exacting</u> science and good taste is easily learned. In timely fashion I present for you, The Science of Personal Dress.

ACKNOWLEDGEMENTS

Even though this subject has kept me interested and intrigued for many years, it has been an evolving process supported by many, many people—knowingly and perhaps not so knowingly. I thank every person who has passed by and helped to validate the consistent order and harmony of the principles explained in this work. The following individuals have consciously given their support and input beyond measure:

Marilyn Sandon, the very first person to see the value and invest and train as a colorist. For her hours editing this eBook, valuable insights and *The Science of Personal Dress* title concept; and mostly for her enduring, patient friendship for 45 years.

Jana Riter Raleigh, my daughter, for invaluable designing development and continually setting a high standard of professionalism as well as business acuity with strong ideals; she loyally stood by always offering her support and artistic expertise.

Marian Chapman, my sister, for editing and working with me in presenting the material in a practical step by step format with knowledgeable insights keeping it simple as the concepts evolved, always faithfully there as an astute sounding board for discussion.

Jerry Lyman, brilliant physicist and mathematician, for guidance in moving the data into the computer-age world of technology, seeing the value of the work and taking it to the next level by designing presentation formats and giving me his strong input and love.

Birdean Larsen for introducing me to color analysis in the first place, being by my side at the printing presses through four successive programs and being my quiet long enduring friend and confident for so many years.

Kristen Riter, my daughter for expressing her talent and wise support with the videos and constant feedback; to her husband Eddy Erpelding, clothing manufacturer and designer providing the opportunity to work with his wonderful *Lily Farouche* clothing in Germany as I learned to apply the principles to another level of couture design.

Linda Denise for taking my teachings literally and proceeding to prove the lines of clothing were universally applicable at even greater depth.

Daryl Vanderhaar owner of Ironwood Lithographers for the thousands of books they printed giving us the opportunity to express complicated color layouts even before six color presses were available.

Loc Huynh, computer instructor extraordinaire and technical expert making this book possible with his very much needed timely and patient support.

My 4 sons, Steven (square) **Cary** (oval) **Gregory** (triangle) and **Michael** (circle) were classic examples of the four body shapes: who years ago were the perfect models for the 4 men's body-shape drawings in this book. My whole family provided the perfect workshop to reveal practical insights into color Inter-seasons because they represented the perfect mixtures and combinations for the work. Synchronicity? For sure!

It is not possible to name all the hundreds of colorists who have been trained, and who have trained in return. We were all in this together but I had the fun of keeping track as it progressed by illustrating and writing it down. If some of the pictured examples are dated…well, it has been a long intoxicating journey.   Blessings of beauty to all, Irenee

THE SCIENCE OF PERSONAL DRESS

"The Earth Speaks To Us In The Deepest Language We Know"

UNIVERSAL ARCHETYPE LANGUAGE OF COLOR AND LINE

The Universe has an archetype language that has symbols, lines and colors which give meaning and form to our lives. The order and harmony of the Universe expresses its beauty through four different templates, or energies. These specific energies are illustrated in the four seasons—each adding to the balance of the whole.

Based on *The Law of Attraction*, this work is offered for those wanting to go beyond conventional systems into a new paradigm of color and body analysis. Even though primarily focused on personal dress as a practical first approach, the principles ultimately apply to all art forms providing a conceptual framework from which to even further expand. Written and illustrated in an unfolding step-by-step format, this study is considered the in-depth manual for color and line education and acts as a reference guide based on scientifically based principles—The Universal Language of Color and Line. Because these principles are sound and unchanging, they are classic in every sense and meet the criteria of on-going studies in all creative art associated areas.

PURPOSE FOR THIS WORK

The purpose for this work is to bring to conscious awareness that there is absolute order and beauty to everyone's embodiment. Our bodies follow the natural lines and colors represented by nature and are not a hap-hazard mix of genes. One doesn't just happen to have blue eyes thrown in with any-which color of skin or hair—our color schemes have been orchestrated to perfection. One doesn't just happen to have sloping shoulders or high-set hip bones or tapered fingers—our forms have been balanced perfectly. We are infinitely part of the deliberate order we find in our universe and this teaching reinforces this order by applying proven, common sense principles of color and line to the beauty of personal dress. A deeper understanding of what underlies form and color brings a greater syntax of language giving one cognition of the more refined nuances of body and dress. With this, one is more likely to make perceptive assessments. The English romantic painter, John Constable vested his paintings with intensity and affection saying one must learn how to look at things properly. He claimed,

"There is nothing ugly; I never saw an ugly thing in my life, for let the form of an object be what it may — light, shade and perspective will always make it beautiful."

Isaac Mizrahi makes an interesting comment on the importance of clothing. He says,

".....it's just that every single human being wants beautiful clothes, I think. And if they don't, it's fine. But somewhere they're lying, I'm sorry, somewhere they're lying."

George Dearborn, one of the early theorists on the psychology of clothes, found that clothes help to protect us from fears; fear of ridicule, of the estimation of inefficiency, or lack of taste, or lack of charm.

"Protection and relief from such fears.....I take to be the real reason and purpose of wearing clothes. And that is of importance."

Marjorie Barslow Greenbie, a keen observer of human nature, wrote,

"There is undoubtedly a confused, half apologetic manner—a reduction of the personality to something negative and vague which comes from not realizing completely and to one's satisfaction, one's picture of one's outward self."

A FOUNDATION ART COURSE

The material covered in The Science of Personal Dress is the same 90 hour course Irenee taught at the Academy Of Art in San Francisco to fashion design and art students from all over the world. Going beyond conventional color analysis, the students worked with advanced testing tools, techniques and *The Science of Personal Dress* master reference manual. The refinements from these prepared lessons and the high interest surrounding these concepts made it obvious that it was time to present them on a web site for everyone.

From that format the teaching has now progressed into printed form—*The Science of Personal Dress Complete Study.* From this classic teaching evolved a shorter version for Women and Girls, an even shorter version for Men and Boys, *The Universal Language of Face Analysis*, and *Impeccably Sharp* – a thesis on etiquette, manners and dress covering what wise men know and young men can learn.

Not only fashion students, but this study applies to art classes, photography, interior design, architecture, advertising illustration, sculpture as well as all fine arts. The following are comments from students at the Academy of Art in San Francisco:

"I think this class is vital to anyone studying fashion design, interior design, architecture or really anything in the arts."
Felicity Squire, Fashion Design Major, England

"Seasons! I had absolutely no idea that everything revolved around the 4 seasons. I learned how color can change feelings. Body types!! I thought it was hereditary. I thought as a circle body type, if I lost weight I'd become an oval (loose curves.) Untrue! I'd just be a smaller circle! I now understand the significance of it all."
Rachel Arakaki, Fashion Major, Hawaii

"The best thing I learned is the balanced picture, the importance of framing hair and shoe colors, and using balanced colors for designing because they look good on so many people." **Melissa Bennett, Fashion Design, New York**

"My textile projects highly depend on color training background. I believe my color ability has greatly improved because of this class."
Liang-Yuan Chen, Textile Major, Taiwan

"Personally, I have a new perspective of life and use your theory as a sort of special meditation. I think learning your system makes creativity a piece of cake!"
Antoinette Ayon, Fashion Major, San Francisco

NEW PRACTICAL APPROACH TO COLOR AND BODY ANALYSIS

Overall, right colors do make a big difference but there are more elements to dress than the color involved. The body shape is the vehicle for all the colors and lines and needs to be understood, honored and framed in beauty, comfort and relevant practical expression. This stimulating study addresses aspects of dress not commonly covered:

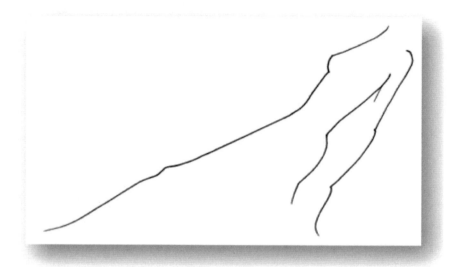

- LINES — Right lines are more important to how you feel than right colors.

- LIGHTING — Colors are dramatically altered by lighting; day-light vs. artificial night-light.

- TEXTURE SHADOWS — Textures in fabric cause shadows and make colors appear darker.

- SHINY REFLECTIONS — A color can appear brighter because of shiny reflections from tightly twisted threads in woven fabric.

- SPECIAL OCCASIONS — An occasion may call for more color than a person's own "best" colors can deliver.

STUDY ADVICE: If studied step by step in sequential order, each concept builds upon the preceding one for complete understanding. There are parts that may seem to be repeated but it is necessary to reinforce certain connections so that all the parts come wholly together. By the end of the study you will have a very advanced understanding of this subject and it is guaranteed to serve you throughout your life.

So to begin, as already seen there are more aspects to dress than at first expected. In fact there are five.

THE 5 ASPECTS OF PERSONAL DRESS

1. YOUR RIGHT COLORS
Determined with the Questionnaire and Hair and Eye Color Charts. This will indicate if you wear bright, muted, light, dark, warm, cool or in-between-balanced colors (flattering to your natural skin, hair and eye colors.)

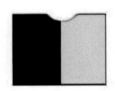

2. YOUR RIGHT COMBINATIONS
Instructions on how to enhance and combine your colors properly. The darkest contrast value in your natural coloring will be repeated (to avoid looking blurred and out of focus.)

3. YOUR RIGHT OUTSIDE CLOTHING LINES
Line-wise, you will learn the outside silhouette of your body shape so that clothing lines will fit and ride easy on your form (wonderful feeling not having to tuck, pull, adjust or pull in your tummy.)

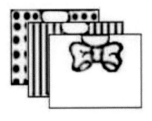

4. YOUR RIGHT INSIDE CLOTHING LINES
Determined by your Keysize which indicates if you need small, medium small, medium, medium large, large or can handle extra-large inside lines (size of cuffs, collars, buttons, bows, pleats, flaps, patterns, accessories; all the inside detail lines of clothing.)

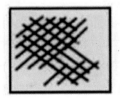

5. YOUR RIGHT TEXTURES/PATTERNS
Understanding the textures and weight of fabrics and materials, as well as choice of patterns will be in harmony with your color category, body shape, head shape and features.

COLOR AND LIGHT SCIENCE

Everything in the Universe is in motion and has a unique rate of vibration. Color is one of the many vibrations of our earth. For a better perspective of where color fits into the scheme of things, think of solid matter as the slowest and lowest form of vibratory motion. As the frequency of vibrations increase, matter changes form to become liquids and gases. Then the Electromagnetic Spectrum begins and is comprised of sound, electricity, heat, the Visible Light Spectrum (which is our Rainbow colors,) ultra-violet, x-rays, gamma and cosmic rays.

Electromagnetic Spectrum

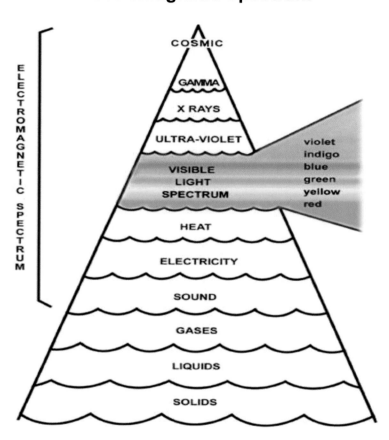

About 300 years ago, man began to unravel the mysteries of color and is still on the threshold of understanding the fundamentals. Much of our knowledge is based on the experiments of Sir Isaac Newton in 1665. He passed a beam of sunlight through a triangular prism and the white light split into a multicolored beam consisting of red, orange, yellow, green, blue, indigo and violet. This was the discovery that white light is a combination of all colors.

Scientists have put all the many types of radiation (energy that gives off rays) into a single category which they have labeled the Electromagnetic Spectrum. That portion of the electromagnetic spectrum we see is the Visible Light Spectrum.

Although it has been established that light is a form of energy which radiates or gives off rays in all directions (similar to a pebble creating waves when dropped into water) no one is really certain what light is. Scientists are unable to decide upon a single theory of light. They accept the idea that light is a form of energy or radiation produced by the photon (energy particle of the atom) and travels like a wave. Through quantum physics it is now recognized that light also has discrete particle properties—thus light is a particle-wave duality. Research continues.

HOW COLOR COMES FROM LIGHT

Each color of the spectrum has its own wave length and can be measured by a special instrument called a Spectroscope. The **red light wave** is twenty-eight millionths of an inch in length; on the other end of the spectrum, the **violet light wave** is about half as long as red—or sixteen millionths of an inch.

Only in the presence of light do we see color. According to scientists, neither black nor white are really colors even though we sense them as colors. White is the presence of all the colors of sunlight, while black is the absence of light or color.

An opaque object will reflect certain colors and absorb the rest. In daylight the leaves of trees appear green because they reflect green light waves of sunlight and absorb the rest. Those leaves at night appear black because there is no light that they can reflect. The color that is **"not"** absorbed is the color you see. Further examples are: a **red apple absorbs every color except red**; red paints or dyes are special compounds that have been mixed to reflect red light waves while absorbing the other light waves from the sun or from artificial light.

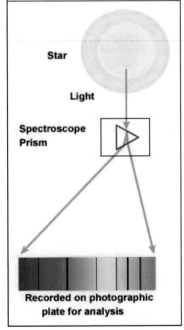

Color has had a profound impact on science through the use of the Spectroscope. This important instrument can detect and identify traces of elements and analyze them qualitatively and quantitatively. It gives us a greater understanding of the "behind the scenes" drama that color is playing out in our universe.

All substance has a characteristic spectrum, revealed when the substance is made to emit light by subjecting it to heat or electricity. The light that is dispersed creates a distinctive color spectrum which can be measured with a Spectroscope. Common uses of the Spectroscope are; astronomers estimate stars' motion and group the stars by their spectra (red is coolest, yellow and white are the hottest;) chemists determine the elementary composition of substance and expose the presence of copper, zinc, etc. in foods; doctors diagnose certain diseases; criminologists detect the presence of poisons in cadavers; metallurgists locate impurities in steel; archeologists can analyze pigments of old masters paintings and ancient Egyptian embalming fluids. The rainbow we see in the spectroscope has miraculously taken the universe apart down to the most infinitesimal detail.

THREE ASPECTS OR FORMS OF COLOR

There are three ways of looking at color. Each of these three forms of color has its own unique laws and phenomena:

LIGHT: The primary colors of light are red, green and blue-violet. Mixtures of these colors are additive and work toward white. These three "light" colors when mixed together produce white light.

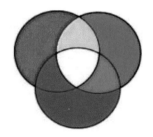

PIGMENT: The primary colors of pigments, paints and dyes are red, yellow and blue. Mixtures of these colors are subtractive and work toward black. These colors mixed together produce black.

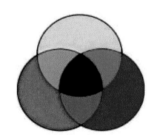

SENSATION: The sensory aspect of color is visual and embraces both physiology and psychology. The human eye discerns four primary colors; red, yellow, green and blue. Mixtures generally tend to work toward a neutral gray.

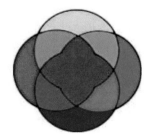

VISIBLE LIGHT SPECTRUM

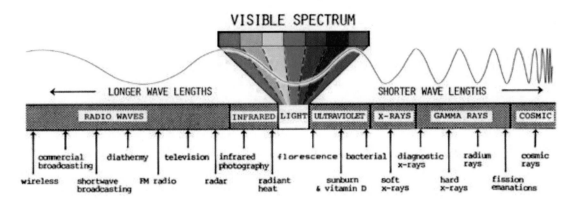

Looking more closely at the Visible Light Spectrum we see that each color has its own rate of vibration. Moving up the scale from the lowest vibration to the highest; red, orange, yellow, green, blue, indigo and then into violet. After the color spectrum comes the invisible ultra-violet rays, X-rays, gamma rays and cosmic rays.

EACH PERSON VIBRATES COLOR AND LIGHT

Every individual has an energy field of color and line interpreted through the five senses as vibration. Hair, skin and eye colors, feature lines and body shape are all part of the person's energy field. Clothing colors and lines affect this energy field with added vibrations. "Bare naked" a person is completely balanced in color and line. When we begin to add clothing, textures, makeup and accessories, we have the opportunity to enhance, add beauty, variety, change and excitement to the body. Since each person has a unique vibrational field, there will be specific colors and lines which vibrate in perfect harmony.

CLOTHING ALSO VIBRATES COLOR AND LINE

If certain colors vibrate well with a given person, they will also vibrate well with each other. Because of this there will be a common quality, coherence or undertone running through all the person's best colors regardless of the hue. If a clear **bluish** red looks good then it automatically follows that the same **bluish**-undertone will be best in other colors as well; **bluish**-green, **blue**-gray, **bluish**-dark brown rather than yellow-brown, **bluish** pink rather than coral-pink, **bluish**-silver rather than gold etc. The attuned colors will synchronize and vibrate together as though a certain "pitch" or "tone" is satisfying a harmonious chord running throughout the wardrobe.

When clothing, accessories and makeup colors are selected on this basis, they will all match or complement each other—this is the real value in knowing your colors and lines. It simplifies shopping, saves money and provides a versatile, efficient wardrobe. This is especially important for people who are usually on the move and who need the added confidence of being well-turned out and put-together. Let's take a deep look into how Nature vibrates harmoniously through the energies of color and line.

SEASONS ALSO VIBRATE COLOR AND LINE AS ENERGY

The Universe has an archetype language that has symbols, lines and colors which give meaning and form to our lives. The order and harmony of the Universe expresses its beauty through four different templates or energies. You can see these specific energies illustrated in the four seasons—each adding to the balance of the whole.

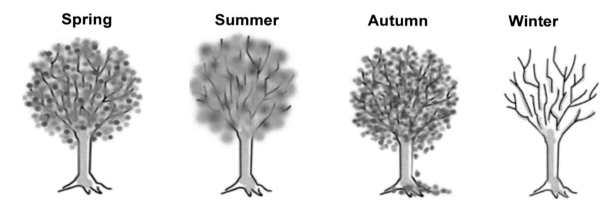

| Spring | Summer | Autumn | Winter |

The same four energies expressed in Nature are in the lines, shapes and coloring of our own bodies. It is all connected. There actually is an archetype language of beauty and order that we can access. There are Universal tools of art with which one can create.

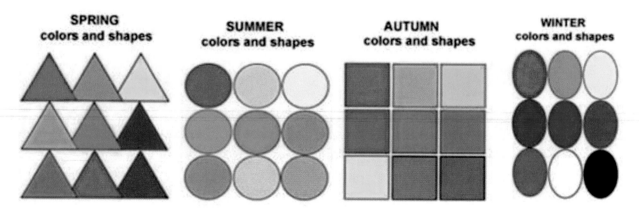

18

WHAT THE 4 ENERGIES DO

"Seasons" are used merely as a teaching tool presented here in a simplistic manner, and if considered will prove to be extremely beneficial and accurate in translating energy into the selection of clothing, makeup and all aspects of personal appearance. The energy associations provided on the following drop down chart give a whole new understanding of the correlation between color and form based on the co-esthetic relationship observed in Nature. These associations give one the foundation to know what effect each of the four energies create: what it expresses as, feels like, is colored as, and forms as...

SPRING ENERGY EXPRESSES AS...	SUMMER ENERGY EXPRESSES AS...	AUTUMN ENERGY EXPRESSES AS...	WINTER ENERGY EXPRESSES AS...
In the Spring the newly blossomed tree stands out singular and unique. Nature seems too beautiful to be true ...almost unreal. The light is brilliant with acrylic color accents everywhere. It is as though a bouquet of flowers tossed in the air spontaneously and dramatically alights. There is the movement of life, borders of flowers, butterflies bursting into color as crisp, clear, fresh air picks up the spirit.	As Summer emerges, the Spring bloom becomes sun-struck and softens the colors into subtle beauty. Lacy leaves mingle with full-bloom flowers. Patterns become "cameo-like" in watercolor tone-on-tone blends and monochromatic color schemes. Genteel elegance is savored as a precious flavor. The fantasy and innocence of youth beckons us to play and relax.	As the lazy Summer fades away, the tree bursts into multi-faceted Autumn busyness. Harvest begins as mature grain, fruit and nuts are gathered in for storage. School begins and life becomes enriched and practical. Light is more diffused with rich oil painted patterns and warmly colored paisley "true-to-life" scenes of nature emerge. Comfortable, cozy feelings of security and enrichment.	As the Autumn leaves drop away, the regal simplicity of Winter poise remains. Nature lays down her brush and pens a fine etching in black and white. There is lack of color distraction. Color is used for contrast rather than design. Lines are kept even and patterns are duplicated as everything becomes still, set and distinct. Balance reigns throughout this long lasting season of solitude and peace.

SPRING ENERGY FEELS LIKE...	SUMMER ENERGY FEELS LIKE...	AUTUMN ENERGY FEELS LIKE...	WINTER ENERGY FEELS LIKE...
Early morning light... bright, vibrant color, vivid, exaggerated, caricature, unreal, bigger-than-life, animated, unusual, crisp, original, dramatic, colorful, accentuated, bold, fleeting, changeable, temporary, spontaneous, flamboyant, vital, costume effect.	High noon light............ sun-struck, watercolor, monochromatic, blends, open-bloom, delicate, subtle, gentle, fragile, graceful, feminine, sensual, curved, youthful, small, thin, fine, dainty, lacy, elegant, refined.	Early evening light....... muted, multifaceted color, warm, earthy, natural, enriched, harvest, busy, dependable, secured, efficient, mature, masculine, realistic, genuine, true-to-life, practical, sturdy, coarse, textured, richly comfortable.	Evening light.............. cool, single color focus, sharp contrast, stark, frozen, still, set, solitary, calm, peaceful, simple, distinct, poised, proper, stately, sophisticated, even, formal, serene, regal, classic, finished, style with restraint.
SPRING ENERGY IS COLORED AS...	SUMMER ENERGY IS COLORED AS...	AUTUMN ENERGY IS COLORED AS...	WINTER ENERGY IS COLORED AS...
SPRING ENERGY FORMS AS... exciting angle lines	SUMMER ENERGY FORMS AS... feminine soft lines	AUTUMN ENERGY FORMS AS... masculine stable lines	WINTER ENERGY FORMS AS... balanced regal lines

COLORS AND LINES CREATE YOUR PERSONAL STYLE

We begin this study by focusing on you—your coloring, your body and your clothing. You can deliberately express different aspects of your personality through the use of color and line to create a personal style. You want to be able to look at anything, even a rubber sole on a shoe, and be able to identify what it is communicating and know what feeling it is expressing. This will give you practical tools to become your own clothing expert.

wedge   **French**   **stacked**   **classic**

For example, a colorful, canvas wedge communicates a playful, temporary trendy Spring feeling; a curved French heel communicates a dressy feminine light Summer feeling; a wooden stacked heel communicates a practical, comfortable Autumn feeling; a classic medium heel communicates an enduring, sophisticated Winter feeling.

THREE KEYWORDS DESCRIBE EACH SEASON ENERGY

These highlighted aspects from each Season show what is needed to deliberately create whatever effect you desire. Remember, you are molding energy just as artists mold and manipulate their mediums in paint, clay, wood, iron, fabric, rocks, feathers, beads, jewels and plants.

These four easels display 3 Keywords for each energy. Know the imagery, color modifications and the particular details of these Keywords and you have it all!

SPRING KEYWORDS
ACCENT
EXAGGERATE
ANIMATE

SUMMER KEYWORDS
SOFTEN
CURVE
BLEND

AUTUMN KEYWORDS
NATURAL
BUSY
ENRICH

WINTER KEYWORDS
STILL
SET
BALANCE

ARTISTIC CREATIVE TOOLS FOR EACH SEASON

There are specific items in each set of creative tools that are unique to that set of tools. Anytime one of these "tools" is used the energy of that season is being expressed. Compare the compartments in each toolbox carefully. This gives great insight into all creative endeavors!

SPRING TOOLS

Keywords: accent exaggerate animate	triangle forms	angled lines
fem + masc energy	bright warm colors	shiny crisp textures
accented contrast	3 or more colors	extra large size

SUMMER TOOLS

Keywords: soften curve blend	circle forms	curved lines
feminine energy	light cool colors	thin delicate textures
low contrast	mono-chromatic colors	small size

AUTUMN TOOLS

Keywords: natural busy enrich	square forms	straight lines
masculine energy	muted warm colors	heavy coarse textures
medium contrast	two colors	large size

WINTER TOOLS

Keywords: still set balance	oval forms	even lines
masc + fem energy	dark cool colors	medium fine textures
high contrast	one color	medium size

GOOD TASTE CAN BE LEARNED…ABSOLUTELY!

With this study the principles of good dress are orderly and reliable. The *Science of Personal Dress* teachings, training, tools and techniques gives one the ability to apply proven color and line principles for a tremendous feeling of well-being. Women begin feeling classically sensual and men feel smooth and put together. A most important aspect of color is the deep psychological depth of color meanings. When these nuances are considered, greater refinement of assessments can be made.

PSYCHOLOGICAL ASPECTS OF COLOR

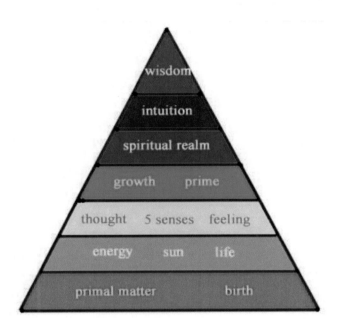

The study of color is as much a psychological as a mental science. Intuitively we associate color with *feelings, emotions and states of being*—both consciously and subconsciously. The story of the symbolism of the seven colors of the spectrum has been built upon many centuries of history, tradition, religion and superstition.

To some extent the colors of the Rainbow trace the archetype of human life here on earth. Allegorically speaking, in the color **RED** we see beginnings, birth and actual primal matter. The next successive color is **ORANGE** bringing energy, the warmth of the sun, the pulse of the earth and life is born. **YELLOW** brings thought, sensitivity, awareness of the five senses and a feeling of Self. With **GREEN** comes growth, youth, the prime of the physical body bursting with feelings and enthusiasm. **BLUE** introduces the spiritual realm and the infinite possibilities at our command. **INDIGO** awakens the inner world of intuition and knowingness. The last color is **VIOLET**, and here red is reintroduced to the blue bringing us again full circle, but with more understanding and wisdom as we are spiraled upward into the next cycle.

The colors have not "died" but have gone beyond our apparent ability to see them (much like there are sounds in upper octaves we cannot hear.) Faber Birren, one of the foremost authorities on color in this age, states that this remarkable sequence of colors beginning with red and ending with blue-red (violet) indicates another beginning on a higher plane and **"inspires awe in the heart of the researcher and magic in the heart of the child within us all."**

COLOR AWARENESS IS EVOLVING

Actually, man has not always been sensitive to color—color was simply not readily available for his use. The struggle to distill the colors from nature was, and still is, a continuous process. Before modern times people worked more on the land and materials had to be practical. Colored things were rare and only the rich could afford the expensive color dyes, materials and jewels.

THE AGE OF COLOR

With the advent of less expensive chemical synthetic dyes and materials we are now surrounded by color; colored printing, color in home decor and the workplace, color television, movies and now the internet, plus the extensive use of color in individual creative endeavors.

| print | decour | color | color | color |

When psychedelic colors emerged, the impact was felt as a kind of "color wave shock," but exposure to more color has resulted in a keener perception and acceptance of a broader range and quality of color. Now we experiment constantly with color. This new awareness of the power of color has ushered in the Age of Color with expanding fields of endeavor, including personal color analysis.

Sir Winston Churchill said,

"When I get to heaven, I shall require a still greater palette than I yet have below. I expect orange and vermilion will be the darkest, dullest upon it, and beyond these will be a whole range of wonderful new colors which will delight the celestial eye."

EVERYDAY PSYCHOLOGICAL ASSOCIATIONS

Consider the everyday psychological associations we have with color. Policemen wear authoritative, intimidating black or dark colors—they don't wear baby-yellow uniforms and get out of pink patrol cars carrying lavender pistols.

On the other hand, babies don't wear black baby-dresses. Race cars are painted in psychedelic energy-packed colors or fierce, dark threatening ones—they are not ordinarily painted in sweet pastels.

COLOR AND FOOD

Realize that foods are mostly colored in appetizing warm colors.

Warm Browns	nuts, bread, meat, grain
Warm Reds	cherries, rhubarb, strawberries
Warm Oranges	oranges, apricots, carrots, yams
Warm Yellows	bananas, squash, grapefuiit, lemons

Candy and sweet things are often in pastels—children usually have to be coaxed into eating dark cool colors like blueberries, prunes, eggplant and olives.

COLOR AND SYMBOLS

Even the common signal lights speak to us in color symbols of:

Red = "stop"
Green = "go"
Yellow = "caution"

Warning signs on steps are yellow because yellow in paint has the highest visibility vibration. Children's school buses are yellow for the same reason.

COLOR AND MARKETING

Marketing people know that "low cost" is associated with bright yellow and black signs and packaging. Psychedelic colors often make people uneasy because these colors have been associated with exaggerated loud music, drugs and shocking colored hair and dress—these colors are more easily accepted in the theater or circus arena where excitement is encouraged. Observe that a car or dress can look very rich in one color and ordinary or cheap in another. A taupe-colored car is "richer" or more sophisticated looking than a lime green car.

The following example of a yellow-red dress and a blue-red dress illustrates the different energy expressed by each—the bright red dress communicates a hot, attention-getting dress, whereas the cranberry dress is more sophisticated. If the cranberry dress had long sleeves the sophisticated energy would be doubled.

Bright red dress communicates a "hot" attention-getting affect.
The other subdued cranberry dress gives a more sophisticated format effect.

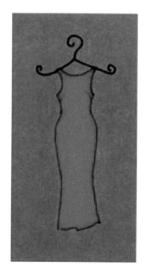 

26

COLOR AND MUSIC

Nearly 300 years ago Newton *saw* vibration in tones of the music scale:

red   = C
orange = D
yellow = E
green   = F
blue   = G
indigo = A
violet   = B

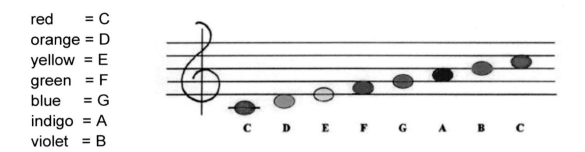

Color and music share vocabulary and freely exchange terms such as *tone, pitch, intensity, volume, color and chromatic.* Beethoven, Wagner, Schubert and other composers related their music to color. Liszt had pet terms such as, "more pink here," "this is too black" and "I want it all azure." To Rimsky-Korsakov, F sharp was strawberry red and sunlight was C major.

Another interesting fact, music also aligns with the energy of the Seasons. —Consider the following:

Winter = Classical Music
Summer = Waltz Music
Autumn = March Music
Spring = Jazz Music

COLOR AND THEATER

The psychological reactions to color are mainly associated with two modes: the *warm* active, exciting qualities of red, orange and yellow; the *cool* passive, calming qualities of green, blue and purple. In the theater, lighting and costumes portray and stimulate definite emotions.

Associated with Comedy   **Associated with Tragedy**

COLOR AND HEALTH

Sunlight, containing all the colors of the spectrum is a nutrient. Scientists observe that all living things tend to orient themselves toward light or brightness—when energy stimulation goes up, the response tendency goes with it. It appears that muscular activities perform well in warm light and surroundings; mental tasks are better performed with softer, deep colors. The study of human muscular strength and movement verifies the body's need for the right vibration in color. A person's normal muscle strength is weakened by wearing colors that are incompatible with their coloring.

The body absorbs energy vibrations from colored water and colored materials. This is undoubtedly one reason man has universally enjoyed sleeping under grandmother's multi-colored patchwork quilts. When one looks at color, the vibration strikes the eye and is transferred throughout the body. We may be well advised to "look" at the roses as well as to "smell" the roses.

COLOR ANALOGIES

Truly, and not to be underestimated, the quickest way to really understand and know how to use color deliberately is to get a deep feeling for the meaning of each color. The following analogies are gathered from commonly used, everyday terms and associations with color. Understanding these associations give a powerful tool which is vital knowledge for students of all art disciplines.

Red — Begins the color spectrum. The name *Adam* means "red clay." Red is the primal color produced by long wave lengths of low frequency and is nearest to infrared waves which produce the sensation of heat; thus red is very stimulating. It is "bossy" and grabs attention. Red stands out as a party dress, stop-sign, a package on a supermarket shelf and on lips. Eve was attracted to the red apple and restaurant owners have long known that vivid red goblets, tablecloths and rugs stimulate both the appetite and mood of diners. Red is the color of passion, vigor, courage, excitement, sensuality, and also symbolizes anger, lust, seeing red, red-letter days, red ink, red tape, red-light districts and blood on the man being caught "red-handed." Children and bulls are attracted to this heavy attention-getting vibration.

Orange — The most energetic of all the colors, symbol of the sun and radiant energy. If autumn had a color it would be orange. Orange is a secondary color and plays second fiddle to red because red hair, red clay, red fire and red sky are all arguably *orange.* It connotes endurance and strength and is the color of fun, joviality, clowns and friendship. Fast food restaurants use orange to get customers to "eat and run" for quick turnover. Orange virtually has no negative associations; no one gets orange with rage, orange with envy or has a nasty orange streak. Usually children or people with high energy wear orange.

Yellow — The brightest color of the spectrum and we associate it with the intellect. Because it is a mental stimulant, yellow is the color of legal scratch pads, yellow pencils, caution signs for school buses, maintenance trucks and warning hazards on step edges. In its pure form, yellow represents inspiration and a sunny disposition, yet it sullies easily just as a negative thought ruins dispositions. Yellow is a favorite of advertisers and stands for a "bright idea" (light bulb) cheerfulness (yellow kitchens) and the enlightened Buddhists who wear yellow saffron robes. Negative associations are cowardly with a yellow streak down the back. Yellow is a difficult color for people to wear because of the basic warm undertone color of skintones.

Green — Is the midpoint of the spectrum and divides the warm and cool colors; being a mixture of happy yellow and tranquil blue it represents emotional balance. Green is the color of money and represents the resources of a nation. It rests the eye and counterbalances cause and effect. Green is ambivalent—being the color of mold, sickness, bruises and poisoning; yet it is nature's greatest healing color in grass, trees, parks and herbs for rest and refreshment. The dual nature of green signifies freshness yet decay, a color of great visibility as well as the color of camouflage, the green-thumb of the gardener contrasting the green hand of the novice sailor. Green is used for the surgeon's gown to neutralize the after-image of the patient's red blood (green and red are complementary colors.) Green is reputable, civilized, and stands for the rebirth in the spring and the silent abiding power of nature.

Blue — The coolest of all the colors and reminiscent of the sky which is transparent and intangible. Blue is spiritually related without the sensuality of red or the intellect of yellow. It is fundamentally beneficial, even its negative meanings are merely extensions of its positive traits; cool taken to cold, solitude to isolation and tranquility to inertia. Blue skies are a patent cure for the blues, sorrow ultimately being transcended into heaven, singing or listening to the blues brings relief and pleasure. Blue bears dirt more gracefully than other colors, has a calming effect, people receive "bolts from the blue," being true-blue represents high value as blue-ribbons, blue chips and *blue-blood* meaning "high born." The pigment ultramarine, processed from lapis lazuli was originally as costly as gold, but after it was chemically synthesized it became so common it was even used for laundry bluing to keep things bright and white. In clothing, the color blue flatters nearly everyone because blue is complementary to warm skin.

Indigo — The deepest of all the colors, an ultramarine color with just a hint of red like the midnight sky or the deep clear ocean. A mysterious color, historically references to the color are virtually nonexistent. Isaac Newton couldn't even detect the color in the rainbow so had to get his younger assistant to verify the color. Before synthetic dyes, navy blue was made from the indigo plant which furnished the world's only blue dye and was the official color of the Royal Navy. The universal "Levi" pant was made from this dye. Indigo is the closest color to black which has the ability to absorb all light rays. Because of its intensity and depth of color indigo is associated with the misery of the human condition known as "the blues."

Purple / Violet — The shortest ray of the visible spectrum, the highest vibratory color and is used to represent high rank and royalty. In medieval days it was against the law for commoners to wear purple. Purple is a mixed color (a bit darker than violet) and violet is a pure spectral hue. There is no real evidence that early man saw violet as we do today (color sensitivity seems to be evolutionary.) People have mixed and varied feelings about purple as it seems to psychologically affect people to an extreme of delight or aversion. Being the last color of the spectrum it is associated with death, but being arranged in a circle between indigo and red indicates it also suggests transmutation and new beginnings. Artists and creative people are more attracted to this high vibratory color. Color-wise, purple and violet are flattering to all skintones.

Pink — Anytime white is added to a color the vibration is refined and lifted higher. Add white to dynamic red, and instead of passionate love we have the pinker rose-red of the valentine or the delicate pink symbol of babies. Pink is always positive suggesting high spirits and tip-top condition—if you're "in the pink" everything is rosy.

Black — Black is the subtractive absorption of all color and light. In reality there is only light; black is merely the absence of light. Symbolically, it is associated with authority and discipline. Positive associations begin with black as part of the creative process, the seed needing dark to germinate. Positive associations are: formal, sophisticated (tuxedo and basic black dress,) sexy, black lace, black satin sheets and the dark lighting desired by romantics. Negative are grief, despair, evil, black-ball and blackmail.

White — White symbolizes God, totality and "Oneness." All the colors of the light spectrum added together create white light. Positive associations are purity, goodness, all-knowing, ascension, "white lies," angels and cosmic consciousness. Negative associations express the vanity of the Caucasian race in casting aspersion on red, black and yellow man. To say a "man is white" or one is a "fair-haired boy" infers superiority.

CO-ESTHETIC RELATIONSHIP OF COLOR AND LINE

The reason each color is related to a specific symbol is because of how the eye perceives the color-vibration filling into the edges of the form. For example, yellow paint is highly visible to the eye and can fill in the sharp angles of the triangle, whereas blue creates a blurred image in the eye lending itself to softer round shapes.

COLOR	NAME	SYMBOL	ASSOCIATION
Red	Square		Red has the lowest vibration rate. It is hot, dry, opaque, solid and substantial. It is visible to the eye – lends itself to structural planes and sharp angles.
Orange	Rectangle or Trapezoid		Orange is less earthy than red. It is more incandescent and is clearly focused by the eye – lends itself to angles and points.
Yellow	Triangle		Yellow is more celestial than worldly, lacks substance and weight. It is the color of highest visibility in the spectrum – lends itself to sharp angles and points.
Green	Hexagon		Green is the midpoint of the spectrum with qualities of both sides. It is cool, fresh, soft and not sharply focused by the eye – does not lend itself to angularity.
Blue	Circle		Blue is cold, wet, transparent, celestial, has a retiring quality and creates a blurred image on the retina – therefore, it lends itself to soft or round shapes.
Indigo	Spherical Triangle		Indigo is obscure, mysterious and shows depth. It has the lowest visibility in the spectrum – lends itself to vague forms.
Purple/Violet	Ellipse		Purple has the highest vibration in the spectrum. The added red makes it cling more to the earth than blue. It is associated with the highest universal oval form – lends itself to graceful, regal lines and shapes.

SYMBOLS USED TO DEFINE SHAPES

Symbols are used to simplify a concept and aid in making it comprehensible, thereby adding to the richness of the language of color and line. Using the symbols of the three primary colors—red, yellow and blue—plus violet, every other color in the spectrum is represented. The four also represent all the basic shapes—the square, triangle, circle and oval. These four shapes encompass all the basic lines needed to create and depict designs; a straight line, a circle, points of angles, squared lines and curved lines:

The 3 KEYWORDS associated with these symbols are from Webster's dictionary and perfectly describe the symbolic expression of each.

SYMBOL FOR THE EXAGGERATION OF "LIFE"

The triangle, point up, is expressive of evolution. Symbol of the triune Godhead; body, mind and spirit; the father, mother, child; super-conscious, conscious, subconscious. The three masculine straight lines enclose an implied circle giving a feeling of feminine/masculine combined. The accompanying lightning bolt symbol suggests a thrust of activity, a surprise angle for an instant, and then dramatic growth or thrust to be left off-center or asymmetrical—note the backward or sharp downward motion, the second thought, the pause, review or effort to achieve counter-balance that is indicated before continuing, and then onward with renewed confidence. The symbols represent the spark of life, the birth and beginning of growth in Spring. 3 KEYWORDS associated with this symbol are:

ACCENT — A distinguishing style or expression. A striking or prominent feature; an object of detail that lends emphasis as by contrast to that which surrounds it; special attention. To set apart and emphasize; drawing a line around; bringing up color.

EXAGGERATE— To make larger, therefore to be more noticeable; intensify; to enlarge or increase or to an extreme or abnormal degree; overemphasize.

ANIMATE — Making "not real to life" replica for emphasis; to make alive, fill with breath, give life to; to make gay, energetic, spirited; to stimulate to action or creative effort; inspire; to give motion to; put into action; to make move so as to seem "lifelike." Implies making alive or lively; to quicken to action that which is inert.

SYMBOL FOR THE FEMININITY OF "BEAUTY"

The circle represents unmanifested Deity, perfect and complete before creation; including everything and wanting nothing; without beginning or end. Neither first nor last; timeless; absolute; eternal. A perfect heavenly shape; encircling; suggests the womb, the next, nurturing and mothering. The accompanying S curve symbol is feminine and is emphasized by the repeat of circles in the graceful figure. The symbols represent the innocent perfection of the child; angels and the angelic; bubbles; fantasies before coming to grips with the "real world" and the growth and expansion of life in the summer. 3 KEYWORDS associated with this symbol are:

SOFTEN — Implies an absence or reduction of all that is harsh, rough, too intense, etc. so as to be pleasing to the senses; gentle; being pleasantly soothing or tranquil.

CURVE — Suggests a swerving or deflection in a line that approximates or follows the arc or a circle; a line having no straight part; to form a curve by bending.

BLEND — To mix; to glimmer indistinctly; to mix or to mingle so as to produce a desired flavor, color, grade etc.; to pass gradually or imperceptivity into each other.

SYMBOL FOR THE MASCULINITY OF "STRENGTH"

The square is always symbolic of the earth. Of man on the earth, the material plane, reason and regularity; all that is stable and enduring on the earth plane; the four corners of the earth; the four seasons; the four winds; and then the four elements—earth, air, fire and water. This symbol is made up of straight masculine lines. The square is symbolic of a box or bag which gives a feeling of being constrained, inhibited, "boxed in" or grounded to the earth. The accompanying stair-step zigzag symbol has square angles which show the line of the masculine thrust, always coming back to earth for grounding and stability. The symbols represent work, matter, gravity; the maturity of the adult; comfort; the harvest in Autumn. The 3 KEYWORDS associated with this symbol are:

NATURAL — Of or arising from nature; not artificial or manufactured; of the real or physical world as distinguished from a spiritual, intellectual or imaginary world; innate; normal or usual; customarily accepted or expected; free from affectation or artificiality.

BUSY   — Full of activity; characterized by much action or motion; having much detail and variety of color; occupied; diligent.

ENRICH   — To make rich or richer; to give greater value, effectiveness, so as to increase in value; importance.

SYMBOL FOR THE BALANCE OF "POISE"

The oval or ellipsoid shape suggests the creative feminine circle, elongated to show the effect of the creative masculine power standing erect. The accompanying straight line figure shows the masculine/ feminine combined and balanced. The most evolved forms of life resemble the oval. The vital part of the body is the head (oval shaped.) The heart and the organ of the body which gives the power of sight is the eye —both ovular in shape. A most important part of the wheat is the germ (oval shaped.) Eggs, seeds and nuts are ellipsoidal. The orbit of the earth, the orbits of the sun and moon are all elliptic in shape. Even the highest elected position in the land resides in the Oval Office. Rocks refine down to ovals—not triangles, squares or circles. This symbol represents the result of much hard work and experience to achieve balance, perfection and the well deserved rest of Winter; only to begin again on a new cycle ever evolving into greater spheres of consciousness. The ancient Egyptians used the sacred "Eye of Horus" ellipsoidal symbol for protection, royal power and good health. The all seeing *Third Eye* (also known as the Inner Eye) is the depicted seal on the one-dollar bill and represents a non-dualistic perspective and the all seeing eye of God. In eastern spiritual traditions the "eye" refers in part to the brow chakra opening to enlightenment and having deeply personal spiritual or psychological significance. **It is interesting to note that the most appropriate shape for the displays of color in this work, to be *seen* properly, turned out to be an oval-shaped format.** The 3 KEYWORDS associated with this symbol are:

STILL   — Implies the absence of sound or movement; quiet; silent; hushed; at rest; stationary; characterized by little agitation or disturbance; calm serene; tranquil; not effervescent or bubbling.

SET   — To place in the proper or designated place; to cause to lie or become; put in order; to adjust so as to be in a desired position for use; to regulate; deliberate; fixed in advance; purposeful.

BALANCE   — A state of equilibrium or equipoise; mental and emotional stability; poise; harmony of various elements; steady; pleasing harmonious proportions.

COLOR THEORY REGARDING DRESS

THE LAW OF ATTRACTION

The reason colors are so important to dress is because any color worn accentuates the same pigment colors in your eyes, hair and skintones. The powerful *Law of Attraction* is in play here causing changes from effects. The *Law of Attraction* says that "like attracts like." This phenomenon of color interaction makes colors that are alike draw towards and accentuate each other. In the Matisse painting below, each colored frame accentuates the same "like" color in its picture: i.e. the teal frame brings out teal in the picture, the red frame brings forward red, orange tends to match the orange, purple accents purple, yellow accents yellow and periwinkle accentuates the blue and darks.

USING THE LAW OF ATTRACTION

Because of this law, some colors make you look better than others. The colors in your skin, hair and eyes are affected by the colors you wear. Everyone knows that blue eyes change color depending on the color being worn; the same thing happens to the skin and hair.

EYE COLORS
Eye colors appear to change and match the color being worn— blue-green eyes look bluer when wearing blue and greener when wearing green.

SKIN COLORS
Any color worn around the face will accentuate similar pigment colors in the skintone—wearing yellow will make the skin appear more yellow; wearing red will make the skin appear more red.

HAIR COLORS
Colors can change the appearance of hair color—wearing dark colors will accentuate the dark tones in hair; wearing light colors will accent the lighter tones in the hair.

HOW COLORS ARE CREATED

All colors are derived from 3 Primary Colors: blue which is cool and dark; yellow which is warm and bright; and red (blood red) which is more balanced than the other two extremes. Secondary colors (and all other colors) are mixtures of these 3 Primary colors: red + yellow = orange; yellow + blue = green; and blue + red = purple.

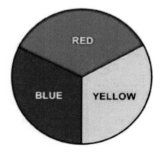 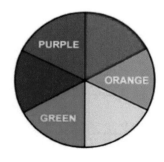

PRIMARY COLORS   **SECONDARY COLORS**

THE QUALITIES OF WARM, COOL AND BALANCED COLORS

Understanding how colors are created helps use *The Law of Attraction* to great advantage. All colors have varying proportions of red, yellow and blue. These 3 primary colors also have a 3-dimenionsal (3D) quality because each has a different degree of luminosity or brightness. Yellow is the brightest, then red, and then the least bright is blue in a corresponding proportional ratio of 8: 6: 3.

These two factors, along with light and dark values, combine in many ways to create the entire world's color: red warms color, yellow brightens color, and blue darkens color.

`RED` is the most basic color—it makes colors warm. It is important to point out that red is used more than the other two primary colors. It is the most common basic color in many areas: color mixtures more commonly include red than they do yellow or blue. Skintones all have red (blood) in common. Generally speaking red is more flattering to skintones than yellow or blue. Red is the basic color for lip and cheek colors. The incandescent light bulb gives off predominantly red light, warming our world.

`YELLOW` is the most luminous color—it makes colors bright. For example, "hot pink" is made by adding yellow to regular pink. Yellow also adds warmth.

`BLUE` is the darkest color—added to other colors it makes them darker and cooler. In paint pigments it is the only way a color can be cooled. Fluorescent light is cool and therefore is not as flattering to skin-tones as warmer incandescent light.

COLORS CAN BE SLIGHTLY CHANGED OR ADJUSTED

Any color can be adjusted. A color can be made relatively more cool and dark by adding blue; more warm and balanced by adding red; and more warm and bright by adding yellow.

Adding `BLUE`	Adding `RED`	Adding `YELLOW`
cools and darkens	warms and balances	warms and brightens

THE COLOR PYRAMID

The colors on the following pyramid show another example of how colors are relatively warmer or cooler compared to each other. To explain: Yellow is basically a warm color but adding blue cools it down. Green is basically a cool color but by adding blue it becomes even cooler; green becomes warmer by adding yellow.

`BLUE` is the coldest color on the color wheel—it is impossible to have a warm blue because adding yellow to warm it merely turns it into a greenish-blue which is balanced. There are no warm blues....period! (See X below) Purples test very well on people because purple is a mixture of red, yellow and blue making it balanced.

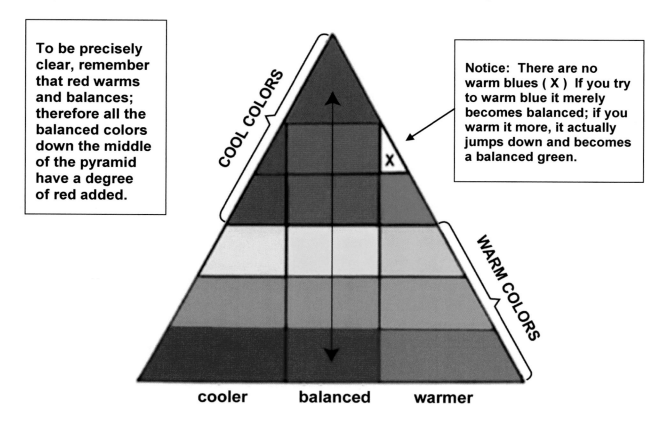

To be precisely clear, remember that red warms and balances; therefore all the balanced colors down the middle of the pyramid have a degree of red added.

Notice: There are no warm blues (X) If you try to warm blue it merely becomes balanced; if you warm it more, it actually jumps down and becomes a balanced green.

COOL COLORS

WARM COLORS

X

cooler   balanced   warmer

IMPORTANT NOTE: Keep in mind that in color analysis we are not testing a white wall; we are testing warm skintones. All skintones are basically warm derived from the orange color family. Even though green is considered to be a basically cool color, on skintones all greens test out to be balanced (i.e. hunter green or mint green) or they turn out to be relatively warm (i.e. olive green or lime green.) Blue is a purely cool color, and when testing on basically warm skintones blue remains a cool color (royal blue, powder blue, French blue) while all other greenish-blues (teal-blue, turquoise, aquamarine) test out to be balanced. One exception is navy-blue which is a balanced blue-red-yellow combination, but there are relatively cooler and warmer navy blues as well as yellowed-navy, grayed-navy, light and dark navy blues.

white wall

skin

Most people can wear balanced colors—all blue-greens and green-blues are balanced. Only a very warm skintone can wear a cool blue, and only a very cool skintone can wear olive or lime green.

COMPLEMENTARY COLORS

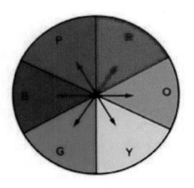

On the color wheel, warm colors are opposite cool colors. Each warm/cool pair (red/green, blue/orange, yellow/violet) is <u>complementary,</u> otherwise complete. Why? Because each pair consists of mixtures which contain all 3 Primary colors. Notice that secondary colors are all mixtures of two primary colors, then when added to the opposite color on the wheel, all 3 primary colors are equally present.

yellow + blue = green — therefore, green + red = all 3 ▮▯▮ Primary colors

yellow + red = orange — therefore, orange + blue = all 3 ▮▯▮ Primary colors

red + blue = purple — therefore, purple + yellow = all 3 ▮▯▮ Primary colors

The reason complementary colors are important is because they have the same components that the combined 3 primary colors do—they bring equilibrium to the eye. When all three primary colors are present, the eye is at ease and sees harmony. When one is missing, the eye becomes stimulated or disquieted...excited, but not at ease.

THE SIGNIFICANCE OF GRAY

For the eye to be at ease it needs to see "gray." And, gray is produced in the eye by the combination of the 3 primary colors, or by the combination of a complementary pair.

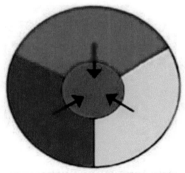

PRIMARY COLORS MIX TO GRAY   COMPLEMENTARY COLORS MIX TO GRAY

Complementary colors complete each other and the eye wants to see "gray" for comfortable balance. It is significant that both complementary-pairs and primary-colors mix to gray. And the reason gray is so significant is because it satisfies the basic rule of all color harmony:

Gray has so many interesting qualities. It tends to take on the hue of any color it is combined with or next to—this is why gray eye-shadow makeup is the basic eye-shadow color. Look around. Notice all shadows and lines are various shades of gray. Face features are defined by gray and even blonde hair has charcoal-gray shadowing between strands. Gray is the color which defines the texture and weave of fabrics. In fact, gray is the basic canvas color of our entire world. Artists often begin with a medium gray canvas as a base painting before adding lights, darks and colors. In dress, everyone can wear charcoal, but make sure it is combined with basic Homebase colors because it will take on the tone of colors which surround it.

Another phenomenon of complementary colors that occurs is the fact that when two complementary colors are side-by-side they incite each other to bright-maximum-vividness; however when mixed together they do the very opposite—they annihilate each other and turn into gray.

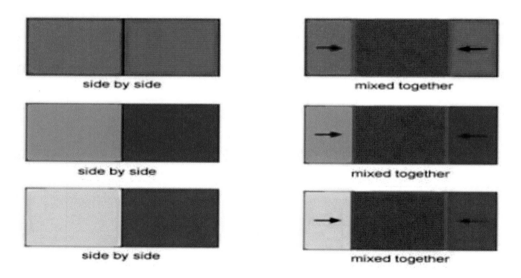

side by side   mixed together

side by side   mixed together

side by side   mixed together

Christmas colors are bright because red and green are complementary. Orange earth looks brilliant against blue skies, and costumes are more alive and dramatic utilizing complementary colors together. Artists know that if they put touches of a color's complementary color next to it for accent, paintings spark and come alive. A touch of complementary color in a tie or scarf can heighten the look and add a dash of interest to the attire. This is something clothiers should know and can use to great benefit.

INTERESTING POINT: Complementary colors are opposite of each other, yet they require each other to make a perfect whole. The eye will even spontaneously generate the complementary color if it is not present. If you stare at a red square for some time, then close your eyes, you will see a complementary green square "after image." The reason the eye posits the complementary color is that it has to create gray to maintain its equilibrium. Gray generates a state of complete equilibrium in the eye—when missing, the eye becomes disquieted. Thus, the eye will create gray for balance. Try it for yourself.

EXPERIMENT: Stare at this red square for a minute, and then close your eyes and you will see a green square "after-image."

IMAGE

"AFTER-IMAGE"

NATURE CREATES COMPLEMENTARY BALANCE

Nature uses both warm and cool colors to balance and "complete" her pictures. Notice how nature alternates between the warm and cool colors to establish harmony and balance in our seasons, in landscapes and in people:

IN SEASONS . . . .

First the warm-bright colors of Spring

Then cool sun-struck colors of Summer

Next, the warm-muted colors of Autumn

Then with the cool-dark colors of Winter

IN LANDSCAPE . . . .

Warm red-brown earth tones are cooled by their complementary color of green grass and trees, blue skies, water and clouds.

IN PEOPLE . . . .

People with *classic* red hair have complementary green eyes. People with ruddy "orangey" skintones have complementary cool, blue eyes just as an example.

One common example of this principle: If a person's hair begins to look greenish from chlorine, dyes or sun-bleaching, its complementary color of red will restore the hair to its original color.

PEOPLE ARE CREATED WITH COMPLEMENTARY BALANCE

Here is the scientific orderly principle behind human coloring—warm-skin has cool-hair and cool-skin has warm-hair—<u>the hair and skin are not the same</u>—they are opposite! *The Law of Attraction* will always accentuate the dominant pigment color in skin and hair. This is nature's way of bringing balance to our coloring (using warm/cool complementary colors together for balance.) Misunderstanding this has caused much confusion and must be seen clearly for successful analysis. This is proven and valid. This principle is so precise that the eye color magically fills in anything necessary to complete the whole perfect complementary color scheme of red, yellow, blue pigments.

A predominately warm-skin undertone is balanced with a cool undertone in the hair—and wears cool colors.	A predominately cool-skin undertone is balanced with a warm undertone in the hair—and wears warm colors.	A warm or cool skintone may be less extreme and lean toward more of the balanced colors —thus balanced colors can be added to their Homebase colors.

SUROUNDED BY WRONG VERSUS RIGHT COLORS

WRONG (warm skin with warm colors)

RIGHT (warm skin with cool colors)

WRONG (cool skin with cool colors)

RIGHT (cool skin with warm colors)

WRONG (balanced skin with ?????)

RIGHT (balanced skin with balanced color)

HOW COLORS AFFECT AND ALTER EACH OTHER

The Science of Personal Dress is based on the most powerful law in the Universe and impacts everything—the action of *The Law of Attraction.* This law causes a color to draw color like itself forward and accentuates itself in other colors; like attracts like. However colors can be manipulated to appear differently just by juxtaposition—putting different colors side by side. This is termed **simultaneous contrast.**

An eye can be "fooled" into seeing a color a certain way by comparing it against another color. Examples: Below, the center watermelon color looks very pink against orange, but more orange against pink; periwinkle (a mixture of blue and purple) appears very purple against royal blue, but very blue against purple.

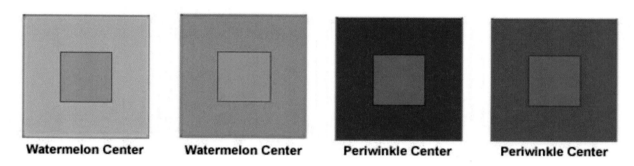

| Watermelon Center | Watermelon Center | Periwinkle Center | Periwinkle Center |

This may seem contradictory and one may ask, "Why doesn't *The Law of Attraction* make the periwinkle appear bluer in the blue frame and more purple in the purple frame?"

Here is the reason. When two extreme colors come together and are too vibrationaly apart for a match they automatically <u>flip-over and become opposite</u>; as opposites they become polarized. Even though there is not a match, they are held together by the same *Law of Attraction*; pulled together to create a virtual whole. In the periwinkle example, the colors of the frame and center mix together in the eye and achieve a comfortable complementary balance. The universe is set up to bring about expansion and completeness through complementaries. The word complementary is derived from the word "complete" and the eye adjusts to complete its complement for counterbalance.

THE FLIP-OVER PHENOMENON

It is true that colors can be augmented or drawn forward by *The Law of Attraction*—a color can be made to appear darker, lighter, bluer, grayer, redder etc. However, if this is pushed too far or exaggerated by contrast, a reverse effect is created. Rather than pulling together and matching, the colors will separate causing contrast rather than similarity. This is simultaneous contrast and we can describe this as a "flip-over" color reaction. This flip-over phenomenon is very apparent when working with black and white on skintones. Charcoal (a light black) will draw dark tones forward in the skin, and it should follow that black-black would draw forward even more dark tones in the skin—but black at an extreme point will actually flip-over creating contrast which causes the skin to appear lighter. The same thing happens with stark white; stark white should draw light tones forward in the skin and it does to a point, but against dark skin, stark white will cause the skintone to flip-over and become darker in contrast to the white. This phenomenon is experienced after sun-tanning all day and then going out in the evening wearing stark white which makes the tan look more pronounced.

EXPLANATION:

The darkest point of any shadow is at the edge where the light begins. Carefully look at the diagram at the right. Where the white bands cross, the "cross spots" look gray because the light is diffused and there is less contrast. At any point away from the crossing of the white, the lines become more surrounded by more black—this causes more contrast which results in the white looking brighter and whiter, and the black looking darker and blacker.

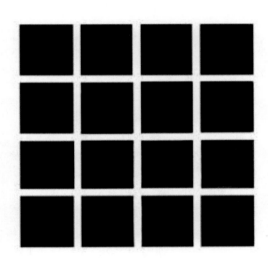

FLIP-OVER PHENOMENON APPLIED TO PERSONAL COLORING

Understanding this color interaction is very important and can often be used to advantage. Simultaneous contrast, or the flip-over phenomenon can clear up skintones.

Red-heads have a cool bluish-pink undertone in their skin and If a bluish red is worn the skin appears more bluish and the effect is unattractive (*Law of Attraction*.) However, if a brighter more extreme red is used, the flip-over phenomenon will occur and clear out the ruddy tones of the skin.

10 COLOR FAMILIES IN HARMONIC SEQUENCE

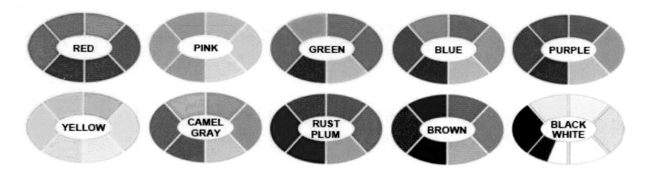

To generate all colors into harmonics, every conceivable color was sorted and arranged into harmonic sequence which turned out to be 10 basic color families. The green and pink color families are shown here as examples representing all possible shades of color arranged in graduated sequences of color.

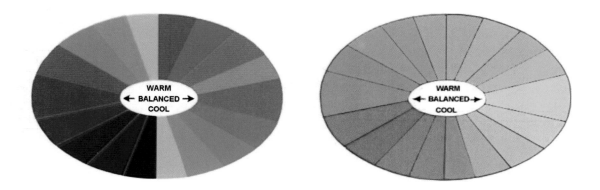

Further sorting only resulted in redundant duplication; reds ran into the plums, plums crossed over into the browns, browns then began crossing over into rusts and rusts back into reds etc. This further substantiates the validity of 9 groups. The only exception was the red family which was separated into two families—red and pink (making 10.) Because the red family is so prevalent in the world and involved in so many aspects it was necessary to expand into the pinks to address makeup colors. The other light color variations are represented through icy and pastel colors illustrated later in this work.

HARMONIC COLOR FAMILIES REDUCED TO 6 COLORS

To simplify, each color family has been reduced to 6 major colors. This practical 6 color format also represents the basic 4 seasons: Spring, Autumn, Summer and Winter. Keep in mind there are many shades in each category and the color shown is only representative of the color group to which it belongs. The advantage of this format is that one can learn quickly by comparisons—including knowing what colors not to wear.

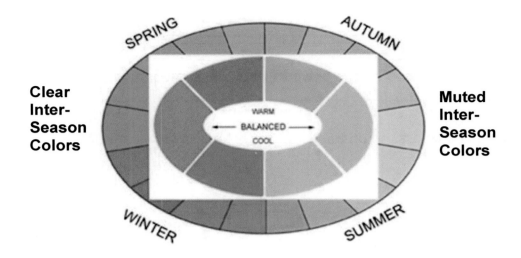

INTRODUCING BALANCED INTER-SEASON COLORS

Arranging colors into harmonic sequences of color revealed the concept of *balanced colors* and was key to understanding colors on skintones. Using the oval-shaped format (ancient symbol of the "eye") colors were sorted and grouped together by vibration beginning with warm colors on top and cool colors on the bottom. Other colors added in succession automatically filled in the gap by virtue of a connecting bridge. These in-between colors provided the missing link colorists were looking for—balanced colors. Notice balanced colors fall on both end sides of the color ovals and are situated in-between the warm and cool colors.

Balanced colors cleared up the confusion connected with the limited four-season approach into Inter-seasons. The extremely *warm* and extremely *cool* colors can be adjusted and modified into balanced colors allowing one to wear an extended range.

Balanced Inter-season colors finally made color analysis make sense. Over and over when people see there has been good reason for their perplexity, they feel validated and are intrigued and want to learn more. If you have felt limited by one season, you are right. You do have a broader range of colors. Many people discover the *Goldilocks* syndrome; "this one is too hot, this one is too cold, but this one is juuust right!" There is a broader range of colors; for instance, if pink is too cool and coral is too warm, balanced pinky-coral is going to be the best color.

HOW THE COLORS HAVE BEEN SORTED

The following is a breakdown of how the colors on the oval format have been sorted and arranged in harmonic sequences of warm, cool and balanced colors:

1. WARM/COOL Colors Warm yellowed colors are on the top half, cool blued colors are on the bottom.	warm / cool
2. CLEAR/SOFT Colors Clearer colors are on the left side; colors which have been softened, dulled, grayed or muted are on the right.	clear / soft
3. BALANCED Colors Mixtures of both warm and cool colors (balanced) are on the sides of the ovals; clear balanced colors on the left, and soft balanced colors on the right.	
4. BRIGHT This section represents the true colors of Spring. The color qualities are warm, clear and bright. They have more yellow and red in them causing the colors to appear more ORANGE	
5. MUTED This section represents the true colors of Autumn. The color qualities are warm, muddy and neutral. They have more red, yellow and black than the other seasons, causing them to appear more BROWN	
6. LIGHT This section represents the true colors of Summer. The color qualities are cool, light and soft. They have more blue, red and white causing them to appear more BLUE	
7. DARK This section represents the true colors of Winter. The color qualities are cool, clear and dark. They have more red, blue and black causing them to appear more PURPLE	

THE BASIC COLOR LAYOUT FOR ALL HUMAN COLORING

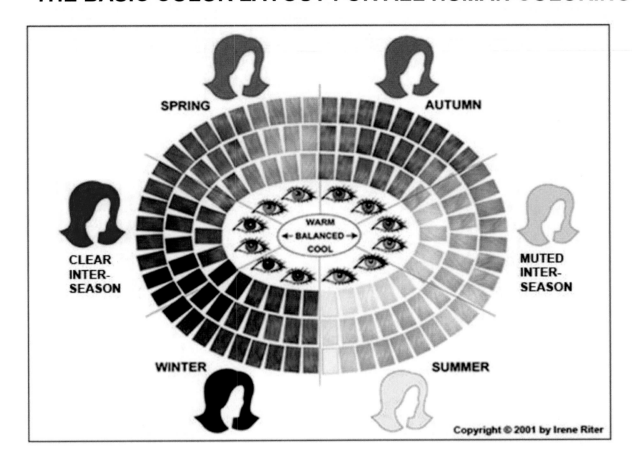

THE HOMEBASE

Everyone has a Homebase group of colors which resonates with their coloring; either a Spring, Summer, Autumn or Winter. These colors are grouped harmonically by energy-vibration and also resonate with each other. This gives a solid basic foundation of colors upon which to build a smart, connected, economically practical and striking wardrobe.

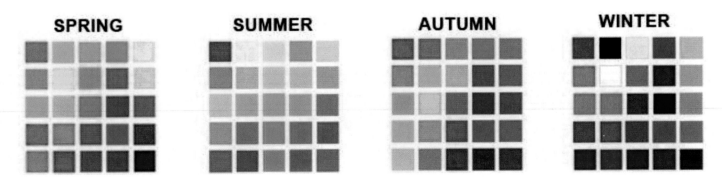

CLASSIC SPRING "HOMEBASE" COLORS AND TRAITS

Everything about this person is vibrant, colorful and exaggerated. **Traits** include glowing skin, peaches and cream, and flushes or blushes easily. Red hair, warm color hair and eyes, green eyes. Freckles or bushy eyebrows add exaggerated accent. Eyes are clear, electric, intense or translucent as if looking down into a pool.

CLASSIC SUMMER "HOMEBASE" COLORS AND TRAITS

Everything about this person is light and more delicate and has less contrast between hair and skin—just like these Summer colors. **Traits** include lighter colored hair, blonde or taupe colored hair, fine hair, wavy or curly hair. Light eye colors, blue or gray eyes. Lighter coloring gives balance to olive or light skin that has a warm undertone.

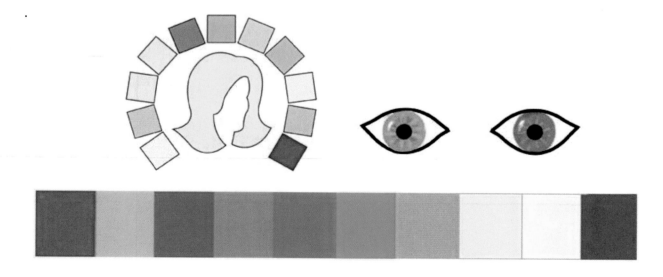

CLASSIC AUTUMN "HOMEBASE" COLORS AND TRAITS

Everything about this person is warm, muted and natural. **Traits** include all shades of medium or darker warm brown hair, rust or dark camel hair and eyes. Brown and Autumn colored hazel or dusty khaki eyes. Skin is very cool and lacks red showing; natural warm hair adds warmth to balance with the skin.

CLASSIC WINTER "HOMEBASE" COLORS AND TRAITS

Everything about this person requires striking contrast. **Traits** include dark or light skin contrasted against dark hair and eyes. Black hair, black or very dark appearing eyes or eyebrows show contrast. White teeth or eye-whites even give contrast. Soft black, dark ash-brown hair and dark brown eyes are Winter variables.

BEST COLORS OCCUPY SAME POSITION

In each color family there is one color that best vibrates in balance and harmony with your vibration. When you discover the position of your best red, the same best position will <u>mathematically</u> follow in all 10 color families as well.

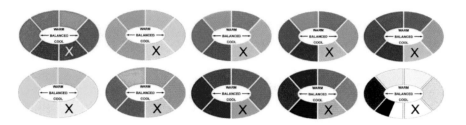

Keep in mind that if a certain hunter green is indicated it isn't always practical or even possible to try to match it exactly. There can be variances as long as the color is within range. For example, a hunter green could be a bit bluer or not, but for all practical purposes a basically dark hunter-green would work—certainly better than olive or lime.

Just seeing how best Homebase colors compare against the opposite colors is a good step. We often learn as much from seeing what not to wear as seeing what to wear. How can one know what would be better if not compared with something?

The following 3 sets of colors show all 10 color families illustrated in 3 different formats:
By Seasons / By Names / By Icy Pastels.

COLORS BY SEASONS

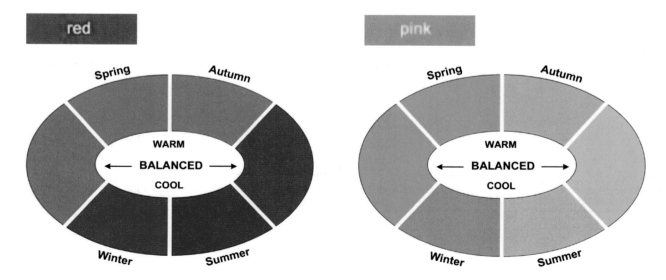

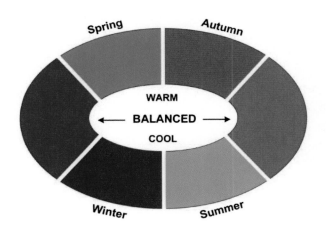

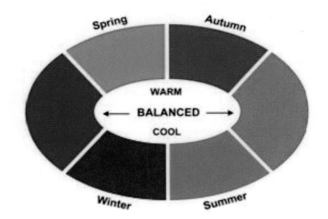

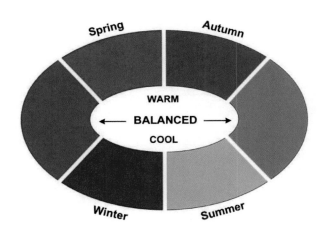

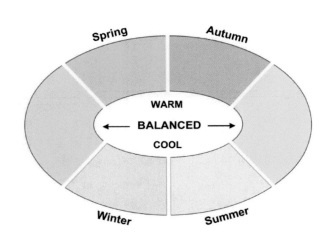

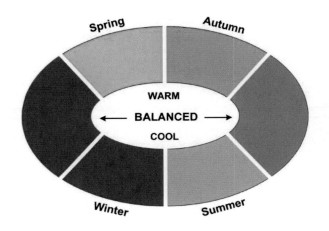

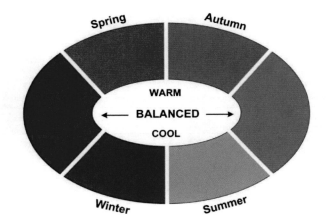

53

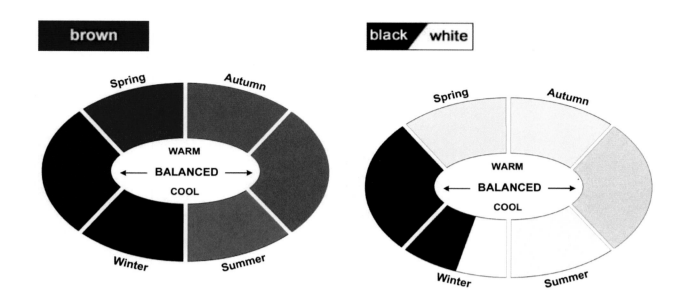

COLORS BY NAMES

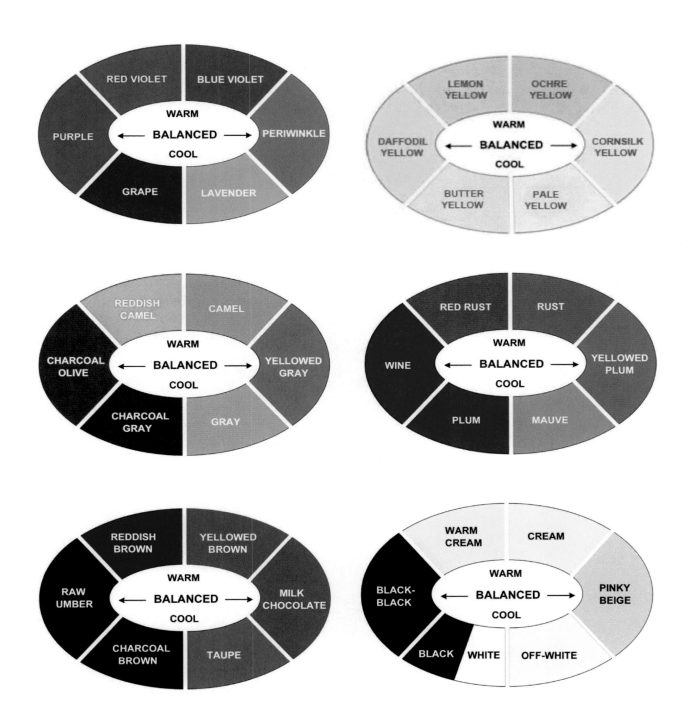

ICY COLORS INSERTED INTO COLOR OVALS

Icy light colors inserted in the ovals do three things: 1. creates contrast, 2. adds light around and to the face, 3. clears ruddy skintones.   True icy colors are found on the bottom of the oval format and fall into the same category as white, but there are light balanced icy-pastel colors as well. (Historically, the word "pastel" refers to pale colors as the result of mixing white caulk with pigment colors in order to lighten them.) Adding white to a color does automatically cool and lighten, but the lightened "icy" colors on the top side of the oval format are still warmer than the icy colors on the bottom. In fact, adding white to a warm color tends to bring it to the point of balance:

The red family is not included here because that family has already been expanded into the light and icy colors of the pink family. Again, the reason for expanding red by demonstrating pinks separately is because red is more abundant in the universe and makeup considerations are important to address. The white and black family displayed above obviously already shows white, bone, cream and warm cream light colors.

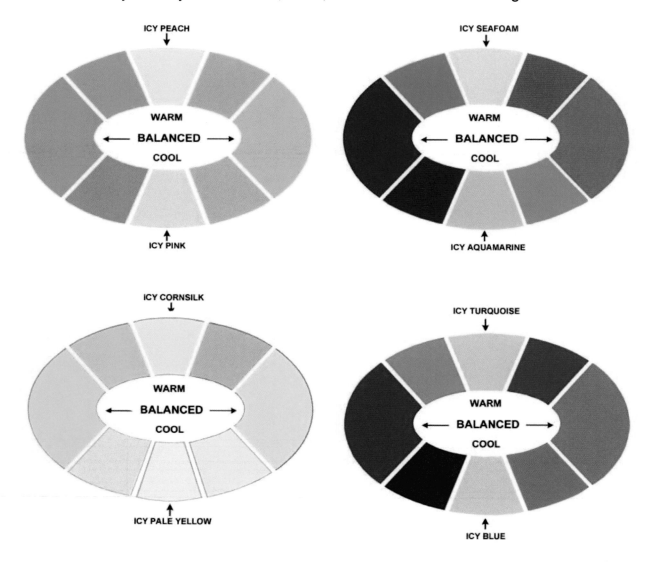

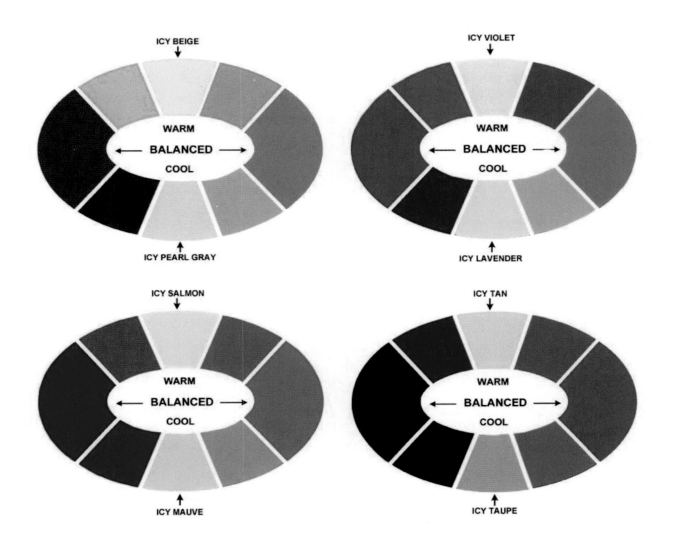

BALANCED COLORS WORN BY EVERYONE

Understand that some color families are inherently more warm or cool to begin with—the yellow family is definitely warmer than the blue family. Even though turquoise and teal are on the warm side of the blue oval-format, they are actually balanced; hunter green is on the cool side of the green oval but is so balanced that nearly everyone can wear it. Balanced medium purples test balanced, but other variables can alter that.

Keep in mind that red (blood-red not orange-red) is balanced between blue and yellow on the primary color wheel. Colors which are composed with more balanced red (such as rust, wine and plum) give greater leeway and are generally more flattering because red accentuates healthy pink and red tones in the skin. All balanced colors have a degree of red involved; some colors are just easier to wear because they are innately relatively balanced.

COLORS FOR UNIFORMS, GROUP COLORS AND MARKETING

Colors which flatter most skintones are balanced colors. These colors are excellent color choices for uniforms, group colors and marketing clothing because the colors will not detract from an individual's natural coloring. Balanced colors are wise choices when choosing gifts to buy for others.

NOTE: These 16 Balanced Colors Are Good For All Seasons

yellowed red	hunter green	turquoise	cornsilk
pinky coral	emerald	purple	charcoal
watermelon	teal	periwinkle	bone or off-white
cherry red	yellowed royal	pinky beige	wine

HOMEBASE MINI QUESTIONNAIRE

The following preliminary questionnaire will give you a good idea of where your Homebase may be so that you can continue to relate to the concepts. An advanced questionnaire for women and men providing an in-depth color and body analysis follows at the end of this book. But for now, this mini questionnaire will give you a good idea of where to look for your Homebase.

This level is especially useful for quick overviews for salespeople, groups and especially for teenagers (both boys and girls.) Young people love to know about themselves and their unique, purposeful place in nature's lineup. No part of this book may be copied or reproduced without prior permission from Irenee Riter. However, if needed, Irenee would welcome your call for an emailed copy and permission.

These questions are based on your "natural" coloring in your prime. Be sure to mark every single trait that could possible apply to you, regardless of the section or how many. The section that has most marks indicates your Homebase category; the section which has the second most marks indicates your secondary Inter-season influence.

MINI HOMEBASE QUESTIONNAIRE

SPRING HOMEBASE

- ☐ peaches and cream skin
- ☐ glowing skin
- ☐ flushes, or blushes easily
- ☐ freckles
- ☐ sunburns easily
- ☐ red hair
- ☐ strawberry blonde
- ☐ bright gold-blonde hair
- ☐ translucent "pool-like" eyes
- ☐ green eyes
- ☐ bushy eyebrows

AUTUMN HOMEBASE

- ☐ pale skin (lack of color)
- ☐ warm brown hair
- ☐ golden chestnut hair
- ☐ light brown hair
- ☐ medium brown hair
- ☐ straight hair
- ☐ medium brown eyes
- ☐ hazel eyes (soft autumn colors)
- ☐ dusty olive (khaki) eyes
- ☐ muted rust eyes

BALANCED CLEAR

- ☐ ruddy or rosy cheeks
- ☐ "Irish" white skin/dark hair
- ☐ Ethnic very warm skin
- ☐ orangy warm skin
- ☐ dark auburn hair
- ☐ very black hair
- ☐ coarse hair
- ☐ defined widow's peak
- ☐ black jet or sparkly eyes
- ☐ vibrant blue or green eyes
- ☐ very black eyebrows
- ☐ very black skin

BALANCED SOFT

- ☐ blonde, not a towhead
- ☐ honey blonde hair
- ☐ champagne colored hair
- ☐ sand colored hair
- ☐ dusty teal eyes
- ☐ soft gray/green eyes
- ☐ soft blue/green eyes
- ☐ dusty brown eyes
- ☐ hair, skin, eyes near same color or value (less contrast)

Spring **Autumn**

# 1 BRIGHT	# 2 WARM
# 6 CLEAR	WARM ← BALANCED → COOL	# 5 SOFT
# 4 DARK	# 3 LIGHT

Winter **Summer**

WINTER HOMEBASE

- ☐ sallow skin
- ☐ tans easily
- ☐ black skin
- ☐ very dark hair
- ☐ dark ash brown hair
- ☐ soft black hair
- ☐ slight widow's peak
- ☐ dark brown eyes
- ☐ black/brown eyes
- ☐ dark appearing eyes
- ☐ dark eyebrows

SUMMER HOMEBASE

- ☐ light porcelain skin
- ☐ olive skin (lacks red)
- ☐ towhead as a child (white blonde)
- ☐ blonde hair
- ☐ taupe or "mousey" hair
- ☐ medium ash brown hair
- ☐ wavy or curly hair
- ☐ baby fine hair
- ☐ blue eyes
- ☐ light gray eyes
- ☐ thin eyebrows

HAIR COLOR STUDY

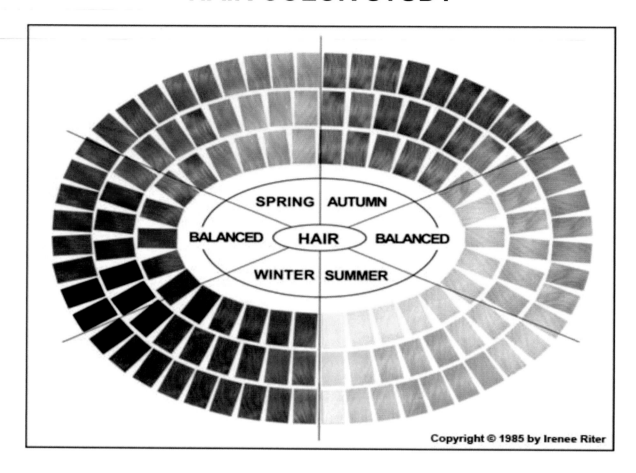

HAIR COLORS ARRANGED IN HARMONIC SEQUENCE

It is interesting to see that hair color can be arranged in the same harmonic sequences of warm, cool and balanced colors. This orderly progression of hair-color demonstrates the underlying consistent order of human coloring.

Warm hair colors are arranged on the top, the cool hair colors are on the bottom with in-between balanced hair colors on the sides—soft blended hair colors are on the right side, and more intense hair colors are on the left side.

Hair colors are easier to see than skintone colors, so we begin determining the Homebase category by establishing where the hair color falls on the hair chart. Even though a person's skintone *ultimately* determines the correct Homebase, the hair color is the biggest clue because we know it is the exact opposite color from the skin undertone color. Provisionally this test is simple and direct because hair generally fits into one of the basic four season categories. If not easily decided then further testing is required to once and for all establish a Homebase.

HAIR COLOR CHANGES DUE TO LIGHT AND CHEMICALS

Even though hair is the "shortcut" way of testing for Homebase colors and gives a quick idea of nature's plans for a person's color scheme, it is easy to see......except:

- Except when the hair is an in-between color; these hair colors are marked with an asterisk in the chart below because they are balanced and can be coaxed into appearing more warm or more cool by *The Law of Attraction.*

- Except when the hair has been sun-bleached.

- Except when hair has become lightened because of permanents.

- Except when hair is very fine, therefore losing color easily.

Under these circumstances examine for new hair close to the scalp. When color is removed from hair (for whatever reason) the hair pigment colors—blue melanin, red hemoglobin and yellow carotenoid—lift out in exactly that order:

1. First, the blue dark pigment lifts out which leaves the hair "redder" looking.

2. The next pigment color to lift out is red which leaves a "brassy" yellow.

3. Then yellow lifts out leaving platinum as the very least and last "no color."

NOTE: In Nature this change of light sequence is the same. As the black sky begins to lighten blue appears, then red is introduced for a purplish hue, yellow takes over and fades back to a white-noontime "fluorescent-like" light. After noon, the color yellow then reappears and mixes with red into orange sunset colors rolling on back into blue as night comes once more. Even in sunlight we see red once again sitting in a balanced position between the two extremes of cool and warm light. When the sun is lower in the sky at sunrise or sunset, sunlight must pass sideways through a much longer and denser section of the earth's atmosphere which scatters most of the "blue" and "green" wavelengths to produce a distinctly yellow or red hue. Sunlight is also reddened by dust storms, ash from volcanic eruptions or the smoke from large fires. Red, the longest wavelength in the spectrum is prevalent and all around us.

IN-DEPTH LOOK AT HAIR COLOR

If unsure, on the following two lists find a color name that corresponds to the natural hair color. The colors that are marked with asterisks * are balanced colors and therefore are more difficult to place, but there is even more helpful information as you proceed.

COOL HAIR COLORS	WARM HAIR COLORS
stark white	yellow gray
blue gray	cream *
platinum	cornsilk yellow *
off white	golden blonde
blonde	warm blonde
pale yellow	corn yellow
flaxen *	medium sand *
ash blonde *	camel
honey blonde *	beige
pearl gray	golden chestnut
gray	warm beige
light taupe	gold
champagne *	strawberry blonde
dishwater blonde	medium brown *
mousy	rust
ash brown	copper
gray brown	redhead
dark ash brown	chestnut brown
charcoal	golden brown
salt and pepper	wine*
steel gray	auburn
dark brown *	dark wine*
very dark hair	red brown
charcoal brown	dark auburn
blue black	brown
black	dark brown *

HAIR COLOR CATEGORIES

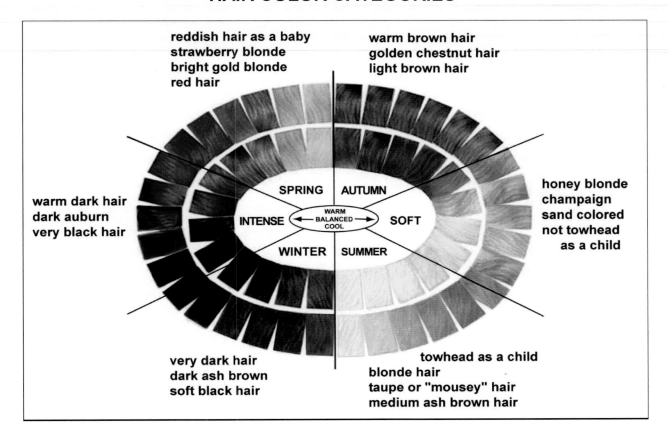

IMPORTANT DISTINCTION CONCERNING BROWN HAIR

The brown hair category is responsible for most mistakes in color analysis and has to be looked at carefully—check near the roots where color has not been lightened by sunlight or permanents. There is a vital difference between warm-brown hair (yellowed) and cool ash-brown hair (blued.) Red, blonde and black categories are obvious and easy to spot, but mistake the browns and the whole Homebase is thrown off.

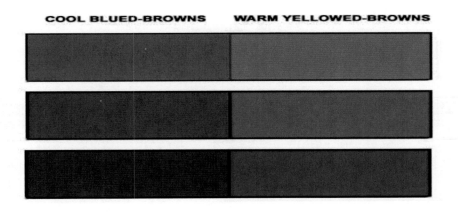

PROPERTIES OF BLUE, RED, AND YELLOW HAIR COLORS

The scientific basis of hair color is derived from the four pigments of nature: melanin, hemoglobin, carotenoid and chlorophyll. **Chlorophyll** is found in plants and used for photosynthesis—the other three pigments comprise our hair, skin and eyes illustrated by the primary colors on the color wheel. Even though a color is in the form of pigment, it is still the color of the light it reflects. Keep in mind, whenever we see color we are seeing colored light, but pigments have a special ability to absorb certain wavelengths from the light and to reflect others to the eye. The rose is red because all the other wavelengths have been absorbed by the rose except red.

For our purpose, it is helpful to understand that we have three pigment colors we work with in color analysis. If there is a problem determining whether the hair is warm or cool the following information will be helpful. Hair colors are divided into three families, each with unique properties—BLUE, RED and YELLOW.

BLUE HAIR FAMILY — darkness and coolness

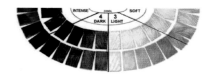

The blue pigment in hair is that which makes it cool or dark and is found on the lower half of the hair chart. Artists always color the highlights in hair blue when depicting a black-haired person. In light colored hair, it is the blue pigment which causes platinum or ash-blonde tones—otherwise the hair would be brassy looking. Ash-brown hair has a blue base.

Blue Highlights

RED HAIR FAMILY — medium value and warmth.

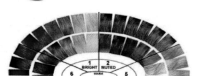

In hair color, it is the degree of red pigment showing which makes hair color warm and is found on the top half of the color chart. All hair colors carry some red tones, but if the hair has natural orangey-red tones then it is a warm color indicator indicating that warm colors are needed in the wardrobe. This will accentuate the warmth in the skintone.

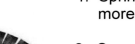 **YELLOW HAIR FAMILY** — lightness and brightness

There are two kinds of blondes:

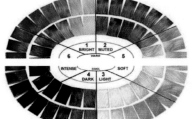

1. Spring Homebase blondes have yellow and more red pigments.

2. Summer Homebase blondes have yellow and more blue pigments.

In the lighter blonde ranges, the least degree of change in hair color can make a vast difference. Explanation: Take a can of medium or dark paint and add a good drop of green and it would not affect the overall color very much—however, that same drop of green put into a can of light yellow paint would immediately alter or sully the color. Lighter colors easily show variances.

Because the changes occur in such a subtle range, many women are unsure whether to bring out the warm gold-tones in their hair or the cool platinum-tones. A common problem when adding highlights or color to blonde hair color is the tendency for it to end up looking too "brassy." Keep in mind that yellow brightens as well as lightens color. The problem is solved by knowing the correct Homebase category.

SOLUTION: If the Homebase is on the top warm side of the oval then it will be easy to use warmer blonde highlights in the hair (platinum would pull all the blue undertones forward in the skintone and not be flattering.) If the Homebase is in the lower cool half of the oval, use ash-blonde highlights to keep hair from looking too brassy.

HINT: If the person was a towhead as a child, their skintones are warm no matter how fair their skintone appears—the Homebase is Summer and they need cool colors.

If the hair color is in the yellow, cornsilk, flaxen, honey, sand or beige range—then it's balanced and the skintone will have a degree of balance regardless of the Homebase. When hair is in this balanced category it will have to be carefully tested to determine whether the Homebase leans toward the warm side or more toward the cool side.

Because sunlight and permanents readily fade blue pigments from hair (especially fine hair) many people who have naturally cool hair think they have warm hair. New hair growth next to the scalp reveals the true hair color and is usually darker than color on the ends. Even if hair has not been altered by chemicals, people are often surprised to discover how dark their natural hair color really is. The darkest tone of the hair is the most important color because it provides contrast required for a striking look. It is necessary to evaluate brown hair carefully to establish the correct Homebase which is vital to know when building a wardrobe. If the wrong brown is chosen it throws the whole color scheme off. This is why when coloring hair it is highly recommended that hair color be kept in its own natural Homebase family. Generally, blue pigment fades out easily from hair leaving redder tones, but an ash-brown rinse or hair color will correct it.

WHITE-GRAY HAIR / CREAMY-GRAY HAIR

When people in the blue-hair family turn gray their hair turns into the most beautiful salt-and-pepper gray whites, even into startling snowy whites that are striking on both men and women. Taupe-colored hair is often referred to as "mousey" but will gray into glistening crowning highlights. It is in this

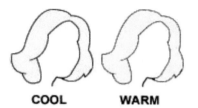

COOL   WARM

category that the dishwater or mousey-colored hair finally comes into its glory—its soft and naturally frosted effect becomes its owner's delight! By the same token, Autumn or Spring Homebased people will gray into lovely streaked creamy-grayed tones which are balanced for their cooler skintone. Nature always supports the correct balance. Careful attention to this subtle difference is important. (For warm hair, it is a big mistake to think creamy-gray is less attractive because it is not a white-gray and then mistakenly try to add blue rinses.) Wonderful gray hair can be optimized by enhancing it with frostings or soft rinses—but keep as close as possible to the natural color scheme.

THE PERSONAL COLOR TESTER

For those interested in fine-tuning, to use professionally, or for pure interest and enlightenment, The Personal Color-Tester is the ultimate color analysis tool. The flip-down color testing process exaggerates the changes of 60 basic families of colors so that the eye can definitely see differences. *The Law of Attraction* easily emphasizes

whatever color is most prevalent in the layers of skintone—the dominant color quickly comes forward. Included in the tester are 20 split testers which show the remarkable difference that combining warm or cool colors can make, and how to balance colors outside of a person's Homebase. This professional color tester is the ultimate tool for determining the exact percentage of shades and tints to highlight and enhance hair color.

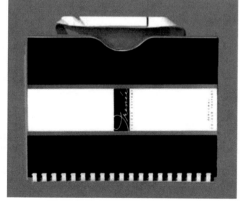

See Personal Color Tester Information online at:
www.thescienceofpersonaldress.com

BODY HAIR HELPS DETERMINE INTER-SEASON

Because blue pigment lifts from the hair so readily, the emerging red often results in incorrect conclusions regarding the amount of warmth required in a person's color scheme. One sure-fire method of double-checking to see if red is *naturally* present in the hair is to compare the color with body hair.

If the body hair is redder than the hair on the head, it indicates that colors tend toward warm; if the body hair is lighter than the hair on the head, it indicates that the colors extend into the lighter range; if it is darker than the hair on the head, the color range will include darker shades. This always holds true when checked and is an indication of the correct extended color range—darker, lighter, warmer or cooler.

HAIR-COLORING BASED ON HOMEBASE COLORS

Hair color choices can be totally flattering if sound color-theory principles are followed. The basic question is, should a person choose warmer red-tones or cooler ash-tones to color their hair. Furthermore, would they look better with streaked or frosted hair (adding lines and patterns) or be better in full intense hair color?

The characteristics of each Homebase category tells exactly what colors and lines are the most flattering. These guidelines work every time because they are based on *The Law of Attraction* and should be taken into consideration by all beauticians.

The Color Tester offered on *The Science of Personal Dress* website is of great assistance in determining the effects pertaining to correct hair color selection. The advantage is that the thick color-coated pages can be flipped down to show actual percentages of chosen colors to simulate the overall plan for color effect. The Tester includes 30 specific hair color testers plus all makeup colors. See uTube demo.

HAIR COLOR TINTS, DYES, STREAKING, FROSTING, WARMER, LIGHTER, COOLER, FULL COLOR OR VARIEGATED TREATMENTS

COLOR KEY TO CHART

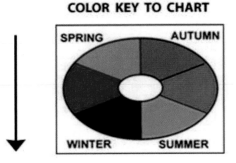

COMPLETE HAIR-COLORING GUIDE CHART

Should the hair color be warmer?		Yes, if most of the Homebase colors are on top of the oval in Spring or Autumn; then encourage or add red, gold or warm hair colors.
Should the hair color be cooler?		Yes, if most of the Homebase colors are on the bottom of the oval in Summer or Winter; encourage or add ash, platinum or cool hair colors.
Should the hair color be lighter?		Yes, if most of the Homebase colors are in Summer; then encourage lighter shades and you can add frostings or cool high-lighters for a special frosted angelic effect.
Should the hair color be darker?		Yes, if most of the Homebase colors are in Winter; then emphasize or add darker shades. Anytime there is dark contrast in the coloring, darker hair tones add striking effect.
Should the hair color be intense full color?		If most of the best colors are on the left side of the oval; then add intense full color. One dramatic accent streak is better than busy streaking or frosting and is usually natural.
Should the hair color be softly variegated		If most of the colors are on the right side of the oval; then encourage or add soft muted color or monochromatic variegated colors.
Should the hair color be frosted?		A cool platinum, bone or soft white frosting is best if the Homebase is in Summer or light colors. Monochromatic color schemes are natural to this category, so frosting light hair gives a flattering monochromatic effect.
Should the hair color be streaked?		Warm cream, sand or beige highlights are best if the Homebase is a soft Autumn. Streaking the hair with lighter highlights will give a warm patterning which is perfectly natural for this category.
What value hair color would be best?	medium med.dark dark light	The Homebase determines the value. Inter-season influence will modify colors: Winter influence goes darker; Summer influence goes lighter; Autumn influence goes more medium-dark; and Spring influence goes medium.

EYE COLOR STUDY

EYE COLORS ARRANGED IN HARMONIC SEQUENCE

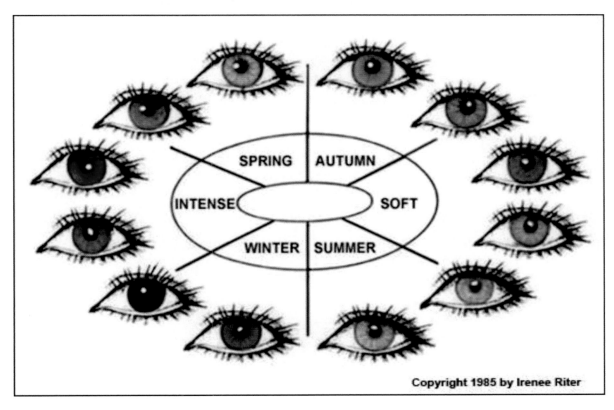

Copyright 1985 by Irenee Riter

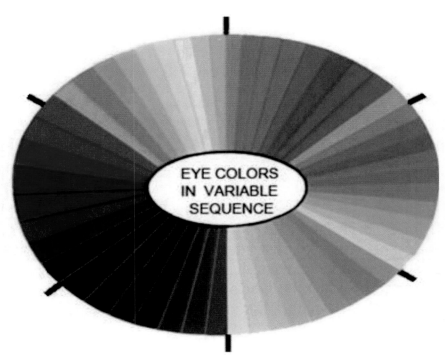

Eye colors can also be arranged in harmonic sequences of warm, cool and balanced colors. See the many variances of eye color possibilities illustrated on the chart above. Of paramount importance is the fact that a person's eye colors are the exact, precise complementary color which completes the even mix of red-yellow-blue pigments in one's overall innate color scheme. Therefore the eye color becomes a secondary basic wardrobe color because it repeats or matches the coloring. This is why it is best to not change basic eye colors when wearing contact lenses.

Eye colors vary from opaque (more like a door) to very transparent (more like a window) in appearance. Opaque eyes are matte-like—they are dusty or muted in appearance. Transparent eyes are more translucent—they are luminous and have an electric quality like "clear pools" you are able to peer into.

NOTE: We define "hazel eyes" as having the coloring of muted soft warm colors seen in autumn colors—not to be confused with dusty teal which is a balanced color in-between blue and green. This is an important distinction.

EYE COLOR CATEGORIES

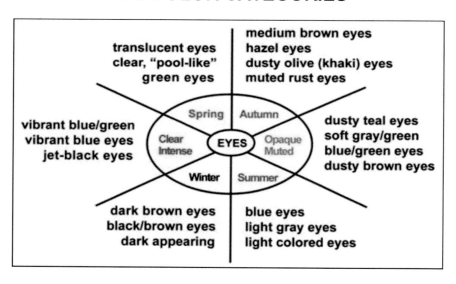

The same definitive harmonic sequence format is valid and consistent when applied to eye colors. Being able to isolate a color from one's own inherent coloring gives another color to work within the wardrobe; just that extra touch of matching and repeating an eye-color somewhere speaks volumes of intentional awareness and class. The eye color plays a key part in offering the precise color which indicates the expanded Inter-season color range—just as skin and hair colors indicate the Homebase.

SKIN COLOR STUDY

PIGMENT COLORS IN SKINTONES

The reason for this information is to explain why there has been much confusion about whether to call skin colors an undertone or overtone. This is because there are complicated elements to skintone; the thickness, thinness, weathered and sun effects, illness and age that all impact skin—so it is good to understand more about the layers.

Skin, as well as hair and eyes, also has varying proportions of red (hemoglobin,) yellow (carotenoid) and blue (melanin) pigments which color it. There are actually seven layers of skin but for our purpose we will address the three main layers of tissue which make up the skin.

Epidermis — This is the layer you see. The surface is actually composed of dead skin cells that were made at the bottom of this layer and have risen to the top. This layer is constantly making new skin. It's also making a substance called melanin which gives the skin its color.

Dermis — Nerve endings are found in this layer of skin and work with the brain and nervous system and allows the ability to feel things and react to them. The dermis is also full of blood vessels and home to oil glands.

Subcutaneous Layer — This layer is made mostly from fat which helps keep one warm and protects the body from damage and varies greatly in people. This layer is also the layer from which hair grows on the body.

EXAMPLE OF PIGMENT PERCENTAGES IN VARIOUS SKINTONES

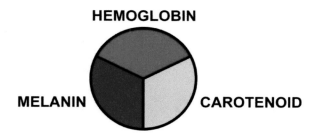

The following diagrams illustrate how dark skintones have a greater percentage of melanin, carotenoid and hemoglobin pigment color—whereas lighter skintones simply have less. Skintones: black, brown, orange, yellow, olive, beige, tan, pink, cream and white all have different percentages of blue, red and yellow pigments.

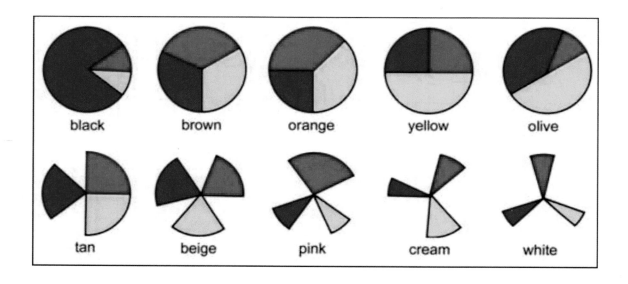

LIGHT AND DARK VALUES IN SKINTONES

light value

medium value

dark value

THICK AND THIN SKIN TYPES

The predominant pigment color in a skin always means that the complementary pigment color (the color opposite on the color wheel) is automatically less. Thus olive skin lacks red, orangey skin lacks blue, yellowed skin lacks red and blue.

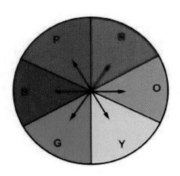

THICK SKIN

Asian, Black, Indian and Hispanic skins have more melanin pigment which tends to cover the red hemoglobin tones underneath. Olive skin falls in this group because it lacks red—the olive tone is a balanced mixture of blue and yellow (green) which gives the skin an olive cast. Sallow skintones have less blue and red (purple) therefore it shows more yellow. This thicker skin has more oil and fat in its layers therefore it has the advantage of having less tendency to wrinkle. However, extra care needs to be taken to clean the skin and hair because this skin may tend to hold body odors.

THIN SKIN

Skintones with less melanin are thinner and show more red—some, so transparent that blushing or flushing occurs from the least exertion. These thin skin people have sensitive faces and necks which can turn red even from an emotional impact, and the chest area turns red at the slightest touch. It is easy to understand why this type skin tends to freckle and sunburn so easily. If rubbing the chest turns it red, it shows a thin-skin category. Thin skin has the disadvantage of a tendency to wrinkle but the advantage of the blood flow near the surface keeping it clean and fresh smelling. And no matter what the Homebase is, it means there is a degree of Spring Influence present because the skin coloring is brighter (especially when compared with most people.)

Thick Skin

Thin Skin

SKINTONE DIAGRAM

Even though we look at hair and eye colors to get a quick take on the probable correct season Homebase, ultimately it is the skin undertone color that tells the true story. And this checks out every single time. Using the 60 page Color Tester with warm, cool and balanced colors, the undertone color can actually be seen which leaves no doubt—thereupon the person's whole color scheme unfolds revealing the complete picture. Luckily, even without the tester we know the complementary color scheme gives a big hint through the hair and eye colors, so we have a pretty good idea.

All skintones are dominantly derived from orange rather than from the other basic colors. This is a very salient fact and explains why colors affect the skin the way they do because all skintones are basically warm. As pointed out earlier, we are not working with a white wall; we are working with a warm base. Of course there are some extreme skintones that lack pigment but no one is actually white-paint white just as there are no black-paint black skins however dark—this is because the skin has seven layers of intricate design full of moving life force.

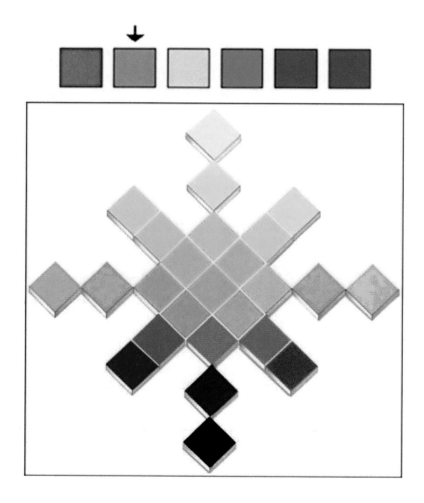

SKIN COLOR CATEGORIES AND CHARACTERISTICS

This chart will help determine into which Homebase skin characteristics fall. Afterward, the following discussion walks through the characteristics and details of each skin type.

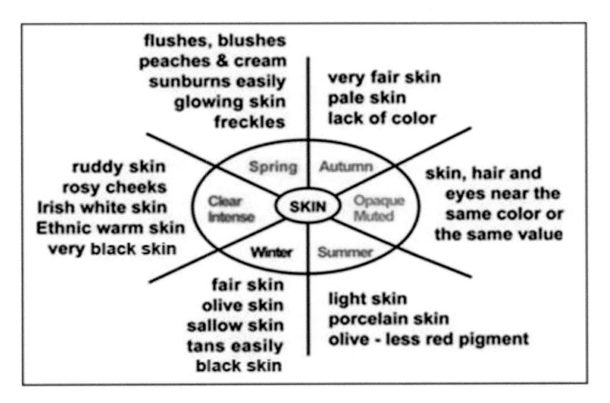

SPRING Skin Characteristics

A classic Spring has very thin skin. Because of this, high color shows easily from emotional blushing and flushing from heat or strain. The term "peaches and cream" is often used to describe this wonderful glowing skin. Very thin skin usually freckles easily which is a characteristic trait of this energy (accent and exaggerate.) If the skin is thicker then it indicates Winter Interseason influence is present. Characteristically, this skin type is extra sensitive due to thin skin and lack of oil present near the surface.

AUTUMN Skin Characteristics

A true Autumn skintone has a blue, cool undertone and lacks color. Their hair is naturally warm to bring about a balance. The warm orangey-brown Autumn colors are necessary to complete and add warmth to the skintone. If the skin has an olive cast this indicates that a Summer Inter-season influence is present.

SUMMER Skin Characteristics

Light or porcelain skin has the characteristic qualities of light Summer colors, but underneath there is the yellow undertone which actually adds vitality and energy to the skin even though the skin may look light (but it is not pale.) The olive skintone listed in this category has very little red (green olive is opposite red) therefore needs the cooled blue-pink Summer colors for balance.

WINTER Skin Characteristics

The warm-based skintones in this category have a broad range of color from very dark to fair but there is definitely a yellow undertone in the skin which needs the cooler blued-colors of the Winter category. Black skintones are rich in all the pigment colors and surprising need to be carefully tested for subtle Inter-season differences. Olive thicker-skins have less red pigments; sallow skintones have even less red and show more yellow. No matter how fair or dark the skin appears, testing will validate if the undertone is warm or cool.

BALANCED-SOFT Skin Characteristics

This balanced soft natural coloring appears to be all medium value—no extreme contrast between the skin, hair and eyes. It is Important to determine the correct Homebase first. The colors needed here are more subdued into richly mellowed, dusty or blended balanced colors.

BALANCED-CLEAR Skin Characteristics

Again, "exaggerated" rosy or ruddy skintones are Spring in feeling, but these skintones are one step down, or away, from needing the actual brightest Spring colors; therefore these skintones only need the *bluer* bright colors. The white skin, rosy cheeks and blued-eye characteristic of the Irish falls into this category. Also, the deeply colored Ethnic, Indian, black or darker skin types are undoubtedly "colorful" and need the fuller intense, bright or balanced colors found in this bejeweled category.

Comment for Dark Skin and Aging: Do not take for granted that all dark skintones are a Winter season Homebase. Yes, most of the world now has dark hair so there is Winter involved, but skin is skin and each variance means something unique to that person. It is enormously satisfying to see distinctive modifications required by each person's coloring. And by the way, a person's color scheme does not change with age; adjustments may be made because of ill health and hair color changes, but not that much—they are still better off coming from their Homebase. Use lighter values of color.

INTRODUCING INTER-SEASONS

The basic 4 Seasons provide an important foundation from which to deliberately expand one's colors into Inter-seasons. Adding colors from another season (and maybe even two seasons) is not done at random—these Inter-season colors are literally a mixture of warm and cool colors thereby creating balanced colors. What is fascinating is that one can scientifically see where the colors come from and how it all works together. These finely-tuned colors are precise, and percentage-wise mathematical.

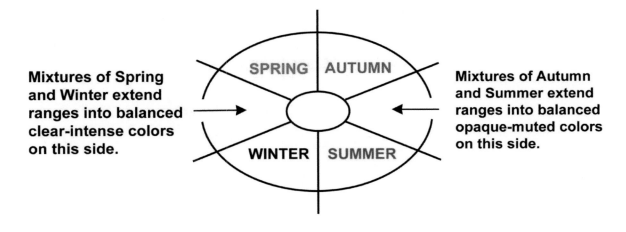

Mixtures of Spring and Winter extend ranges into balanced clear-intense colors on this side.

Mixtures of Autumn and Summer extend ranges into balanced opaque-muted colors on this side.

MIXING WARM AND COOL COLORS

Color is at its hottest at the top of the color oval and then begins to cool down as it becomes more balanced toward the middle. Color is at its coldest at the bottom of the color oval (right between Winter and Summer at the very bottom) and begins to warm up as it rises toward the middle to become balanced.

What is interesting is when two Homebase colors meet and begin mixing; they actually become balanced and can be worn by either side. But here is the trick; balanced colors have to be combined with the Homebase (discussed in-depth later.)

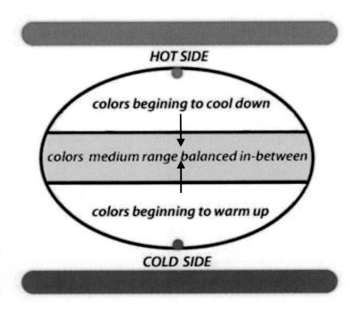

12 INTER-SEASON COLOR GROUPS

The Homebase is ultimately determined by the skintone, however many people need their colors extended by adding the influence of colors from another season. If one season appears too warm or too cool it calls for an adjustment. Therefore, the next step is to fine-tune and extend the color scheme by combining it with Inter-season colors.

This diagram shows the 4 Seasons with 12 sub-groups divided into or Inter-seasons. These 12 Inter-seasons provide color groups which can extend one's Homebase if the person's coloring calls for more warm or cool balancing from another season.

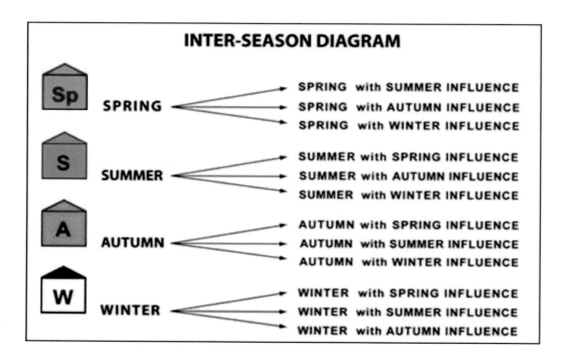

Inter-season colors are based upon energy and the characteristic traits from each season. This is determined by the person's hair and eyes (particularly eye colors) but there is much more to it—there are specific traits that can be traced to a season.

IMPORTANT: If there is one or more traits of any season present it will count as a point. No one has ever had your exact coloring...ever. It is a thrill to see how each person is like a mystery to be unraveled. People are amazed to see parts of themselves they never paid attention to, or may have even viewed as flaws, to be a unique and interesting part of their human design. This means colors can be added to extend Homebase colors which creates a unique color scheme. And this is how you become your own expert because you understand exactly what trait it comes from and why it works.

INTER-SEASON INFLUENCES

Spring Inter-season Influence is present if there is a touch of bright, exaggerated, accented or animated traits—greenish eyes, freckles are "accents," thin skin that sunburns easily, a widow's peak, vibrant colored hair, coarse hair, and glowing, bright or colorful skin.

Summer Inter-season Influence is present if there is a touch of fine, softened, curved, blended, or ethereal-like traits—anything delicate such as fine hair, wavy or curly hair, lighter eyes, lighter hair, and light or even olive skin that needs some pink added back for softening balance.

Autumn Inter-season Influence is present if there is a touch of warm, natural, busy, muted opaque traits—multicolored hair tones, warm brown or autumn colored eyes, more muted not as much contrast, and even lighter skin that needs warmth added back for balance.

Winter Inter-season Influence is present if there is a touch of contrast, symmetry and well defined coloring—dark contrast, dark appearing traits, dark hair, dark eyebrows, very white eye-whites, contrasting white teeth, and even light skin against dark hair which adds contrast.

HOMEBASE AND INTER-SEASON COLOR GROUP LAYOUTS

In the following illustrated color groups, observe how each group and sub-group have the same vibration or quality—they resonate together; bright colors are grouped together, soft blued colors are grouped together, warm muted colors together, etc.

Notice the "brightening" warm effect Spring-Influence whenever mixed or combined. Notice the "softening" cool effect of Summer-Influence whenever mixed or combined. Notice the "muting" warm effect of Autumn-Influence whenever mixed or combined. Notice the "contrasting" cool effect of Winter-Influence whenever mixed or combined.

Now it is timely to see the color layout of each Homebase color group along with its special bonus row of additional colors and subsequent Inter-season groups. If you were to go to a colorist, these are the colors you would receive.

On the following color layouts check HOMEBASE, BONUS COLORS and study INTER-SEASON color categories. How to specifically, and in great detail, combine Inter-season colors with Homebase color follows on page 88. This is an art and expertise worth taking the time to develop.

SPRING HOMEBASE COMPLETE COLOR LAYOUT
plus INTER-SEASON COLORS

SPRING COLORS
(Basic Spring colors used as foundation before Inter-season modifications)

bright red	orange red	dark coral	cherry red	watermelon	pink coral
lemon yellow	dark corn yellow	red rust	rust	straw	chartreuse
kelly green	lime green	light lime green	cream	reddish camel	forest green
bright turquoise	red violet	clear emerald	emerald green	peacock blue	blue violet
dark wine	reddish purple	purple	caramel	reddish brown	dark yellowed gray

BONUS SPRING ACCENT COLORS
(These bright jewel colors may be added and used for fashion, play and accent)

bright royal	bright lime green	bright yellow	dark hot pink	bright orange	bright violet

SPRING WITH SUMMER INFLUENCE
(Additional colors to add lighter, sherbet-like colors for delicate effect)

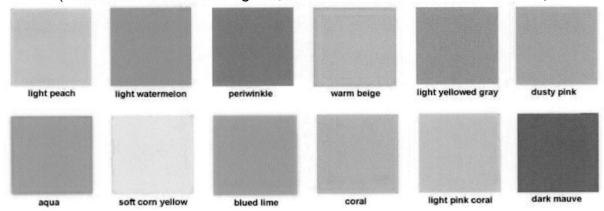

| light peach | light watermelon | periwinkle | warm beige | light yellowed gray | dusty pink |
| aqua | soft corn yellow | blued lime | coral | light pink coral | dark mauve |

SPRING WITH AUTUMN INFLUENCE
(Additional colors to modify brightness and bring in added warmth and texture)

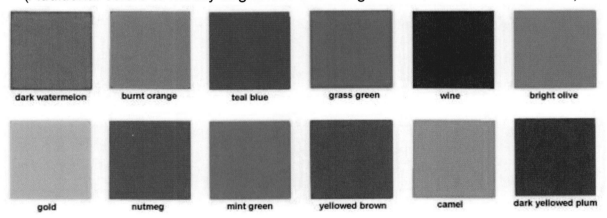

| dark watermelon | burnt orange | teal blue | grass green | wine | bright olive |
| gold | nutmeg | mint green | yellowed brown | camel | dark yellowed plum |

SPRING WITH WINTER INFLUENCE
(Additional colors to modify brightness with striking bold sophisticated contrast)

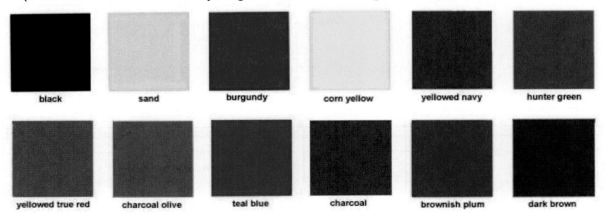

| black | sand | burgundy | corn yellow | yellowed navy | hunter green |
| yellowed true red | charcoal olive | teal blue | charcoal | brownish plum | dark brown |

SUMMER HOMEBASE COMPLETE COLOR LAYOUT
plus INTER-SEASON COLORS

SUMMER HOMEBASE COLORS
(Basic Summer colors used as foundation before Inter-season modifications)

pink	dark pink	off white or bone	dusty pink	teal	aqua
cranberry	light pink	mint green	french blue	blue	turquoise
pale yellow	soft mauve	mauve	medium purple	lavender	light blue
medium gray	light gray	plum	light periwinkle	periwinkle	grayed soft navy
light taupe	medium taupe	taupe	dark taupe	pinky beige	rose beige

BONUS SUMMER ICY CONTRAST COLORS
(These colors may be used to create contrast or monochromatic color schemes)

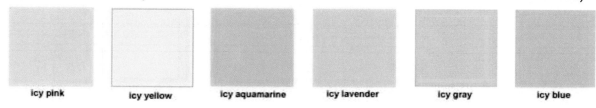

icy pink	icy yellow	icy aquamarine	icy lavender	icy gray	icy blue

SUMMER WITH SPRING INFLUENCE
(Additional colors for play and brighter glowing jewel-like exciting effects)

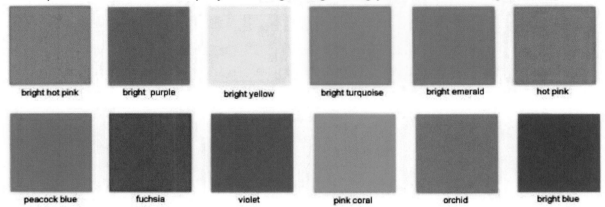

bright hot pink | bright purple | bright yellow | bright turquoise | bright emerald | hot pink

peacock blue | fuchsia | violet | pink coral | orchid | bright blue

SUMMER WITH AUTUMN INFLUENCE
(Additional colors which add warmth and richness for lovely balance)

corn yellow | dusty teal | wine | ecru | light brown | yellowed plum

light pink coral | pistachio | light dusty pink | light peach | yellowed gray | camel

SUMMER WITH WINTER INFLUENCE
(Additional colors for bold striking contrast and more sophisticated statement)

blued red | charcoal | stark white | raspberry | blued hunter green | french blue

dark plum | purple | dark ash olive | burgundy | navy blue | charcoal brown

AUTUMN HOMEBASE COMPLETE COLOR LAYOUT
plus INTER-SEASON COLORS

AUTUMN HOMEBASE COLORS
(Basic Autumn colors used as foundation before Inter-season modifications)

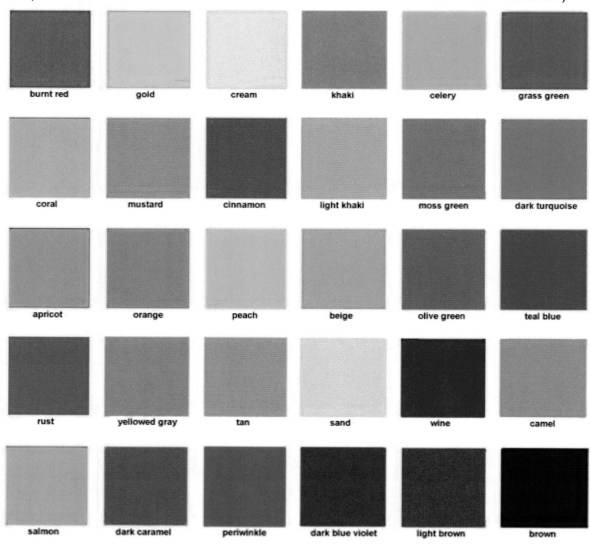

burnt red	gold	cream	khaki	celery	grass green
coral	mustard	cinnamon	light khaki	moss green	dark turquoise
apricot	orange	peach	beige	olive green	teal blue
rust	yellowed gray	tan	sand	wine	camel
salmon	dark caramel	periwinkle	dark blue violet	light brown	brown

BONUS AUTUMN SPECIAL NATURAL COLORS
(Use these balanced neutral colors generously to connect and enrich warm colors)

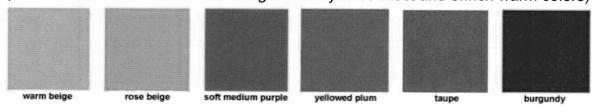

warm beige	rose beige	soft medium purple	yellowed plum	taupe	burgundy

AUTUMN WITH SPRING INFLUENCE
(Additional colors to add brighter spark of life, energy, play and fun)

| bright red | bright gold | purple | peacock blue | dark watermelon | red rust |
| pink coral | spice | dark lime green | nutmeg | bright turquoise | kelly green |

AUTUMN WITH SUMMER INFLUENCE
(Additional colors to soften, beautify and add lightness to modify muddy colors)

| dusty pink | pistachio | light yellowed gray | light peach | aqua | light periwinkle |
| dusty teal | soft corn yellow | light dusty pink | mint green | blue | light salmon |

AUTUMN WITH WINTER INFLUENCE
(Additional colors for striking contrast, sophistication and powerful statement)

| soft black | brownish plum | yellowed true red | dark wine | charcoal olive | charcoal |
| corn yellow | cordovan | soft grape | dark teal | navy | hunter green |

WINTER HOMEBASE COMPLETE COLOR LAYOUT
plus INTER-SEASON COLORS

WINTER HOMEBASE COLORS
(Basic Winter colors used as foundation before Inter-season modifications)

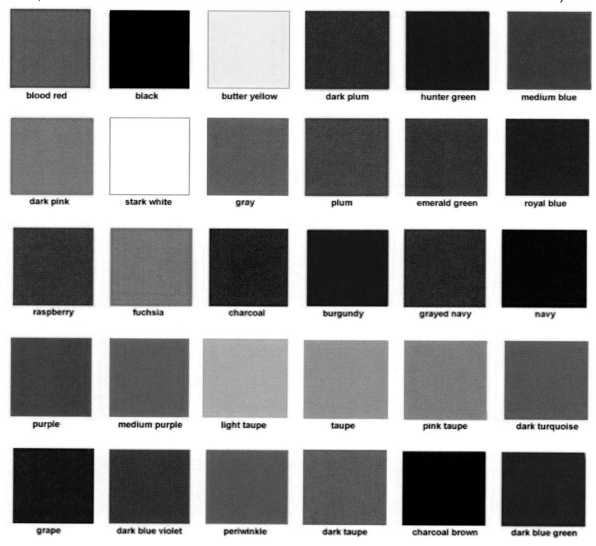

blood red	black	butter yellow	dark plum	hunter green	medium blue
dark pink	stark white	gray	plum	emerald green	royal blue
raspberry	fuchsia	charcoal	burgundy	grayed navy	navy
purple	medium purple	light taupe	taupe	pink taupe	dark turquoise
grape	dark blue violet	periwinkle	dark taupe	charcoal brown	dark blue green

BONUS WINTER ICY CONTRAST COLORS
(Add these colors to provide contrast and to set off striking light and dark effects)

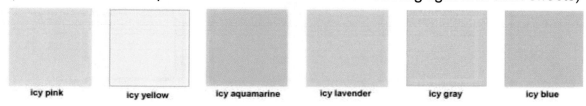

icy pink	icy yellow	icy aquamarine	icy lavender	icy gray	icy blue

WINTER WITH SPRING INFLUENCE
(Additional colors to brighten and accent with blue-based jewel-like energy glow)

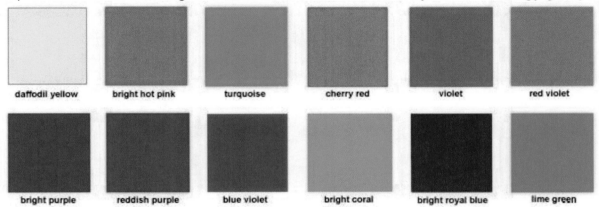

| daffodil yellow | bright hot pink | turquoise | cherry red | violet | red violet |
| bright purple | reddish purple | blue violet | bright coral | bright royal blue | lime green |

WINTER WITH SUMMER INFLUENCE
(Additional colors to soften and smoothly step into more beautiful medium contrast)

| french blue | cranberry | mauve | ash olive | dusty pink | soft hunter green |
| burgundy | light gray | pinky beige | dusty teal | soft butter yellow | soft grape |

WINTER WITH AUTUMN INFLUENCE
(Additional colors to generously enrich and add warmth for striking effect)

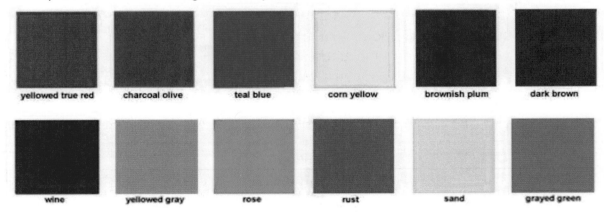

| yellowed true red | charcoal olive | teal blue | corn yellow | brownish plum | dark brown |
| wine | yellowed gray | rose | rust | sand | grayed green |

HOW TO COMBINE SPRING HOMEBASE WITH INTER-SEASONS

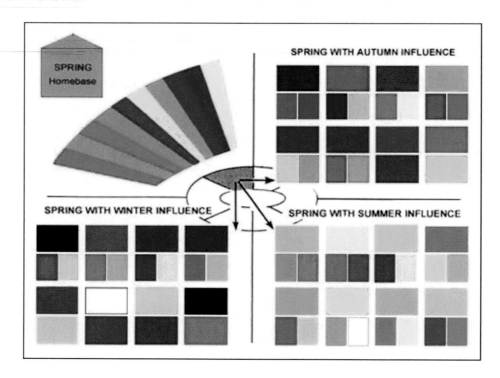

SPRING HOMEBASE WITH AUTUMN INFLUENCE

Brightest Spring colors need to be toned down and the color range extended to include the warmest Autumn colors (orange, bright olive, grass green, gold, and teal.) Emphasize color rather than contrast. Save the very brightest Spring colors (bright red, bright lime green and bright yellow) for accent, casual or evening wear. Autumn patterns are good if there are Spring accent touches of solid bright color. Stark white may be worn with hair color tones. Add some natural Autumn textures, materials and stones. Adapt and add Autumn casual lines and patterns.

ADDITIONAL COLORS: beige, gold, orange, burnt red, teal blue, bright olive, grass green, pumpkin, rust, copper, brown, khaki, blue violet.

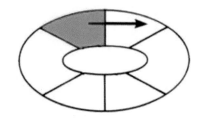

SPRING WITH AUTUMN INFLUENCE

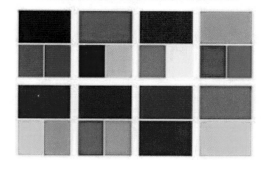

SPRING HOMEBASE WITH SUMMER INFLUENCE

Full bright color combinations are over-powering. Need larger proportions of light colors. Combine lightened "sherbet" colors with bright colors. Cool icy pastels (pink, blue, mauve, lavender, light gray) can be used if combined with a warm cream, camel, tan, brown or rust. Monochromatic color schemes and varied-color Summer blends are excellent. Wear stark white with cream or hair color tones. Gray and charcoal will offer subtle cooling effect; ash olive is superb if eye is greenish. Silver jewelry is excellent when combined with bright or sherbet colors. Adapt and add soft, delicate Summer patterns and lines.

ADDITIONAL COLORS: icy-peach, pinky coral, cornsilk, icy-yellow, icy-blued lime, icy-turquoise, aquamarine, yellowed gray, dark pink coral, lavender, dusty pink, wine.

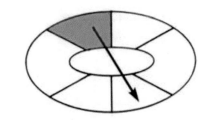

SPRING WITH SUMMER INFLUENCE

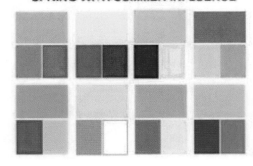

SPRING HOMEBASE WITH WINTER INFLUENCE

Dark colors need to be added to create contrast. Solid colors are emphasized (winter, yellowed-true-red, hunter green, dark teal, reddish brown, charcoal olive, cherry red.) Combine dark cool colors (black, navy, grape, and plum) with warm cream, camel or gold. Use stark white for accent and contrast with warm hair color tones. Use solid color in full dress for a more striking statement or two colors of comparable value together. Dark ash-olive is important if eye color is greenish. Cool silver-jewelry will tone down bright warm colors. Adapt the simplicity of Winter lines and patterns.

ADDITIONAL COLORS: black, yellowed navy, yellowed true red, dark brown, corn yellow, hunter green, yellowed-royal blue, dark teal, dark blood red, burgundy, cherry red, darkened pink, maroon.

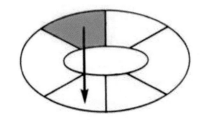

SPRING WITH WINTER INFLUENCE

HOW TO COMBINE SUMMER HOMEBASE WITH INTER-SEASONS

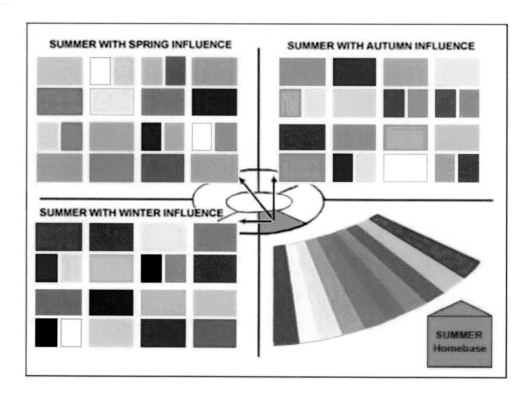

SUMMER HOMEBASE WITH SPRING INFLUENCE

Basic Summer colors are understated in this category—bright "blued" colors can be added for accent and flair. Combine light Summer colors with bright accent colors in the same hue. Bright colors combine well with light hair-color tones (bone, cream, taupe or honey colors.) Combine "icy" colors with solid bright colors. Use stark white to create dramatic contrast. Wear cream and stark white together. Dashes of black or white for accent value. Brighten lip and nail colors. May use gold and rose-gold jewelry for warmth. Adapt and add soft Spring patterns and lines.

ADDITIONAL COLORS: stark white, fuchsia, orchid, pinky coral, bright purple, violet, emerald, peacock blue, turquoise, tulip yellow, red violet, kelly-green, dark pink coral, accent cherry red.

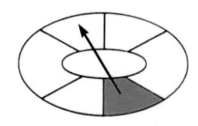

SUMMER WITH SPRING INFLUENCE

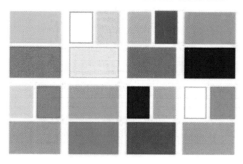

SUMMER HOMEBASE WITH AUTUMN INFLUENCE

Cool Summer colors need to be warmed and balanced.. Combine powder blue, pink, gray, cranberry, mauve or taupe with cream, ecru, camel, cornsilk or soft brown for warmth. Use one Autumn color with two Summer colors (i.e. rust with pearl-gray and silver jewelry.) Use stark white with camel or cornsilk (or hair color tones.) Charcoal is an excellent basic color. Jewelry can be rose-gold, silver set with warm stones or pearls set in gold. Dusty pink is an important color. Adapt some tailored Autumn lines and incorporate soft textures and patterns.

ADDITIONAL COLORS: cream, sand, pinky beige, cornsilk, light peach, yellowed gray, pistachio, light pinky coral, dusty teal, light camel, light brown, maroon, wheat, dusty pink.

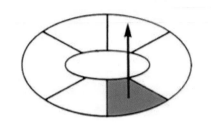

SUMMER WITH AUTUMN INFLUENCE

SUMMER HOMEBASE WITH WINTER INFLUENCE

Touch of dark contrast needs to be added to repeat person's darker contrast. Blends from light to dark are excellent. Use larger areas of light colors with small touches of dark color for contrast. Wear medium value colors for full dress (such as cranberry, French blue, medium gray.) Materials with lighter nub or white thread will soften darker colors. Use stark white instead of black to create contrast. Wear stark white with hair color tones. Adapt small Winter patterns and simplify lines for classic effect. No gold jewelry.

ADDITIONAL COLORS: stark white, charcoal, charcoal brown, soft blood red, hunter green, French blue, dusty teal, soft purple, periwinkle, pinky beige, burgundy, dusty rose.

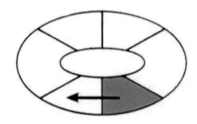

SUMMER WITH WINTER INFLUENCE

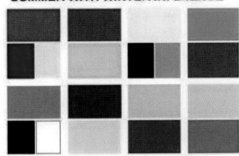

HOW TO COMBINE AUTUMN HOMEBASE WITH INTER-SEASONS

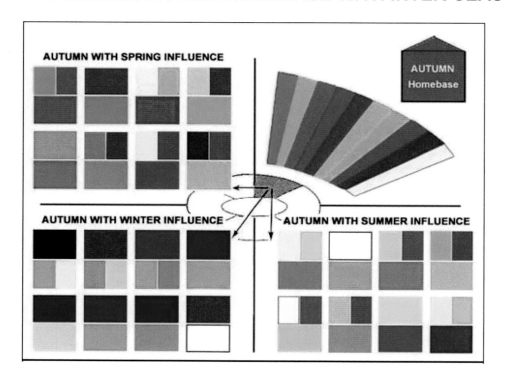

AUTUMN HOMEBASE WITH SPRING INFLUENCE

Autumn colors can be augmented with brighter color for this Inter-season blend. Can use a variety of colors in combinations for the wardrobe. Not as much extreme contrast—use warm colors closer in value (i.e. gold, emerald and purple.) Use animated patterns in muted Autumn colors, or Autumn patterns with accents of bright color. Stark white can be worn with neutral hair color tones. Add unusual pieces of jewelry in copper, brass or bright gold. Adapt Spring lines and patterns for additional flair.

ADDITIONAL COLORS: warm cream, nutmeg, corn yellow, bright gold, bright orange, melon, cherry red, red rust, dark wine, peacock blue, kelly-green, purple and reddish brown.

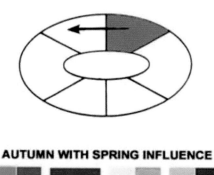

AUTUMN WITH SPRING INFLUENCE

AUTUMN HOMEBASE WITH SUMMER INFLUENCE

Lighter colors and additional pink tones are needed for this coloring. Use soft Autumn colors in monochromatic blends. Use combinations of warm and cool colors; camel can be combined with dusty pink, cream, maroon, cranberry or blue. Combine stark white with camel, brown or neutral hair color tones. Darkest charcoal substitutes for black in this category. Combine light gray with warm colors (peach, khaki, rust or brown) and use silver jewelry. Rose gold is good—no shiny bright gold. Use silver with warm colored stones. Adapt curved Summer lines and soft materials to add touch of delicate energy.

ADDITIONAL COLORS: pinky peach, cranberry, pinky beige, light coral, dusty pink, maroon, light cornsilk, aquamarine, light celery, taupe, oatmeal, pistachio, dusty teal, ecru and bone.

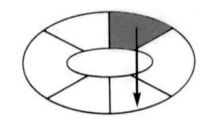

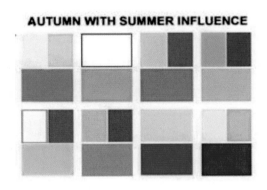

AUTUMN WITH SUMMER INFLUENCE

AUTUMN HOMEBASE WITH WINTER INFLUENCE

Dark contrast is emphasized, and solid balanced colors are important here (yellowed-true red, dark teal, hunter green.) Cool dark colors (black, navy and grape) must be combined with warm colors (cream, camel, beige, sand or tan.) Wear black or stark white with brown, charcoal-olive or rust. White gold or silver jewelry cools down warm colors. Warm stones (coral, turquoise, petrified wood) can be set in silver to create striking balance. Simplify color combinations; use only one or two colors together. Adapt classic Winter lines and patterns.

ADDITIONAL COLORS: soft black, burgundy, yellowed-true-red, soft grape, charcoal olive, browned plum, raw umber, hunter green, maroon, cornsilk, pinky beige, yellowed-navy, dusty pink.

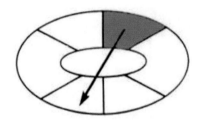

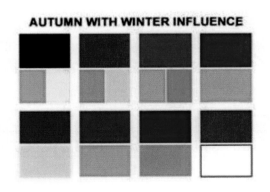

AUTUMN WITH WINTER INFLUENCE

HOW TO COMBINE WINTER COLORS WITH INTER-SEASON COLORS

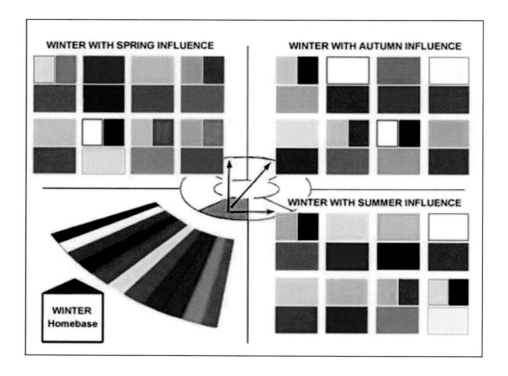

WINTER HOMEBASE WITH SPRING INFLUENCE

Dark colors used together are too cool and stark. Balance with dramatic, clear hues and "blued" bright colors (i.e. fuchsia, peacock, bright purple.) Use icy light colors to contrast darker colors of the same hue. Vibrant colors are more sophisticated when worn alone rather than mixed with other colors. Focus on one outstanding accent (bright lip and nail colors, dramatic streak in hair, or highlights from embossed silk fabrics.) Light skin types can add shiny silver jewelry; warm skin types can add some gold (warm cool comb.) Wear "jewel colors." Adapt Spring lines and patterns for flair and accent. ADDITIONAL COLORS: icy pastels, fuchsia, daffodil yellow, dark pink coral, dark hot pink, reddish purple, red violet, peacock blue, emerald green, grass green, bright blue, blue-violet, yellowed-royal blue, cherry red, accent lime green.

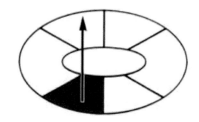

WINTER WITH SPRING INFLUENCE

WINTER HOMEBASE WITH SUMMER INFLUENCE

Darkest colors need to be toned down. According to hair color, charcoal brown or soft black may become the basic neutral color. Lighten or soften extreme cool colors (black, blood red, purple and royal blue.) Combine light with dark colors. Medium value colors such as cranberry, French blue and soft purple are better worn alone as a whole statement. Stark white will provide contrast and is good worn with hair color. Ash olive and dusty pink are excellent. No gold jewelry. Combine small pattern design with solid colors for contrast. Adapt and add soft Summer lines.

ADDITIONAL COLORS: pastels, cranberry, burgundy, dusty pink, pale yellow, pinky-beige, soft plum, dusty teal, blue, ash olive, periwinkle, medium purple, gray, taupe, charcoal brown.

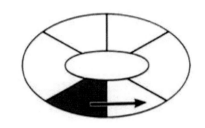

WINTER WITH SUMMER INFLUENCE

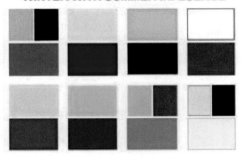

WINTER HOMEBASE WITH AUTUMN INFLUENCE

Dark cool colors (black, navy, grape) need to be balanced with cream, ecru, sand, tan, beige or camel. Charcoal brown becomes additional basic neutral color. Use solid colors (yellowed-true red, hunter green, burgundy, dark teal.) Balanced pastels (pinky peach, aquamarine, pistachio and light pink coral) are good with dark contrasting colors. Use stark white with dark brown. Rust with gray, charcoal and silver jewelry. Add natural stones (petrified wood, green-turquoise, coral) set in silver. Rose gold is excellent. Adapt some casual Autumn lines, textures and ethnic looks.

ADDITIONAL COLORS: cornsilk yellow, rose, ecru, wheat, yellowed gray, charcoal olive, teal blue, dark wine, raw umber, rust, pinky beige, sand, dusty pink, oatmeal, wheat.

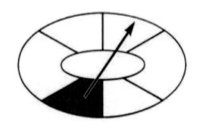

WINTER WITH AUTUMN INFLUENCE

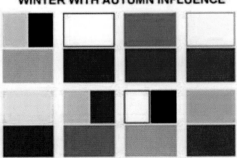

FIVE MOST COMMON INTER-SEASON GROUPS

SUMMER HOMEBASE WITH SPRING INFLUENCE

These types are more vibrant than the classic Summer. One type has thin skin which flushes easily with an electric sparkle to the eye. The medium-dark ash-brown hair types also have a touch of Winter (third Influence) and use black and white for contrast and accent. The other type is a Summer person with more color in their skin (even olive) and warmer honey-blonde hair therefore needing more color. These colors are used for color accent with light Summer colors.

A MIXTURE OF SUMMER AND SPRING COLORS

SPRING HOMEBASE WITH SUMMER INFLUENCE

This person is more fragile than the classic Spring, with Summer characteristics of blue, gray or light colored eyes. Strawberry-blonde hair person who shows more red in the skin (and probably freckles) need light colors to cool off the red "heat." Because Spring is the Homebase, the added lighter colors must be icy-balanced or warmed into more clear "sherbet" colors rather than dusty muted lights.

A MIXTURE OF SPRING AND SUMMER COLORS

SUMMER HOMEBASE WITH AUTUMN INFLUENCE
AUTUMN HOMEBASE WITH SUMMER INFLUENCE

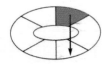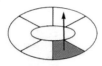

Everything about this person is medium-subtle with a mixture of soft warm/cool blends—just like the following softly balanced colors. This person's eyes are a soft brown or teal color, changing from blue to blue-green depending on the color worn. Hair colors are lighter but more subtle and blended. The hair, skin and eyes are near the same color or value (medium skin, hair and eyes) and the lesser amount of contrast requires softer blended colors. This mixture is more dusty and soft as compared to the "sherbet" quality of the Spring/Summer Inter-season mix.

A MIXTURE OF SUMMER AND AUTUMN COLORS

WINTER HOMEBASE WITH SPRING INFLUENCE

Everything about this person's coloring is more intense—just like these balanced clear colors. There are two types: one type is more colorful with ruddy or Ethnic-warm appearing skin with dark hair and jet-dark eyes. The other coloring type is more clear, vibrant and "jewel-like" as exemplified by the Irish white skin, black hair, intense blue eyes and rosy cheeks—this is dramatic striking coloring. Extremely exaggerated dark eyebrows are in this category. The person wears Winter Homebase colors and bring in jewel-like emeralds and purples to expand and accent their colors.

A MIXTURE OF WINTER AND SPRING COLORS

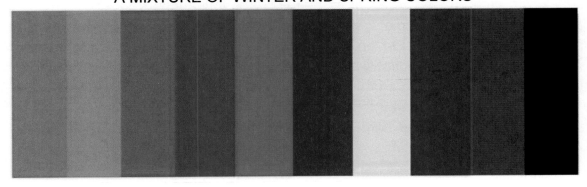

AUTUMN HOMEBASE WITH WINTER INFLUENCE Autumn person with contrast from dark eyes or darker hair need dark colors and more contrast added to their basic colors. These balanced colors will be their "best" colors. (colors pictured below)

WINTER HOMEBASE WITH AUTUMN INFLUENCE Winter Homebase person with sallow skin needs a touch of Autumn warmth added back to colors (Winter over-corrects.) Brown-haired Winter types need this touch of warmth. (colors pictured below)

SPRING HOMEBASE WITH WINTER INFLUENCE

Spring person with striking contrast. Has darker hair or dark eyes and fair skin. Adding dark balanced colors repeats needed contrast. This category is unique because when a Spring Homebase person has Winter Influence from dark eyes or hair, the addition of cool Winter colors tones down much of the brightness inherent in Spring colors. When these people gray they will gray *white* instead of the usual Spring creamy-white. Actually this is mixing warm colors with dark cool colors—thus, the same balanced darker colors apply to all three categories.

MIXTURE OF WINTER, AUTUMN AND SPRING COLORS

THE QUESTION IS...

In addition to Homebase colors, most people have influences from one or two of the other seasons. The extra colors are adjacent to their Homebase, so everyone wears some balanced colors located on the side sections of the ovals. The Questionnaire shows which way the colors flow as the range expands to include balanced colors. The major question is, to swing from the Homebase toward the left into clear intense colors or to the right into dusty soft colors.

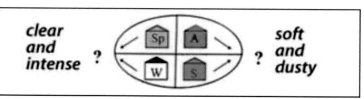

IN-DEPTH COMMENTARY ON CHARACTERISTICS

These comments are included to show the reasoning behind what led to the discovery and specificity of the characteristics of each season. The traits reoccurred over and over until we recognized a consistent pattern and the connection to a universal language of color and line.   Three Keywords summarize each category.

Spring Keywords: exaggerate, animate, accent
Autumn Keywords: natural, busy, enrich

Summer Keywords: soften, curve, blend
Winter Keywords: still, set, balanced

SPRING — Anything that is <u>exaggerated animated or accented</u>. Spring colors say all those things.   Red hair is unusual and is an accent color. Green eyes are the complementary color to red hair. Freckles are an accent. Blushing and the glowing effect of "peaches and cream" complexion comes from an abundance of red easily showing in the skin. Bushy eyebrows, extremely coarse hair or widow's peak show exaggeration. This energy has an androgynous feeling, strong lines tipping toward the colorful bright and cheery feminine aspect.

SUMMER — Anything that is <u>softened, lightened, curved or blended</u>. Summer colors say all those things and are more cool and light. Blonde hair is a light and softer color. Towheads have a sun-lightened or faded no-color effect. "Mousey" hair color comes directly from the summer taupe browns. Dimples are rounding. Curly fine hair is curved and softened. Blue eyes are light and reflect the blue underlying colors of summer. Little contrast between hair, skin and eyes is monochromatic or blended in feeling. This energy is feminine because of the beauty aspect.

AUTUMN — Anything that is <u>natural, busy or enriched</u>. Autumn colors say all those things being more natural and warm. The colors are close in value making busier pattern connections. Warm brown hair. Streaked hair adds lines and texture. No-fuss straight hair. Brown eyes, rust eyes, hazel eyes or eyes with gold in them are suggestive of patterned autumn leaves. Anything "browned" is autumn. This energy is masculine because of the strong stable aspect.

WINTER — Anything that is <u>still, set and balanced</u>. Winter colors say all those things and give an even, quiet, dark effect. Contrast is important in this category. Dark hair and light skin, or dark skin and white teeth and eye-whites give the feeling of winter white and black colors. Symmetric, medium-weight hair stays in place. Very stark white or black hair or dark eyes indicate winter influence. This energy is androgynous tipping toward the side of masculinity because of the classically sophisticated, calm, serene aspect.

SHORTCUT FORMULAS FOR DRESS

REPEAT AND SURROUND YOURSELF IN YOUR OWN COLORS

Everyone has a certain quota of colors they can surround themselves with before looking out of balance. The hair and eye colors can be considered as free because they are merely a repeat of natural coloring and are not counted—repeat them first so the color quota doesn't get used up before adding other colors for variety and fun. Being overwhelmed with too many colors cause a scrambled effect, and classic striking dress usually requires not more than 3 colors (six colors is overdoing it.)

Five special formulas provide common sense short-cuts which make dressing easy. The idea is to provide a color-bridge connecting a person to his or her clothing. These formulas give the ability to deliberately create new looks and even wear colors "outside" of the Homebase. Combining colors correctly develops awareness and style.

THE FIVE SHORTCUT FORMULAS FOR PERSONAL DRESS

FORMULA 1. Repeating Hair Colors

FORMULA 2. Repeating Eye Colors

FORMULA 3. Repeating Color Values

FORMULA 4. Repeating Contrast

FORMULA 5. Combining One, Two or Three Colors

FORMULA 1. REPEATING HAIR COLORS

HAIR COLOR FIRST CHOICE

Simple is best, and offers the most classic striking presentation across the board. A diamond is magnificent sitting on a simple black velvet background; but displayed on a busy pattern, the cut and reflections of the diamond would be diminished or obscured.

 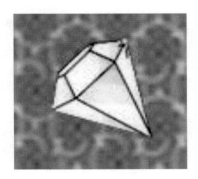

The best advice for putting together a classic wardrobe is simplicity—learning to keep dress streamlined and uncomplicated. The most direct and powerful way to accomplish this is to start by purchasing wardrobe items in colors that come from the Homebase and closely match the hair color. Repeating hair color gives a neutral color or common medium that ties the wardrobe together.

Repeating hair color, starting with shoes, gives an automatic top and bottom basic "frame." You, the center of the picture are then framed in free neutrals without added extra color—not using up the color quota leaves more choices for other possibilities. Once this is recognized the effect that is achieved from closely repeating hair color is so obvious you wonder why you didn't see it before. Think of people you know.   For example:

rust hair / red shoes
auburn hair, wine shoes
"mousey hair" / taupe shoes
sand or beige hair / tan shoes
camel colored hair / camel shoes
light blonde hair / bone shoes
light brown hair / brown shoes
dark brown hair / dark brown shoes
gray hair / charcoal shoes
white hair / white shoes
dark or black hair / black shoes

DISCONNECTED LADIES

Many people do not understand that their hair color establishes the foundation for their whole wardrobe. They disregard their own coloring and often wear clothes that make them appear "disconnected" from their ensembles as pictured below.

Keep the look simple and "uncluttered" by matching the color of shoes to the hair. Accessories purchased in hair colors will feel so natural that they will be the ones used most often (and avoids having to repeatedly change purses.)

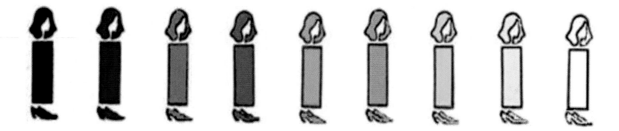

BASIC CLOTHING ITEMS SHOULD MATCH HAIR COLOR

In building a wardrobe, think in terms of repeating the hair color in at least one pair of slacks/pants, shoes, belt, sweater, wallet or purse to establish a basic foundation.

pants   shoes   belts   sweaters   purses

HAIR COLOR GUIDE FOR BASIC NEUTRAL COLORS

It may appear difficult to translate real hair into fabric or leather colors. On the following hair-color-chart choose one that is closest to the hair color.

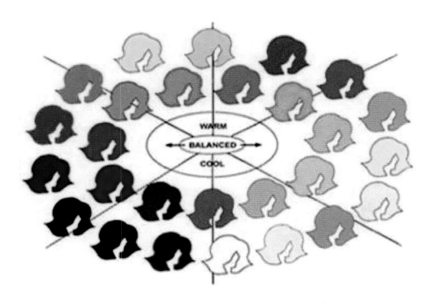

HAIR COLOR SUBSTITUTES

To imagine a particular hair color used as a basic neutral color may sound limiting. But this concept affords remarkable results. There is a wide variety of colors in the Homebase that can repeat, substitute or mimic hair color. Neutral colors include not only the exact color of the hair, but all the colors seen in the hair ranging from the darkest shadow to the lightest sun-tipped end. Look at hair color differently. See the subtle gradations of color that are actually there by looking at them exactly as they flatly project. This is easily observed in magazine photographs.

Red hair has so many warm highlights that the whole warm spectrum from red, rust, orange, brown, gold and cream act as approximate hair color repeats.

"Blondes" can have many tones in their hair, from light-colored outer hair and ends, to darker charcoal tones underneath. Even cream, tan, sand, ecru, bone and soft whites act as repeats.

HAIR COLORS REPEATED IN CLOTHING

This is not a fashion site! The photos on these pages and throughout this work are merely teaching aids presented as examples of specific concepts that can be applied to particular dress.

← This multi-colored sweater is connected to the model by the gold and red tones repeating her hair color in the weaving.

A simple belt ties the model's hair into the picture. A black belt and shoes would totally be out of balance. →

← Hair color is repeated throughout pattern in dress, and the white also acts as contrast. Taupe is part of the brown family which connects to skin color. Black shoes would finish model's look.

The red and yellow in the plaid dress repeats the model's hair color. The black also repeats the dark shadows in her hair. →

FORMULA 2. REPEATING EYE COLORS

EYE COLORS COUNTED AS SECONDARY NEUTRAL COLOR

Repeating eye colors give a magical touch to clothing combinations. This precise genetically determined trait becomes a secondary neutral color. The distinction here is that the eye color fills in and completes the three-way color scheme needed by the skin and hair for complementary balance. It is also the major indicator of the correct influence of an Inter-season—almost like a sign saying "go that-a-way."

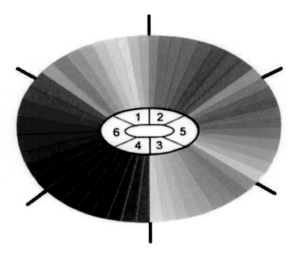

Colors that repeat that eye color are considered a match—therefore they represent secondary neutral colors and can be worn freely. Regardless of the Homebase category, whether warm or cool, it is another matching color to wear and has a valid basis being repeated in clothing.

Eye Colors Are Always Excellent Repeat Colors

GUIDELINES FOR COMBINING WARM AND COOL COLORS

The color combinations illustrated here have been combined specifically for the benefit of those people who have warm/cool coloring (warm hair-cool eyes or the opposite.) Because they are not one classic Homebase season—their coloring is not as obvious and they need to learn how to balance their colors. Understanding how to mix warm and cool colors turns a problem into a solution that works. This may seem like a vague concept at first, but be encouraged. Once people catch on to this, dressing becomes an adventure and they feel rewarded for having figured it out. It makes a dramatic difference between "so-so" dressing and consciously refined taste which is lovely.

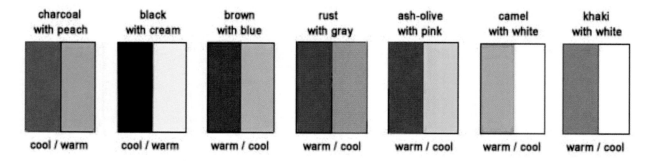

- If basically warm colors are needed but eyes are a cool blue (warm hair/cool eyes)—add cool blues and pastels and combine them with warm Homebase neutral hair colors.

- If basically cool colors and needed but eyes are warm (hazel, greenish or more rust colored)—incorporate pink-rusts, teals, peacock blues and emerald green into the wardrobe.

- If the eye color is in the <u>same</u> category as the hair (i.e. warm hair and eyes)—it emphasizes the need to wear colors in the basic Homebase category. This means that hair and eye colors are both complementary to the skintone.

- If the eye is an intense color (very blue or very green)—add intense vibrant colors which are especially good.

- If the coloring is balanced (camel hair with blue eyes or ash brown hair with green eyes)—wear more of the balanced colors. Learning to combine warm and cool colors is a great asset and produces an astute color sense of dress. This is excellent practice for dramatically increasing an awareness for all artistic endeavors.

REPEATING THE SKINTONE FOR TOUCH OF COLOR ACCENT

This may sound contradictory to the principle of wearing colors that are opposite from the skintone. But using a touch of color that repeats the skintone in a combination of best colors can sometimes add a genius stroke of style and good taste. Deliberately using skin color or tones of it as an accent color offers a clever, innovative touch.

For example, a man with dark hair and Ethnic dark warm skin can wear black and white (his Homebase colors) and have a tie that is black and white with cranberry plus a camel-color-accent in the tie that closely matches his dark skin. First, the warm skintone is balanced with cool white and black, and then the man's skintone color is repeated for a connecting accent.

POSSIBLE SKINTONE COLOR REPEATS

Warm beige, pinky-beige, camel, sand, tan, salmon, charcoal, black and white tones will often actually mimic skintones and create a subtle, well coordinated effect.

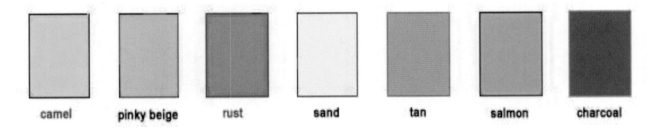

| camel | pinky beige | rust | sand | tan | salmon | charcoal |

COMMENT: To solve a wardrobe problem, immediately look for color tones in the garment that come closest to matching the hair. Then, determine how it can be repeated as part of the ensemble (i.e. in shoes or accessories.) Applying *The Law of Attraction* will surprisingly assist the process; the attractive principle emphasizes a color that is repeated elsewhere.

As a colorist, emphasize a color that is close to the person's hair color and automatically it will connect the outfit to the person making it all appear on purpose. This is a powerful tool and a shortcut to mastering a smooth overall look. Simply tying the person into the picture by not adding anything new reduces complexity, keeping everything classic, simple and connected.

FORMULA 3. REPEATING COLOR VALUES

THE VALUE OF A COLOR CAN ACT AS A COLOR REPEAT

The eye sees color as a match if it is either the <u>same shade</u> or the <u>same value</u> of a color. Subconsciously, the eye will call a color a close match if it has the same value of lightness or darkness. Generally the eye readily discerns the following nine shades of values: white, light-medium-light, medium-light, dark-medium-light, medium, light-medium-dark, medium-dark, dark-medium dark and black.

Value Scale

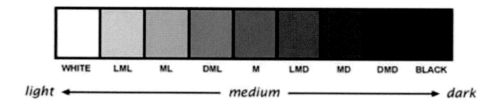

Chromatic Colors Also Have Light and Dark Contrast Values

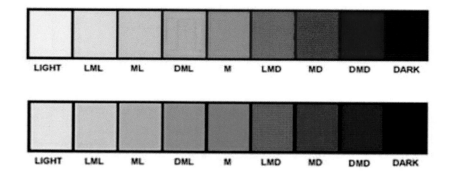

EXAMPLES OF COLOR VALUES REPEATING HAIR COLORS

There are many more colors which can be used to repeat or mimic hair color and give more flexibility to utilize. For example, lavender may not be a "literal" hair color but it appears to harmonize and repeat <u>light</u> hair as the eye scans the overall picture. Medium khaki appears as medium hair values, and navy blue appears as a dark value and substitutes for dark hair.

Light lavender is a light value color, therefore tends to repeat light colored hair.

Navy is a dark color and all very dark colors substitute for for dark dark hair.

Khaki is a medium value color and acts as a repeat color for medium hair. Khaki has the

It is helpful to understand that values are preceived a match.

same value as model's hair, therefore is a substitute hair color and is counted as a neutral "free" color. So she is really only wearing two colors.

LIGHT AND DARK VALUE PLACEMENTS

When combining colors in dress, everyone can wear light colors on the top (blouses, sweaters, shirts and jackets) with dark colors on the bottom (skirts, pants, slack sandshoes.)

For light colored hair (blonde, cream, sand, honey, beige, camel, gray or white,) one of the best looks is to reverse this and wear light colors on the bottom. The point is, light haired people can wear both light and dark colors on the bottom.

For dark haired people, if they wear a light on the bottom part of the ensemble it leaves them top-heavy—it is better for them to wear dark on the bottom which provides a dark foundation to balance with the dark hair top of their "frame."

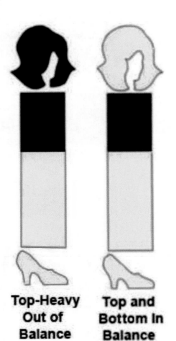

Top-Heavy Out of Balance   **Top and Bottom In Balance**

For dark haired people, dark colors should always be worn on the bottom when combined with light colors. For example, a dark navy jacket with light gray slacks is not as balanced as light jacket combined with dark slacks.

Shoes (especially boots) need to be dark on dark-haired people. As a rule, white shoes are fairly impractical for dark-haired people because they need a dark foundation.

If wearing an all-white ensemble, white shoes with black-edged soles and heels give a finished touch of dark. Follow nature's example; earth has a dark foundation and colors become lighter as they progress upward into grass, trees, sky and clouds.

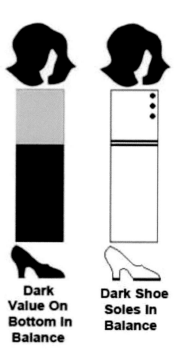

Dark Value On Bottom In Balance

Dark Shoe Soles In Balance

DARK VALUE COLOR SUBSTITUTES

For a dark-haired person, the dark values of navy, grape, brown, plum, wine or hunter can substitute and repeat their dark hair. Fabrics with dark reflections (like velvet and silk) will appear as dark hair color repeats.

| navy | grape | brown | plum | wine | hunter |

GENERAL VALUES OF THE 4 SEASON GROUPS

Summer Colors Are Lighter In Value

Spring Colors Are Medium In Value

Autumn Colors Are Medium Dark In Value

Winter Colors Are Darkest In Value

FORMULA 4. REPEATING CONTRAST

REPEATING CONTRAST KEEPS A CLEAR SHARP FOCUS

If contrast is understood it is the key to combining colors. Contrast is an effect created by very different elements such as colors, shades or textures next to each other. Much like a camera lens, a picture is out-of-focus or blurred when contrast is missing. The sharper the contrast—the sharper the image.

Each person has a given degree of contrast and it is important to repeat the degree of light and dark contrast to keep in focus. This is determined by how much contrast there is between a person's hair, skin and eyes. *The Law Of Attraction* helps define and sharpen lines if enough dark and light values are there to be accentuated. A frame should reflect the degree of contrast value of its picture.

Dark picture requires dark contrast.

Medium picture requires medium contrast.

Light picture requires less contrast.

Try to accentuate as much contrast as possible, keeping in mind that Summer Homebase coloring has a light value, Spring a medium value, Autumn a medium-dark value and Winter the darkest value. The following two photos illustrate how the missing contrast detracts from even getting a good look at the person.

BLURRED FOCUS

SHARP FOCUS

111

FINDING YOUR CONTRAST RANGE

Look at yourself in the mirror and squint your eyes a bit—now find the <u>darkest</u> shade or shadow in your hair, eyes, eyebrows or skin. Whatever expresses the darkest tone is the guide for determining how dark a contrast color can go. Everyone has contrast at least as dark as charcoal gray because everyone has gray shadows in their hair and even in the definition of their features. Dark eyebrows count as dark contrast even if the hair is lighter.

Now look for the <u>lightest</u> shade or tint in your eyes, skin or hair. A contrast range is measured by how light and dark the coloring is. Note: Even if the coloring is light, there are always gray-charcoal shadows in hair that can be repeated for contrast in dress—therefore, again, everyone can wear charcoal combined with Homebase colors.

EXAMPLES OF "MORE" CONTRAST BETWEEN HAIR AND SKIN

Both these models have a fairly wide range of contrast between their skin and hair. They both wear contrast, but for different reasons. The dark haired model in the photo to the left would wear dark colors to repeat her dark hair and light colors to lighten her skin and create striking contrast.

In the photo to the right, the brown-haired model has the same ratio of contrast but is working with the difference between a fair skin and medium-value-hair rather than medium-value-skin and dark-hair. However, this model still does have contrast between hair and skin and needs to emphasize her contrast as much as possible to keep a sharp focus. There are many "brown-haired" Winters who miss this distinction and don't repeat enough contrast (often mistakenly categorized as an Autumn.) Double check carefully for <u>dark ash brown</u> hair because this mistake could throw off the whole color scheme and the person would miss the opportunity for a more striking look.

EXAMPLES OF "LESS" CONTRAST BETWEEN HAIR AND SKIN

Both these models have a smaller range of contrast between their hair and skin. Even though they look entirely different, the model to the left (medium-dark skin and hair) has the same degree of contrast as the model on the right (fair skin and lighter hair.) The model on the left wears medium colors to repeat her hair, combined with light colors to repeat her light eyes and lift her skintone. The model on the right wears medium colors to create a degree of contrast for her eyes and light colors to repeat her fair-skin.

EXAMPLES OF SUBTLE LIGHT AND DARK CONTRAST

Even small amounts of dark contrast have to be repeated to keep a sharp focus. Dark skin and hair tends to emphasize a person's eye-whites and teeth which creates definite contrast; therefore the model on the left can wear light colors to create contrast with her dark Winter colors to enhance this striking appearance. The model to the right also has some Winter influence because of her dark eyebrows and eyes; therefore she needs light colors to repeat her light hair and a touch of dark color to repeat and emphasize her eyes. If this is missed the overall picture is understated.

HOW TO CREATE CONTRAST

 BLACK CREATES CONTRAST

Black makes other colors appear lighter. Black plays a <u>double</u> roll providing contrast (Winter) as well as creating accent (Spring.) The Winter energy is contrast. If a Winter influence is present it means a degree of contrast is needed. If black creates too much contrast (i.e. for a brown-haired Winter) use soft-black or charcoal for contrast instead. Black is also used to create a Spring accent exaggeration or animated touch when used to outline or accentuate designs. A formal, sophisticated feeling is achieved by using black to create striking contrast such as in wearing black tuxedos. If black is an outside color, combine it with a hair color repeat; if the hair color is in the warm ranges then wear warm cream or beige with black.

 WHITE CREATES CONTRAST

White makes other colors appear darker (for instance, wearing stark-white makes tanned skin appear darker.) Stark-white serves as a striking contrast for light-haired people in much the same way that black does for dark-haired people. White also serves as a bright Spring accent by creating contrast just as black creates accent—same difference except coming from the other side of the value chart. Stark-white with medium value camel shows as much contrast as black with camel; the feeling is entirely different but the contrast statement is still made. People with ruddy, hot skintones need stark-white because it cools down red or ruddy tones in the skin.

 BROWN CREATES CONTRAST

An important aspect of brown is its ability to project a casual feeling. Brown combinations are not as dressy as black combinations therefore are especially good for daytime wear. However, cool brown (taupe, gray-brown and charcoal-brown) become elegant when combined with stark-white, pearl gray, icy pink and blue plus silver jewelry. Taupe with black can be combined for a more moderate daytime look. Browns are so versatile that even if warm colors are needed (Autumn or Spring) they can be worn with white or cool pastels. Medium brown will warm these colors enough to balance them for almost everyone. NOTE: If a Homebase is Summer or Winter, be sure to wear silver jewelry with brown because *The Law Of Attraction* will surely accentuate the yellow pigments in brown if worn with yellow-gold jewelry.

LIGHT AND DARK VALUES OF THE SAME COLOR CREATE CONTRAST

Creating light and dark contrast using one color gives a smooth, classic look. For those with lighter coloring, the contrast can be softened into monochromatic color schemes using shades and tints of one color such a hunter-green, graduating to mint green on into aquamarine. This is a good example because everyone can wear this balanced color combination; it all depends on the contrast needed for the individual.

Monochromatic Dark and Light Values   **Dark and Light Values Create Contrast**

COMPLEMENTARY COLORS CREATE CONTRAST

Complementary colors create contrast because used side by side they incite each other to maximal vividness which cause them to appear brighter (i.e. colors opposite from each other on the color wheel such as red/green, blue/orange, yellow/violet.) These color combinations are effective for costumes and party clothes. Knowing how these colors work together gives another tool to use for dramatic brighter effect and creations. Notice that red and brown do create contrast when used together, but red and its complementary green not only create contrast, but bright contrast.

Red and brown create contrast, but red and green create bright maximal contrast as they are a complementary pair.

COLOR VALUES CREATE CONTRAST

Color values play different roles for different people. Medium-dark colors naturally look darker on people with light coloring. In the example below, burgundy appears dark on a blonde but becomes a medium value color on a dark person.

Burgundy is a dark value on a light person.

Burgundy is a medium value on a dark person.

SPACE CREATES CONTRAST

Use less of the color (less space) to give the appearance of the color being lighter.

Use more of the color (more space) to give the appearance of the color being darker.

More contrast or less contrast can be created by extending or limiting either the area, the space or the color. Even for light coloring, if there is a degree of contrast from dark eyes or eyebrows, then a degree of contrast can be added. Wear a smaller amount of dark color in a belt, shoe or halter top—just enough to repeat a touch of dark and give a finished look.

There is a trick to wearing dark contrast in the warm summer-months when more light colors are desired to reflect the heat; something dark can be used to repeat the contrast and reduce the space (perhaps in a sandal or bag.) In the winter-time, a light haired person can wear darker colors but use less space so that the innate light coloring is not over-whelmed.

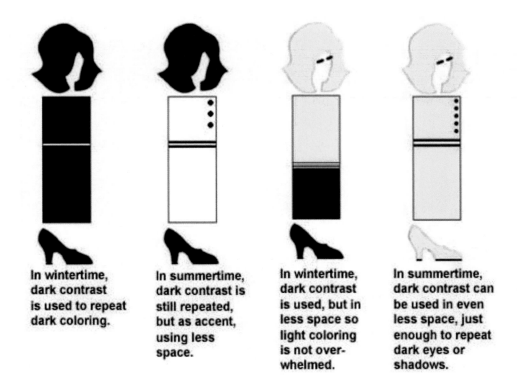

In wintertime, dark contrast is used to repeat dark coloring.

In summertime, dark contrast is still repeated, but as accent, using less space.

In wintertime, dark contrast is used, but in less space so light coloring is not over-whelmed.

In summertime, dark contrast can be used in even less space, just enough to repeat dark eyes or shadows.

HOW BLACK AND WHITE CAN CREATE CONTRAST FOR EVERYONE

In the past, it was thought that only "Winters" could wear stark-white and black. This was obviously limiting for the other seasons because everybody wants to wear black and white. The fact is, only classic Winters can wear black and white together. Other people can wear black and white if they wear them separately. The key to making black and white work, again, lies with hair color.

If a person is not a Winter, wearing black with white creates too much contrast. However, if the person combines either black or white with a color that matches their natural hair color, the combination is automatically adjusted for contrast, warmth and value—all the while providing a connecting color-bridge to the person.

The trick with black or white is to wear it with the specific color of hair. For example, a person with soft black hair needs to wear stark-white with *soft black,* not black-black. To make this work it is best to be precise.

INTERESTING FACT: People with charcoal-gray hair can wear black and white together because the eye sees the black and white colors mixed as gray for a match.

HINT: If the coloring is light and a dramatic effect is desired for evening or costume, merely add dark red lipstick and dark eye makeup for needed contrast.

STARK-WHITE AND BLACK BOTH CREATE CONTRAST

On the following chart the arrows show how the <u>range of contrast</u> for each hair color shifts when combined with black and then with white. Wearing the hair color with black or wearing the hair color with white will magically provide the right degree of contrast—this contrast principle applies to both black and white but in reverse fashion.

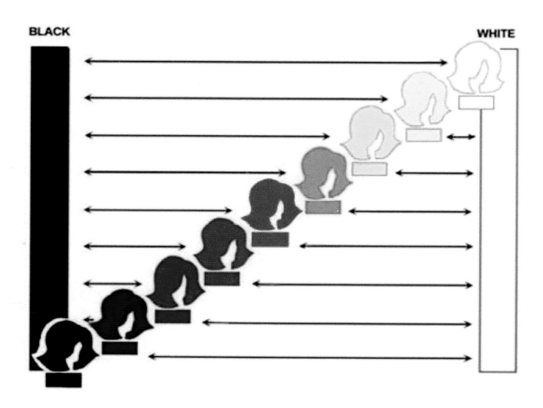

For example, if a person with rust-colored hair wears rust with stark-white the contrast is automatically adjusted perfectly; if a person with rust hair wears rust with black the contrast is also automatically adjusted perfectly.

When a person with cream-colored hair wears cream with stark-white it is a stunning combination. Reversed, that same person can wear cream with black—however, because this person has a light Homebase it might be better to wear more space in cream rather than black, but at least the cream-hair-color repeat with black will work.

This is why everyone can wear black and white—but combined so that the person's coloring is not overwhelmed by too much contrast or understated by lack of contrast. Because a person's skintones are naturally balanced with their hair, the hair color when combined in dress with black or white still works (this concept is similar to the way we handle "outside" colors.)

BROWN CREATES CONTRAST WITH STARK-WHITE OR BLACK

White "outside" color is combined with brown to repeat hair color and create needed contrast.

Black "outside" color worn with camel hair-color repeats and connects to model.

COMBINE STARK-WHITE WITH HAIR COLOR FOR CONTRAST AND BALANCE

Stark-white with hair-color combinations create perfect contrast and are very striking.

Stark-white combined with charcoal gives needed contrast. Charcoal gray substitutes for the model's dark ash-brown hair. This combination is excellent for Winter/Summer coloring.

Stark-white combined with warm coat color repeats this model's hair color, and offers striking contrast. White easily takes the place of black to create contrast.

Stark-white combined with an ash-olive colored skirt repeats value of model's hair and gives needed contrast with the white .

Common Error: Pictured below, model on the left has no repeat of her coloring (medium to light values in her outfit completely miss the contrast of her dark hair.) White with blue is a difficult color combination unless the person has blue eyes and/or white hair. Note: Flag colors (red, white and blue) are a limiting combination for everyone—there simply are not enough color connections to work with for any season category.

NOT ENOUGH CONTRAST   **BETTER CONTRAST**

CONTRAST — A MATTER OF RELATIVE DEGREE

Off-white/black has the same degree of contrast as off-black/white or dark-brown/white. This is helpful to know if you are not exactly a Classic Winter but you still need a very dark contrast. An Inter-season can be striking by using a modified degree of contrast. There are various ways to create dark and light contrast. The chart below illustrates how contrast can be adjusted.

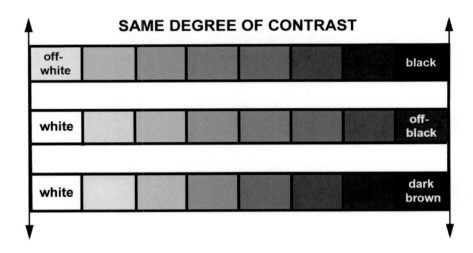

CONTRAST VALUES OF UNIVERSAL NAVY BLUE

Navy blue is a special cool color because it actually tests out to be balanced on skintones. Like the dark firmament, navy is sort of a background color for everyone as is attested to by most of the world wearing light and dark blue jeans with everything. However universal navy is, it is still a good idea to choose navy blues that have a connection with the Homebase. Very, very dark navy for Winter, brighter for Spring, modified with a touch of yellow in it for Autumn, and softened and grayed down for Summer. Navy tends to vibrate with what it is next to, much like charcoal gray. Silver or gold buttons can change the whole look of a navy garment and the color choice for top-stitching is important; rust, gold and orange stitching for warm seasons with white and plum for cool seasons. If a white thread runs through the fabric it softens the look but navy continues to be an important universal color.

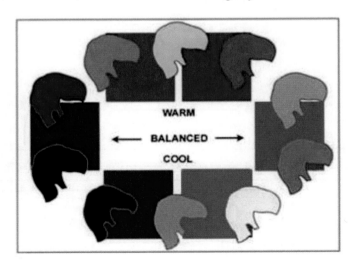

121

FORMULA 5. COMBINING ONE, TWO AND THREE COLORS

SIMPLE, CLASSIC, RICH

HAIR AND EYE COLOR REPEATS FOR PHOTOGRAPHS

As the above picture illustrates, the best photographs are simple repeats of a person's natural coloring. Hair and eye colors frame the person without distracting busyness—and good master photographers know this. Also, the choice of backgrounds for photographs is very important; balanced teals, wines, browns and charcoals are best.

A Spring or Autumn should avoid using cool blue backgrounds in photographs. Unfortunately, children's school pictures are often taken with cool blue backgrounds and then warm-haired children look pale and washed out in their photos. Keep in mind, *The Law of Attraction* brings forward pale blue tones in the skin and can also make warm hair look dull.

Using one, two, three or more colors together makes a great difference in the picture projected. Jewelry stores showcase jewelry on simple one-color backgrounds rather than on busy multi-colored backgrounds that would distract from the piece. For a party celebration, a one color setting would not carry the energy of excitement and fun. Everything vibrates and there is a time and place for a variety of expression. On the race track multi-colored combinations are eye-catching, whereas multiple colored clothing in a symphony would be a distraction when listening and focusing on the music of the orchestra (that is why musicians wear formal black.)

WEARING ONE, TWO OR THREE COLORS

ONE COLOR	Wearing one color is a Winter energy. No matter what the Homebase is, wearing one color always says classic, simple and more formal. One color allows the eye to take in the whole picture without distraction. The hair color is automatically the basic color—repeating it makes one appear more regal and poised. If the whole outfit is in one color, especially when working with a bright color, it will appear more classic.
MONOCHROMATIC	Monochromatic color is a Summer energy, meaning three or more shades or tints of one color. Wearing monochromatic color, or colors close in harmony, remains simple but the feeling becomes softened—more dressy, refined, feminine or genteel. Again, if a monochromatic scheme is a repeat of a person's hair color, no matter what season Homebase, the statement moves into singular classic expression.
TWO COLORS	Two colors are an Autumn energy. Two different colors (no matter what Homebase) begin to give the feeling of casualness. Nature puts two colors together all the time. Autumn colors have many varied shades of earth tones and give the feeling of fewer colors because they come from the same medium value family—no extreme lights or darks. Again, if one of the colors repeats the hair, the color scheme is simplified and leans toward classic energy.
THREE COLORS	Three colors are a Spring energy. Wearing more colors always express costume, exaggeration and accent. When three different colors are combined there is a feeling of fun and aliveness which evokes action and excitement. This is why costumes and party clothes have more colorful combinations. HINT: Be sure to repeat the hair color somewhere or the effect will be disconnected and scrambled.

EXAMPLES OF HOW ONE, TWO OR THREE COLORS ARE USED

It bears repeating that these photos are used to establish specific concepts—they are not intended to illustrate fashion. Because colors and lines have vibratory differences, the expression or mood can be changed merely by adding or subtracting a color or line.

Party or daytime energy. There are five colors in this dress, but six colors are counted because the model's hair color is not repeated, thus it is counted as another color. The floral pattern has busy lines which express moving, exciting energy.

Classic sophisticated energy. One color is counted here. Dark navy is a substitute for dark hair and repeats the hair color, becoming neutral. The pattern is also quiet, even-set polka-dots adding simplicity.

Four colors, actually five colors counting the model's skin color. The blue approaches the hair color and it is borderline to count as a hair color repeat.

Two colors are obvious. The hair is repeated by the white in the suit. The skin is not as obvious but could be counted as another color.

Both of the following pictures are overdone with large over-dramatized bows. However, these examples illustrate how a simple change of hair-color repeat can improve things.

On the left model, there are seven different colors counting hair and skin as two of the colors—a complicated color scheme that is disconnected because not one color ties in the coloring of the model (plus a large Keysize which overwhelms her facial features.)

On the model to the right, warm gold and copper colors in the sweater are "free" connections to her warm coloring. The color scheme becomes more simple and classic merely because the model's hair-colors are repeated.

COLORS CAN CONNECT IF SIMILAR ELEMENTS ARE PRESENT

Important: Wearing numerous colors can be done at times because there are other elements to consider which do make a connection for the overall effect:

- If the fabric is the very same weave there can be a connection made through sameness in texture-shadows such as in gauze, silk, knit or terry cloth.
- If the fabric reflects the same shine or glint as in silk, velvet and satin then there is a connection.
- If the colors have the same light or dark value there is a connection.
- If the occasion is a colorful affair then wearing more colors will add emotional content to be savored, thereby conncting to the theme of the event.

Three or four colors are connected by the same highlighted satin fabric.

Connected by monochromatic color scheme including gauze fabric and the model's coloring.

All similar earth tone colors connected by smooth medium values.

Four colors with the same values and same gauze fabric.

OUTSIDE COLORS

HOW TO WEAR COLORS "OUTSIDE" OF THE HOMEBASE

Yes, "outside" colors can be worn. When wanting to wear a different color, one outside your best range, it can easily be connected by combining it with your Homebase colors. This practical solution is why you want to have your basic shoes, slacks, jackets and suits in neutral hair and eye colors. Therefore there is a formula for how an outside color can be customized. In fact, repeating hair and eye colors will customize all outfits.

THE "OUTSIDE" COLOR RULE

Whenever you wear an outside color, be sure to connect it with two of your Homebase colors — one of them your hair color, and the other could be your eye color or your Homebase jewelry.

HAIR COLORS PLAY A MAJOR ROLL IN CONNECTING COLORS

Notice how many shades and colors are in this model's hair: gold, yellow, camel, brown and charcoal. The light and dark hair-tones set the degree of contrast needed to repeat her coloring. She is wearing a multi-colored scarf of gold, blue, purple and black. The dominant gold in her hair is repeated in the scarf which connects the color scheme of the scarf to her hair. This is a good example of how much difference one color can make—without the gold, the scarf would have a complete "outside" color scheme and would be too dark and therefore totally disconnected.

MULTI-COLORED FABRIC DESIGNS ARE EASILY CONNECTED

People with different coloring can wear the same fabric design, but connect to it in their own way. The following print offers a variety of possible hair-color connections; orange for Spring and Autumn, off-white for Summer, and white, charcoal and black for Winters.

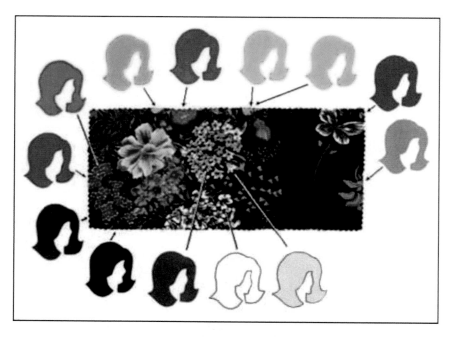

This warm fabric print can be worn by all the Homebase color categories. Spring and Autumn connect to the camel background, but the fabric also has Winter/Summer hair-color repeats. Even dark eyes and warm eyes are repeated in the geometric print.

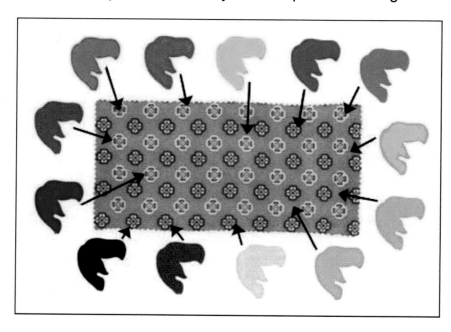

The following print is balanced with a taupe background and offers multiple Inter-season connections: brown, teal and rust for Autumn; white, taupe, rose and light teal for Summer; black, white and dark blackish-teal for Winter; wine, rust and brown for Spring coloring. Eye colors which connect include black, dark brown, dusty teal and brown.

CLOTHING CONNECTS AND DISCONNECTS

Connected: Winter and Autumn man with Summer Inter-season colors are finely tuned and repeated.

Below: Disconnected by too many colors and minimal repeat of the models' own coloring.

CONNECTED:

Pink blouse ties in highlights of brown hair. Yellow blouse ties in highlights of blond hair. Charcoal suits repeat dark shadows in hair.

←———————

———————→

DISCONNECTED:

No tie-in with hair color. (Looks like a light head sitting on a dresser or a dark block.)

DISCONNECTED:

This picture lacks contrast. Colors understate model leaving him out of focus. There is no contrast between the shirt and the shorts. Light colored belt does match skin, but dark leather would be more striking.

←———————

CONNECTED:

Good contrast. Medium value suit is contrasted with stark-white shirt and black handkerchief, buttons and shoes which brings the look back into focus.

———————→

DISCONNECTED:

Wrong colors miss the warm hair color connection. Pinky-beige is balanced but the white pulls it onto the cool side.

CONNECTED:

Glowing coloring of the model is repeated in the warm orange colors. It only takes a dash of high color to tie in a magnetic sparkle. Notice black used as Spring accent to outline and set off the design.

DISCONNECTED:

No hair color repeat. The pink, black and silver jewelry are all "outside" colors and have no connection to the model's warm hair.

CONNCECTED:
Here the embroidery has been changed to repeat and tie in the model's hair color. More attention should be taken to customize avaiable clothing.

A touch of contrast or touch of color can make all the difference. Embroidery over wrong colors, mark or paint over top-stitching, metal-paint over wrong metals, change color thread in centers of buttons, make bead necklaces to tie in colors, add color with nail polish, and even use makeup colors for accent.

DISCONNECTED:

Model to far left does not connect to blue pants when wearing white and red. Dark haired model to left lacks contrast; he has on medium values and would look more striking if he repeated dark hair.

CONNECTED:

Pants repeat model's hair for smoother look.

TOUCH OF COLOR CAN MAKE AN EASY CONNECTION

CONNECTED:
It may only take a touch of color to connect with clothing. The soft brown stripe in the sweater is enough to connect with model's hair.

CONNECTED:
Scarf carries all colors of model's hair; gray fringe connects to gray dress.

CONNECTED:

This medium gray suit is combined with a blue sweater which repeats the model's eye color. Notice this medium value gray/blue combination lacks contrast, however blue adds a strong connection. The charcoal shadows that define the lines of the suit add needed contrast.

CONNECTED:

Subtle connections are important. The color effect of model's hose perfectly match the value and color of her hair. The buttons also match and connect.

CONNECTED:
Yellow accent colors in tie repeat blonde highlights in hair. Brown colors connect to darker tones in hair.

CONNECTED:
Triple connect. Pants connect to blue eyes (brown sandals to brown hair.) Cornsilk yellow is balanced for all seasons.

DISCONNECTED LADIES...THEN SWITCHED, RE-CONNECTED AND BALANCED

Disconnected

The Earth

Connected

NO FOUNDATION

Nature shows us a pattern for comfortable balance, going from dark colored earth, medium colored grass and trees, a light blue sky and then to white clouds.

So often, women with dark hair don't realize that light shoes make them appear top-heavy, lacking a solid foundation. A dark-haired person looks better with dark shoes and boots: burgundy, wine, dark-brown navy or at least a shoe with a black sole for a finished look.

Light haired people can wear either dark <u>or</u> light colors on the bottom; light colored shoes repeat light hair, and yet darker shoes also work because they offer a good foundation. Light shoes are better for casual wear.

Men naturally wear darker shoes, and being men just need a firm foundation. Even if their Homebase is Summer, they still wear dark shoes as a matter of course. Light-haired men and white-haired men have the advantage of wearing light colored shoes for casual wear because the top and bottom of the frame match.

HOW TO WEAR YELLOW

Yellow is a difficult color to wear for two reasons. (1) *The Law of Attraction* is especially apparent when trying to combine yellow in clothing combinations. The property of yellow is readily altered—a dollop of green paint in a bucket of yellow paint it is immediately sullied. The same thing happens when yellow is combined with greens or browns in clothing making the colors appear muddy. (2) Another reason yellow is difficult to wear is because our skintones are already basically warm, and yellow accentuates the yellow in skintones. Consequently yellow is not as flattering as the pink and red tones we use for makeup and accent.

However, there are some very nice combinations that do work with yellow and give a wonderful uplift and change for a wardrobe—black, charcoal, white, navy and all blues combine well with yellow:

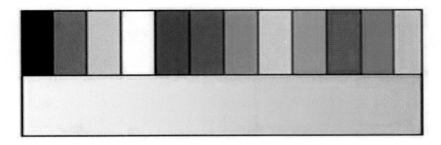

First of all, balanced cornsilk can be worn by everyone so add it to the wardrobe and wear with Homebase blues. Combine Homebase-yellow with one of the above colors: if hair is dark then combine yellow with black or navy; if it is medium in value then use charcoal or a softer navy. Yellow is very compatible with either dark or faded navy blue jeans. Let the stitching on pants be in the Homebase family; otherwise, orange, rust or gold stitching for Spring and Autumn, and white, plum or blue stitching for Summers and Winters. Since purple is the complementary to yellow, when worn together this gives a bright complementary touch.

If the eyes are blue, then yellow with blue is definitely good. If the eyes are teal then combine Homebase yellow with dark and light teals as well as turquoise and aquamarine. Autumns can wear their Homebase yellow with their hair color or colors that have the same contrast value as their hair. (pictured below)

Yellow is an excellent accent color in men's ties and patterns. Regardless of the Homebase, yellow with soft black, charcoal, gray, white or navy are good combinations. Just be sure to combine them with yellow from the Homebase category.

| Winter | Summer | Autumn | Classic Repeat |

- The Winter lady above wears black and stark-white with Homebase yellow. (For fun, cover her white sleeves with your fingers and see how the picture drops into medium value and ruins the striking black and white Winter contrast. This shows the important need for right contrast.)

- The Summer lady (top photo) wears stark-white with Homebase yellow; the Summer/Autumn lady beneath wears stark-white with balanced cornsilk yellow.

- Autumn wears gold with substitute hair colors that would mimic hair by being the same value. Special mention for Autumn is balanced cornsilk yellow.

- The young man pictured above shows the classic repeat which simply allows the eye to take in the whole picture without distraction. Highlights of the hair are repeated in the yellow sweater, and the value of the shadows in the hair is repeated by the shirt and slacks.

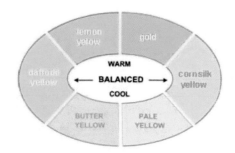

Cornsilk yellow is easy to wear by most people because it has some red in it and is balanced.

A lighter shade of cornsilk is particularly good on people.

MAKEUP COLORS IN HARMONIC SEQUENCE

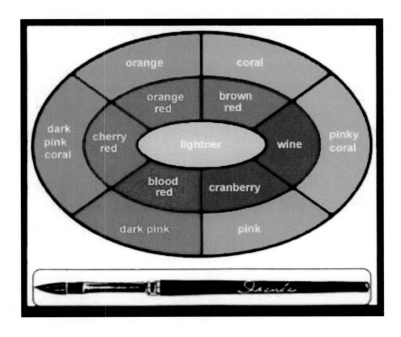

Again, lip colors have been organized into harmonic sequence which helps determine what the best lip and cheek colors are according to the Homebase; this shows the exact makeup color-recipe. Seeing the basis for this order also offers a guide for balancing makeup according to different occasions and different lighting effects.

For all the exotic names and countless shades of lip colors available, lip colors surprisingly fall into only six basic categories—yellow red, blue red, coral, pink, plum and wine. Actually, nearly any lip color can be mixed with just 4 colors: cool blue-red, warm yellow-red, brown and very light dusty pink. This 4 in 1 concept is depicted here:

BASIC LIP COLOR PALETTE

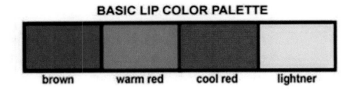

Most people do not realize how much brown is mixed into lip and cheek color formulas; it is surprising to see how brown lipsticks and cheek colors actually are when marked on a white piece of paper. And this is a good thing because the brown brings extreme reds and pinks into closer connection with skintones. Remember all skintones are coming from the orange family. (Review skintones page 74)

HOW TO ADJUST MAKEUP COLORS

When lip-color is correctly applied it portrays a small *portrait* of one's entire color scheme. This becomes a formula "recipe" and indicates the exact needed amount of contrast (dark lip color or liner,) how much warm or cool medium value is required, and tells if a touch of light is needed for uplift. Lip colors depict a complete picture of right proportions of warm-cool-light-dark and are applicable to the person's entire 10 Homebase color families. This formula is key and should be applied and repeated in combinations throughout the whole wardrobe

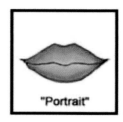

"Portrait"

In practice, if someone wears a color that is too cool for their skintone, they can add a touch of coral for warmth to their makeup and it works. If a color is too warm, then add a touch of pink. Evening light requires a more intense dramatic touch of color.

[diagram: oval labeled WARM, COOL, BALANCED, BALANCED]	**Adjust To Natural Coloring**
	Best reds and pinks are represented by the person's Homebase colors:
	    Cool skintones need warm makeup colors.
	    Warm skintones need cool makeup colors.
	    Balanced skintones need balanced colors.

[diagram: oval labeled WARM, COOL]	**Adjust To Wardrobe Colors** Wardrobe colors that are outside the basic Homebase colors can be balanced by adjusting the lip color. If a garment is too cool for the skintone, balance it with a touch of warm lip color. If a garment is too warm, balance it with a touch of cool lip color.
[diagram: oval labeled NIGHTTIME, DAYTIME]	**Adjust To Lighting Conditions** Makeup colors look different from day to night. Evening light is diffused and warm, so use colors from the left to clear and brighten. Daylight is white and cool, so use more colors from the right half of the color-oval to warm and soften the makeup. Fluorescent lighting is also cool, therefore requires warmer makeup.

[diagram: oval labeled DRAMATIC, CASUAL, DRESSY, NATURAL, FORMAL, DELICATE]	**Adjust For Various Occasions And Moods**
	    For dramatic - add clear bright red/orange
	    For casual - add brown and coral
	    For natural - add browned pinky-coral
	    For delicate - add dusty pink/cranberry
	    For formal - add blood red/dark pink
	    For dressy - add cherry red/dark coral

FOUNDATION-BASE MAKEUP COLORS

Foundation makeup should be so subtle it is not noticeable. If the skintone is balanced, match it as closely as possible. If the skin is more sallow or yellow, a cooler touch of pink- tones in the foundation will bring subtle balance; if the skintone is very cool, then the warmer color tones fill in a bit for balance. Add whatever is missing to bring the skintone into overall moderate natural balance. Otherwise, do not add *more* yellow-beige tones to an already warm skintone which would double the yellow effect. Foundation base colors should merely blend with skintones for a smoother, unblemished look.

MEN WEAR "MAKEUP" COLORS IN THEIR TIES

Women wear flattering pinks and reds in their makeup—men wear flattering pink and red accent colors in their ties and shirts. This adds healthy color to their skintones. Hopefully men will become aware of their Homebase pink and red colors and repeat them in ties as well as sweaters, shirts and in color schemes throughout their wardrobe.

WINTER	SUMMER	AUTUMN	SPRING
blood red	cranberry red	burnt red	bright red
hot pink	pink	coral	orange red
maroon	maroon	rust	rust
dusty pink	dusty pink	wine	wine
silver accent	silver accent	gold accent	gold accent

EYE SHADOW COLORS IN HARMONIC SEQUENCE

It is important to state here that charcoal gray is the basic eye shadow color for all the Homebase categories. The color gray plays a very important role in adding definition to eye contours because gray is also the color of the contours of the face and hair tones. Gray is the basic balanced eye color because complementary colors mixed together create gray. Gray tends to take on tones of whatever color it is next to—therefore it merely repeats and fills in without taking away from a classic striking appearance. Colored eye shadow can be worn in the evening or for emphasis when in costume. Notice, even though grayed down, the colors are still arranged in harmonic sequence.

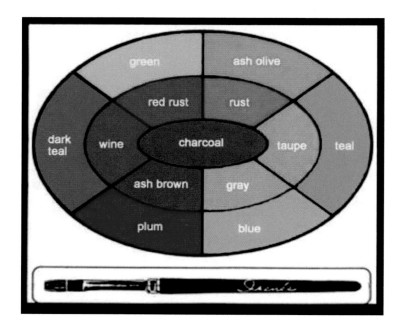

EYEBROW ALIGNMENT

The brow line sets the contours and expression of the whole face. The eyebrow line can make one look mad, unhappy, surprised, worried etc...expressions not wished to unintentionally project. Lines are powerful and can change and alter the whole feeling.

What appears to be a perpetual scowl can be erased by eliminating a few hairs or allowing a few to grow in. Follow these guidelines to redefine the natural brow line. No matter what shape the face is, these guidelines are universally classic and always work in proportion to each unique face structure. Do not underestimate how important these subtle instructions are—people are amazed when they see the results.

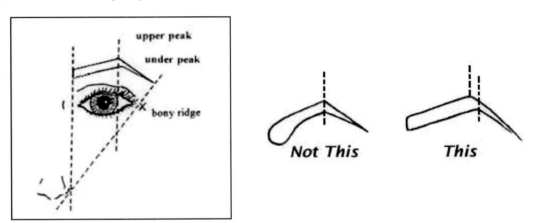

Width through the forehead is set by the upper peak on the eyebrow; consequently be sure to emphasize these peaks with a pencil if the hair in the eyebrow is very light. The turn is at the outside point of the iris—it can be further out (especially on people needing Spring colors or having exaggerated dramatic feature lines) but never closer.

The tail should be longer than usually shown in makeup books, if only by a thin line of hair or pencil. The eye needs to have a complete and natural frame (especially viewed from the side) and not end too abruptly by fly-away ends. This is important.

The eye will now be opened up and lifted by the underside peak of the brow—the under-side peak must be a little bit further out than the peak on the top side. If the upper and lower peaks turn down at the same point the eyes get a scrunched-together look. This little trick of keeping the under peak moved out makes a lovely, classic balanced brow line on everyone. Even a few hairs moved over (and out) make a big difference.

HINT: Buy a *Design* Ebony Art Pencil 14420 Jet Black Extra Smooth in an art store to trace and fill in the brow line. The pencil is not lead, it is just a soft charcoal color on the skin and if any Winter influence is present it will appear natural looking; if the pencil line is obvious then there is no Winter influence and taupe or soft brown is needed.

NO BLEACH PLEASE. People with very light hair and dark eyebrows make a big mistake bleaching their dark eyebrows lighter. This throws everything out of balance. They not only lose much of their expression but give up the one dark contrast accent to repeat in their frame for a striking appearance. There is a reason for everything, and dark eyebrows with light hair is a very unusual beautiful expression—don't ruin it!

SPECIAL RED COLOR DAY

We have discovered something interesting about what to wear when one doesn't have time to redo hair or makeup but needs to look presentable. It is nice to know a technique which can immediately remedy this using *The Law of Attraction.* Have something easy to slip into (like a jumpsuit, shift, easy dress, sweater, special T-shirt, lounging robe, blouse or velour outfit) specifically for when these times come up. But the trick is, it has to be in the most flattering Homebase red or balanced **red based color.** This will add the blush and flush of well-being-health in much the same way that adding red or pink makeup does to freshen up a look.

A burgundy or wine outfit makes skin and hair immediately take on a flattering overall connected full-color look—quickly warm and attractive. It is surprising to see what a difference just wearing a red-based color can make. Experiment with colors until the "dirty hair special" is zeroed in on by choosing from among the red and wine ranges.

JEWELRY COLORS IN HARMONIC SEQUENCE

Understanding this order helps to deliberately use jewelry to complement the colors worn. Gold and brass jewelry will make dress colors appear more yellow and warm. Silver or white-gold jewelry will make dress colors appear more blue and cool.

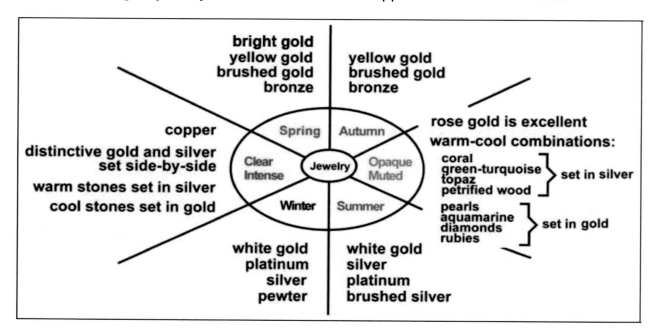

HOW TO COMBINE JEWELRY WITH HOMEBASE COLORS

Jewelry can adjust colors in much the same way as makeup—and the same rules apply. Because of *The Law of Attraction* the jewelry worn will accentuate its color in the clothing. Notice how navy, brown and red change when combined with silver as compared when combined with gold. This is how jewelry can be used to manipulate colors to advantage.

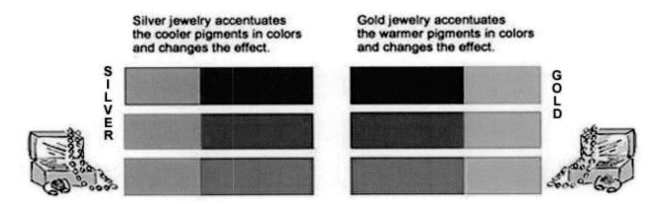

Silver jewelry accentuates the cooler pigments in colors and changes the effect.

Gold jewelry accentuates the warmer pigments in colors and changes the effect.

EXTREME COLORS OF EACH SEASON

It is important to know about extreme colors. The reason colors have been grouped into four season categories is because of a common vibration—either bright, light, muted or dark. In each category, however, there are <u>3 colors</u> which vibrate the most extreme energy of that category. Only a person who tests to be a true Classic Homebase can wear those 3 extreme colors easily. If a person tests best in most of the colors in a Homebase but these 3 extreme colors do not test well, the person automatically has Inter-season influences and must modify and balance extreme colors when worn.

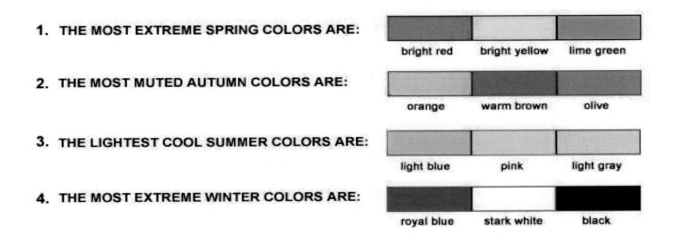

1. THE MOST EXTREME SPRING COLORS ARE:

bright red   bright yellow   lime green

2. THE MOST MUTED AUTUMN COLORS ARE:

orange   warm brown   olive

3. THE LIGHTEST COOL SUMMER COLORS ARE:

light blue   pink   light gray

4. THE MOST EXTREME WINTER COLORS ARE:

royal blue   stark white   black

HOW TO BALANCE EXTREME COLORS

There are 3 ways to modify extreme colors—with jewelry, with makeup or by combining colors.

1. Adding Inter-season Jewelry:

- If extreme Spring colors are too bright, then balance them with silver/white-gold or with warm/cool combinations; i.e. warm stones set in silver or cool stones set in gold.

- If extreme Autumn colors are too dull or muddy, then pick them up with warm stones set in silver or cool stones set in rose-gold. See suggestions on the chart previously diagramed.

- If extreme Summer colors are too cold, then warm those with rose-gold and warm/cool combinations. See suggestions on previously diagramed chart.

- If extreme Winter colors are too stark and cold then warm them with softer warm metals like pewter, rose-gold, white and rose-gold combined, copper or warm stones such as petrified wood or topaz stones set in silver.

2. Adjusting Makeup:

- Add touch of cool-pink to makeup to balance extreme Spring or Autumn.
- Add touch of warm-coral to makeup to balance extreme Summer or Winter colors.

3. Combining Colors: Warm and cool colors can balance the extreme colors.

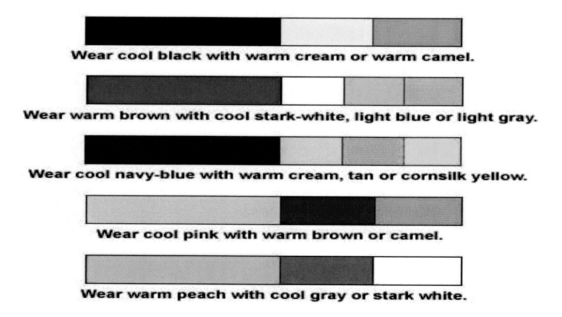

Wear cool black with warm cream or warm camel.

Wear warm brown with cool stark-white, light blue or light gray.

Wear cool navy-blue with warm cream, tan or cornsilk yellow.

Wear cool pink with warm brown or camel.

Wear warm peach with cool gray or stark white.

WOMEN'S SUITS AND COLOR COMBINATIONS

All businesswomen look wonderful in well-fitted classic suits. This is of special mention for a number of reasons. For men, suits are derivatives of the military uniform which technically is the apex of all attire being decorous, functional, dignified and perfectly cut as well as comfortable. For women and men, regardless of body type, classic suits which have set-in sleeves are the most flattering suit design for every body type

Of course in the case of women, beautifully cut blouses and accessories take the suit into another dimension of taste and femininity and goes far beyond awkward bare arms, cleavage and show of legs making one self-conscious and detracts from a beautiful classic appearance. Unfortunately, many women on television miss this vision.

And…it is all in the fitting: The sleeves have to be set at the top of the shoulder pivot; the sleeves cannot be too long (this ruins a youthful look); the skirt length has to flatter the leg line; the cut has to be according to the shape of the waist; and slacks have to have the proper darts and pleats (and most importantly no pleats for certain shapes.) A woman has to understand the lines and colors that are meant for her body type.

Along with lovely suits in a woman's neutral hair color tones, everyone can wear basic black, charcoal and navy colored suits. However, it is important to wear the right accessories and accent colors which connect the person to the outfit. Keeping accessory colors within Homebase colors will serve efficiently and distinctively without having to guess and make mistakes.

An "outside color" can be exciting for variety and to give a fresh energy, but ruined if it is not tied in properly. A light-haired Summer or Autumn Homebase person may wish to wear a Spring colored red-orange blouse; fine, but wear it with a pair of slacks in balanced honey, sand or very light camel to at least approximate a value-repeat of the hair color. Also, there are other elements that can be adjusted; the important correct fit, buttons carefully chosen to repeat Homebase color category, a touch of makeup for balance, or repeated hair-shoe match to smooth the connection.

The Law of Attraction will assist in connecting a suit if the hair and eye colors are used somewhere in the accessories. In the examples below, the three classic suit colors can be adapted for each Homebase merely by wearing blouses, tops, sweaters and scarves chosen in colors, tints and shades from the personal Homebase and Inter-season colors.

WINTER HOMEBASE

Notice the striking statement of "poise" these Winter colors make as *The Law of Attraction* connection draws forth and brings out cool color changes and adds contrast.

AUTUMN HOMEBASE

Notice the casual statement of "strength" these Autumn colors make as *The Law of Attraction* connection draws forth and brings out warmer color changes and adds medium value contrast.

SUMMER HOMEBASE

Notice the subtle statement of "beauty" these Summer colors make as *The Law of Attraction* connection draws forth and brings out cooler changes and adds light value contrast.

SPRING HOMEBASE

Notice the colorful statement of "life" these Spring colors make as *The Law of Attraction* connection draws forth and brings out warm color changes and adds bright value contrast. See **"A Description Of How Many Women Feel About Shopping"** for clothes by Joan Fabrique, businesswoman extraordinaire who shares her vision of the need for a comfortable dress formula for women on page 304 at the end of this book.

INTER-SEASON DISCUSSION ABOUT BALANCED COLORS

Balanced colors are easy to wear and test out so well on skintones that a person may limit himself or herself and not continue further on to determine a Homebase. It is important to begin from a legitimate Homebase before fine-tuning Inter-season colors. Just standing in the middle of the chart is confusing, and will leave one without a solid homebase foundation from which to even begin adjusting colors.

There is a very good reason to have a good vision by looking outward from one's Homebase. There is so much more to consider than just colors. The energy of each Homebase includes vibrating movement of color, lines, and shapes all in coherence with the season (to be aesthetically consistent so that all the separate parts fit together and add up to a harmonious or credible whole.) This gives even greater possibility of expression

If most of the best balanced colors are on the left intense-clear side of the chart, the Homebase is going to be Winter, Spring or Autumn. If most of the best balanced colors are on the right soft-opaque side then the Homebase will be Summer, Autumn or Spring. NOTE: Albeit these will call for strong Inter-season Influence colors.

Careful attention to characteristic traits will be helpful guides to establish a true Homebase. Look for traits like a sparkly eye, magnetic glow to the skin, dark eyebrows, freckles, widow's peak, low contrast, high contrast, even light eyebrows, curly hair, and thin skin. Check Questionnaire lists of traits for more clues. Everyone has a Homebase for sure. In fact, there are classic Homebase individuals who do not even wear balanced colors at all.

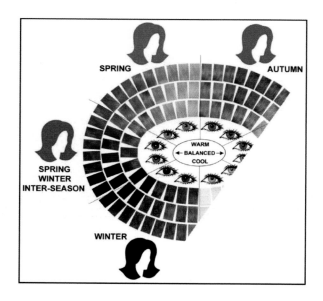 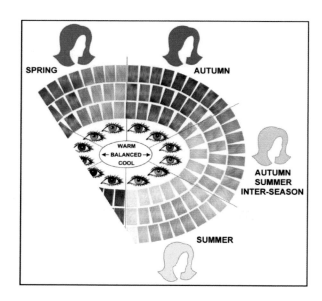

BODY SHAPES

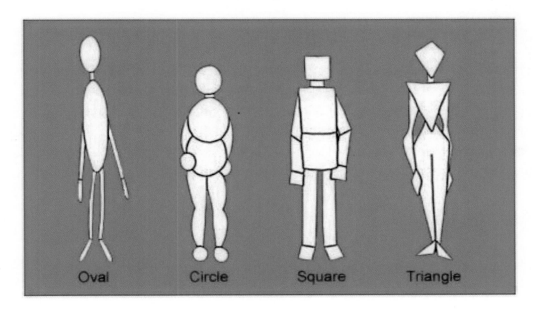

Oval   Circle   Square   Triangle

These exaggerated caricature illustrations show how people fall into 4 basic body types. This significant new concept makes it easy to choose clothing according to the shape of the body. This study shows if a person is basically an oval, circle, square or triangle body shape. And more importantly, exactly which silhouette lines of clothing are most flattering and compatible with their frame—regardless of weight or size.

BODY SHAPES TRANSLATED INTO FEMALE BODY TYPES

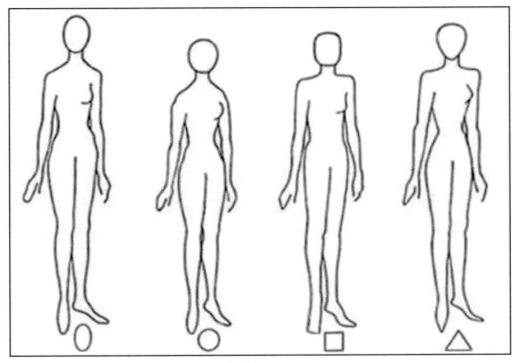

GENERAL DESCRIPTIONS OF THE 4 BASIC BODY SHAPES

OVAL STATURE LINES

This shape expresses through balance, even-set lines and equal proportions. It is centered, stately and symmetric with simple, smooth flowing lines which communicate good balance. All tall people automatically express this energy if the woman is at least 5" 7" and the man is 6' tall or over. The smaller oval figure will actually "appear" taller. This category is defined as overall well-proportioned and is more classic and sophisticated than the other body types.

CIRCLE STATURE LINES

This shape is expressed through any curved, round lines on the figure. A small-boned, short, slight or petite figure can expresses this energy, but round lines can also be robust. The figure will appear taller than it actually is if the proportions are more evenly balanced. When a person has extra weight, the figure tends to look roundish and sometimes even shorter. On the figure, the Reubenesque curve is associated with femininity.

SQUARE STATURE LINES

Type 1 This shape is expressed through any square, straight, or sturdy lines on the figure. Well-set proportions that are solid, express this strong energy. The body, neck, arms or legs are not as curved, and the body parts appear more square. **Type 2** Rectangles are taller and usually thinner and have sleek lines which bode well in modeling clothes; longer arms and legs allow classic styles.

TRIANGLE STATURE LINES

This shape is expressed through angled straight lines, points and asymmetry. **Type 1** has straighter across shoulders and angles down in a V silhouette toward a small waist and angles out again to the thighs; straight shoulders are good for modeling clothing as well. **Type 2** has broad shoulders and angles down in a V silhouette from the shoulders to the waist, and straighter past the thighs down to the ankles; the waist is not as small but the thighs are slim and do not angle out.

GEOMETRIC SHAPES FORM BODY TYPES

This chart is added to show how the body reflects the 4 basic season geometric shapes. The red lines indicate different shapes found on the body. These shapes are precise and have an impact on how we experience life.

For instance, breasts have shapes and that is why some bras fit better than others; triangle feet taper down and adapt to thongs better than other shaped feet; shoulder-strap bags keep slipping off sloping shoulders but are comfortable for square shoulders. The square and triangle heads wear hats better than oval and circle heads. It is all mathematical and makes sense upon consideration. Oval and circle planes express differently on the body than flat straight surfaces. Notice the natural form of an oval is geometrically taller than the other three forms.

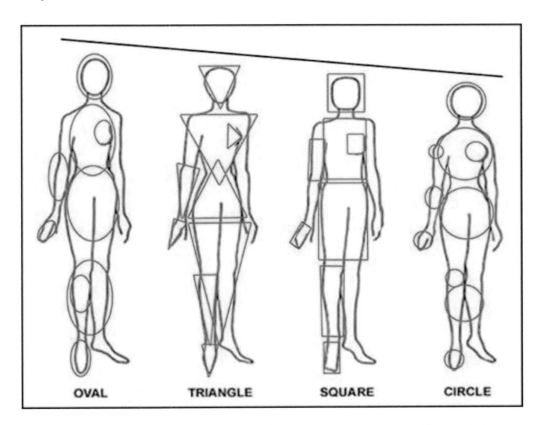

| OVAL | TRIANGLE | SQUARE | CIRCLE |

ILLUSTRATED OVERVIEW OF THE FOUR BODY SHAPES

Complicated body measurement methods fall away when better information is obtained simply from observing what shapes communicate in terms of appearance. On the following pages are illustrated diagrams of the four body shapes. Begin to distinguish the differences between the body forms by comparing the details signified by the arrows. The drawings are exaggerated to help you connect with the significance.

The Oval Body Shape
(less muscular type)

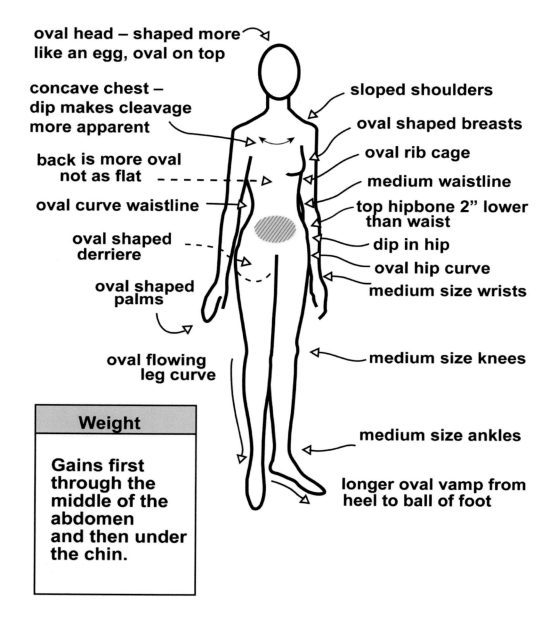

oval head – shaped more
like an egg, oval on top

concave chest –
dip makes cleavage
more apparent

back is more oval
not as flat

oval curve waistline

oval shaped
derriere

oval shaped
palms

oval flowing
leg curve

sloped shoulders

oval shaped breasts

oval rib cage

medium waistline

top hipbone 2" lower
than waist

dip in hip

oval hip curve

medium size wrists

medium size knees

medium size ankles

longer oval vamp from
heel to ball of foot

Weight
Gains first through the middle of the abdomen and then under the chin.

154

The Circle Body Shape
(less muscular type)

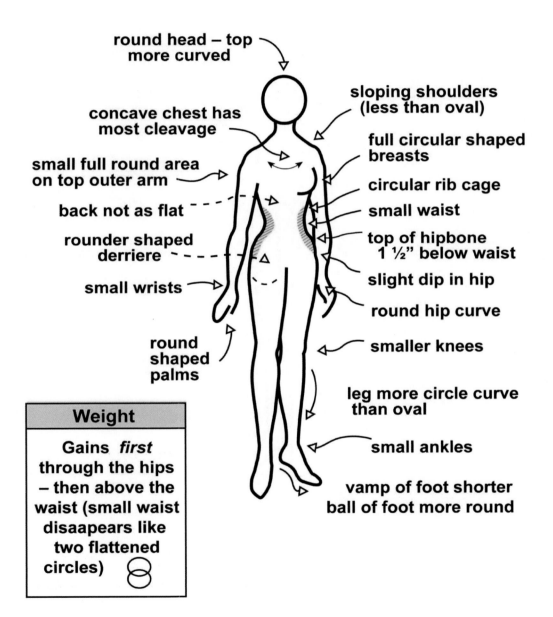

round head – top more curved

sloping shoulders (less than oval)

concave chest has most cleavage

full circular shaped breasts

small full round area on top outer arm

circular rib cage

back not as flat

small waist

rounder shaped derriere

top of hipbone 1 ½" below waist

small wrists

slight dip in hip

round hip curve

round shaped palms

smaller knees

leg more circle curve than oval

small ankles

vamp of foot shorter ball of foot more round

Weight
Gains *first* through the hips – then above the waist (small waist disaapears like two flattened circles)

The Square Body Shape
(more muscular type)

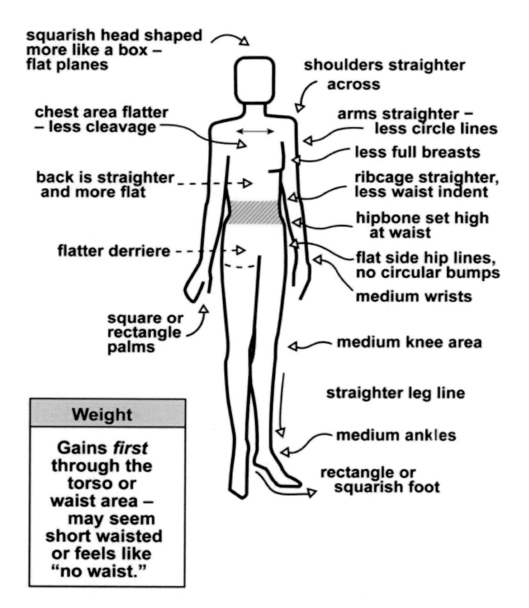

squarish head shaped more like a box – flat planes

shoulders straighter across

chest area flatter – less cleavage

arms straighter – less circle lines

less full breasts

back is straighter and more flat

ribcage straighter, less waist indent

hipbone set high at waist

flatter derriere

flat side hip lines, no circular bumps

medium wrists

square or rectangle palms

medium knee area

straighter leg line

medium ankles

rectangle or squarish foot

Weight
Gains *first* through the torso or waist area – may seem short waisted or feels like "no waist."

The Triangle Body Type
(more muscular type)

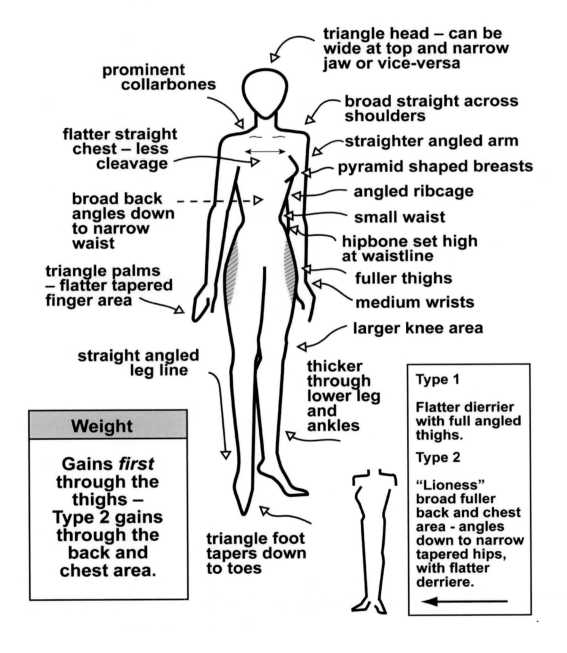

triangle head – can be wide at top and narrow jaw or vice-versa

prominent collarbones

broad straight across shoulders

flatter straight chest – less cleavage

straighter angled arm

pyramid shaped breasts

angled ribcage

broad back angles down to narrow waist

small waist

hipbone set high at waistline

triangle palms – flatter tapered finger area

fuller thighs

medium wrists

larger knee area

straight angled leg line

thicker through lower leg and ankles

Weight

Gains *first* through the thighs – Type 2 gains through the back and chest area.

triangle foot tapers down to toes

Type 1

Flatter dierrier with full angled thighs.

Type 2

"Lioness" broad fuller back and chest area - angles down to narrow tapered hips, with flatter derriere.

THERE IS NOT JUST ONE BEST BODY TYPE

There are four. It is a mistake to assume that there is an ideal body shape, and that if one loses weight or exercises they can attain the ideal. People judge themselves not understanding this. Each body type is special and has advantages which can be emphasized. This is why we make a study of body shapes—to actually see the relationships of points, lines, angles, curves, surfaces and solids. To see the way different parts geometrically fit together in relation to other characteristics of the body. Through this we see the correlation of nature's four season templates being expressed through the structure of the ever consistent universal language of line and shape.

The Position of a Line Conveys a Definite Meaning

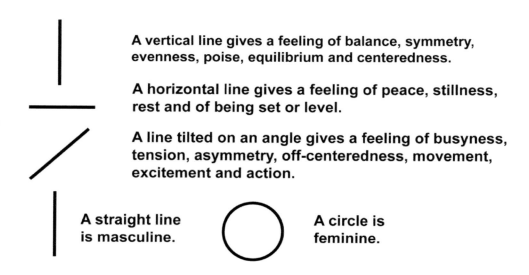

A vertical line gives a feeling of balance, symmetry, evenness, poise, equilibrium and centeredness.

A horizontal line gives a feeling of peace, stillness, rest and of being set or level.

A line tilted on an angle gives a feeling of busyness, tension, asymmetry, off-centeredness, movement, excitement and action.

A straight line is masculine.

A circle is feminine.

MALE FEMALE PERFECT "10"

There are many analogies to support the perfect 10 correlation beginning with the symbolic male straight line and female circle represented by these symbols which stand for being connected, whole and complete. Notice that the male always projects outward (yang) and the female receives inwardly (yin.) Besides the obvious sexual connotation there are all sorts of male and female fittings and adapters; screws and nuts, electrical plugs and sockets, positive and negative batteries and cables. In sports the active ball always goes into the stationary hole. In music, round feminine notes sit on masculine straight lined staffs and of course all numbers, letters, glyphs and languages are based on the line and circle. Count on consistency on this point—there are masculine and feminine associations and feelings about lines, shapes and colors.

Genders Associated With Body Shapes

Square lines are masculine, created by straight strong lines.
Square shapes are masculine because they are boxlike and grounded.

Circle lines are feminine, created by circular lines.
Circle shapes are feminine because they are softened and flowing.

Triangle lines are androgenious, masculine lines in feminine connected circle.
Triangle shapes are straight masculine lines but have an angled feminine flair.

Oval lines are andgrogenous, have feminine curves and masculine length.
Oval shapes are both female and male, curved but with straight strong stand.

A BODY TYPE CAN BE ANY SIZE

Every body type can be any size; they can be large or small, but they will still be in proportion to their specific body shape or in some cases a combination of body shapes.

The Oval template is the tallest of the figures, based on the geometric form of the oval. Examples are: Debra Winger, Celine Dion, Jerry Seinfeld, Kevin Costner, Jimmy Stewart, Prince Charles, Jon Stewart.

The Circle template is shorter geometrically: Sally Field, Barbra Streisand, Marilyn Monroe, Elizabeth Taylor, Hilary Clinton, Ethan Lane, Elvis Costello. But keep in mind there are large and small circles—Pavarotti is a large circle type.

Square types come in two types also: Type 1 is a taller rectangular type: Gwyneth Paltrow, Diane Keaton, Carrie Underwood, Paul Newman, Stephen Colbert, George Clooney. Type 2 is the shorter square stocky shape: Julia Dreyfus, Robin Williams.

Triangle types come in two template types: Type 1 is the typical in-and-out triangle form: Christy Brinkley, Shania Twain, Jane Fonda, Audrey Hepburn, Clint Eastwood, Fred Astaire, Gregory Peck. Type 2 is an inverted triangle which gives a broad breasted Lion or Lioness look: Bette Midler, Judy Garland are excellent examples.

Check out the perfect examples of the 4 classic body types on the *Seinfeld* TV Show: Jerry is an Oval, Elaine is a Square, George is a Circle and Kramer is a Triangle.

> *Seinfeld*
> TV
> Show

THE OVAL FORM IS KEY TO BODY SHAPE MEASUREMENTS

The Oval (ellipsoid) form is the basic structure or shape which is used for measuring lines and shapes. It is necessary to have knowledge of 1 INCH before recognizing what 3/4" 1½" or 2" quantifies. To understand anything there has to be a bench-mark that can be used as a measure with which to compare. The Oval shape provides a basic, medium, non-extreme standard which helps to recognize other shapes and forms—it is key to finding out what the body type is and how to dress it.

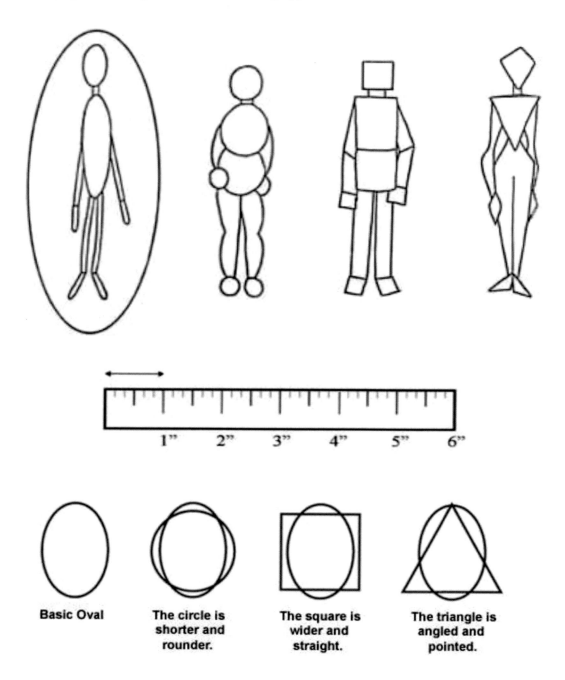

Basic Oval   The circle is   The square is   The triangle is
                    shorter and   wider and   angled and
                    rounder.   straight.   pointed.

BODY WEIGHT INDICATES BODY TYPE

Everyone can put on weight. The question here is where is the weight gain *first* noticed —where on the body is weight the first to come and the last to go. This is a big clue in determining a body type.

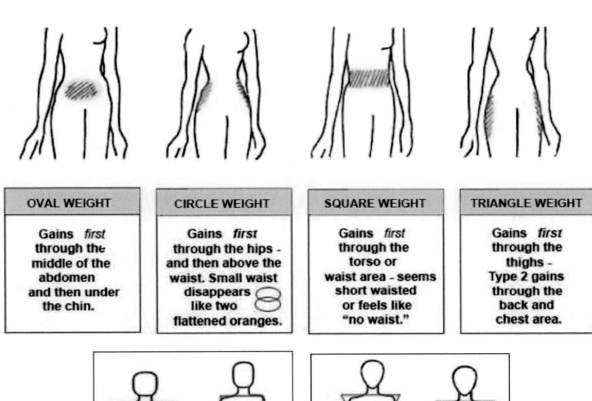

OVAL WEIGHT	CIRCLE WEIGHT	SQUARE WEIGHT	TRIANGLE WEIGHT
Gains *first* through the middle of the abdomen and then under the chin.	Gains *first* through the hips - and then above the waist. Small waist disappears like two flattened oranges.	Gains *first* through the torso or waist area - seems short waisted or feels like "no waist."	Gains *first* through the thighs - Type 2 gains through the back and chest area.

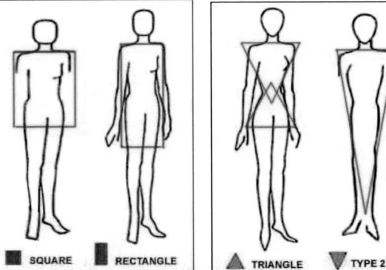

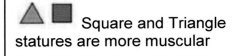 Square and Triangle statures are more muscular

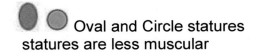 Oval and Circle statures are less muscular

COMBINATION BODY TYPES

Just as an Inter-season person needs a combination of colors from several seasons, a person may be a combination of several body types. However, all shapes are still derived from the basic 4 archetype body shapes so several clothing categories can be incorporated. This body study system is not ambiguous with terms such as "pear shape" to describe a body shape which gives no solid geometric basis for comparison. Note the specific suggestions below on how to adjust and expand clothing selections for these body combinations.

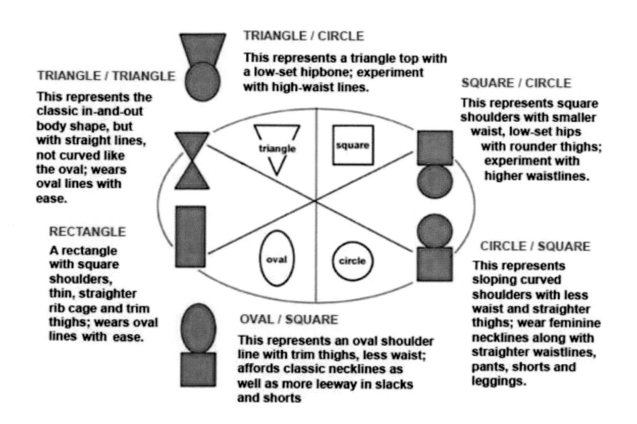

TRIANGLE / CIRCLE

This represents a triangle top with a low-set hipbone; experiment with high-waist lines.

TRIANGLE / TRIANGLE

This represents the classic in-and-out body shape, but with straight lines, not curved like the oval; wears oval lines with ease.

SQUARE / CIRCLE

This represents square shoulders with smaller waist, low-set hips with rounder thighs; experiment with higher waistlines.

RECTANGLE

A rectangle with square shoulders, thin, straighter rib cage and trim thighs; wears oval lines with ease.

CIRCLE / SQUARE

This represents sloping curved shoulders with less waist and straighter thighs; wear feminine necklines along with straighter waistlines, pants, shorts and leggings.

OVAL / SQUARE

This represents an oval shoulder line with trim thighs, less waist; affords classic necklines as well as more leeway in slacks and shorts

COMMENT: The body type drawings have been proven out to be <u>factual</u>. Notice the shoulder slope on the oval figure is more extreme than the circle. The fullness on the upper arm on the circle figure is valid. The angles on the triangle rib cage are accurate and know that the top of the hipbone is immediately at the waistline. The legs on the triangle figure suggest fullness in the lower leg and ankle area (inverted straight pyramid line.) Even hands and feet tend to follow the body form. The square body drawing reflects more of the longer lines of the square-rectangle—the actual square body shape would of course have wider, squarer cube shapes. It has been noted that triangle shoulders may not be quite as straight across as square shoulders.

CLOTHING LINES STUDY

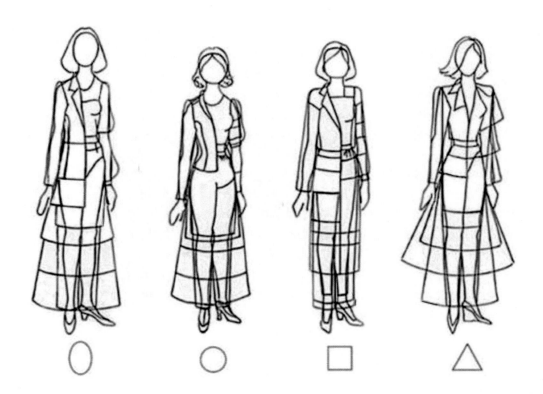

SCIENTIFIC FORMULA FOR CLOTHING LINES

There is a scientific, precise mathematical basis for each person's clothing lines. It is vital that clothing lines fit the body structure so that clothing can ride easily on the form of the frame. Right clothing lines are perhaps more important to a feeling of well-being than right colors. The feeling of things being not quite right, of having to pull the tummy in all the time, or the need to constantly re-tuck, pull-up or re-adjust clothing comes from wearing garments that do not fit the body shape. Discordant lines between the body and clothing can cause one to emotionally feel self-conscious, uncomfortable and even judgmental or unloving toward oneself.

If It Doesn't Feel Right…It Isn't!

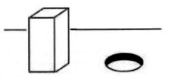

Favorite clothes are flattering because they are right for the shape of the body. It makes sense that round flowing bodies require softer flowing fabrics, and angled or straight bodies can handle crisp, stiff fabrics. When the shape of clothing matches the shape of the body, clothing will ride easy and naturally on the form. No time is wasted trying to *fit a square peg into a round hole!*

DISCORDANT LINES CAN BE FELT

We know when we have had a bad haircut...we feel it! The lines were unflattering because they were out of balance. The same thing happens with clothing. We all know that some clothing makes us feel better than others—like a favorite pair of jeans. Repeatedly changing clothes in an effort to "decide what to wear" is actually the process of eliminating discordant lines until one feels good. This is an attempt to adjust clothing lines, working to get the right balance, often not knowing what causes the difference. This knowledge stops the guessing and deliberately creates right lines.

These concepts make sense. Women with square body shapes often have a dilemma finding wedding dresses—most wedding dresses are made for tiny little waists. Circle types have a hard time finding casual clothes because easy-to-wear, unfitted or loose styles are for square/rectangle bodies. When sewing, it is hard to find patterns for oval and circle bodies; they are not readily available because of the detailed fitting that is required. Classic Triangle bodies have a body shape that can wear most lines and shopping is not a problem. The other body types have a harder time finding clothing that fit their body shape. This new paradigm of information helps us feel good about our bodies, because we understand which clothing lines are most flattering.

THE SAME 4 UNIVERSAL SHAPES CREATE CLOTHING LINES

Just as there are four basic color schemes in nature, there are also four basic shapes —the triangle, the circle, the square and the oval. In art there is a co-esthetic relationship between color and line. The same principles apply equally to color and line.

Shapes are associated with season, color, form and gender: The square is clearly masculine with straight grounded lines, the circle is feminine with curved circular lines, the triangle and oval are androgynous mixtures—the triangle has straight lines with feminine angled flair, and the oval has a feminine curved line with an upright masculine stance.

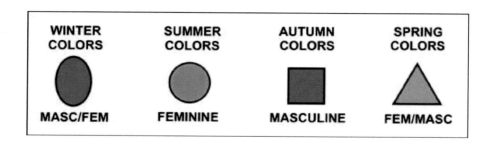

ARTISTIC HINT: It is easier to see shapes in clothing than to learn complicated measuring systems—art students learn proportion by looking at shapes <u>between</u> lines as well as the actual line. Compare the four shapes on the following exaggerated dress caricatures:

- Oval shapes tend to give a classic look
- Round or circular shapes tend to give a youthful, ultra feminine
- Square shapes tend to give a tailored, casual look
- Angled triangular shapes tend to give a flared, exaggerated look

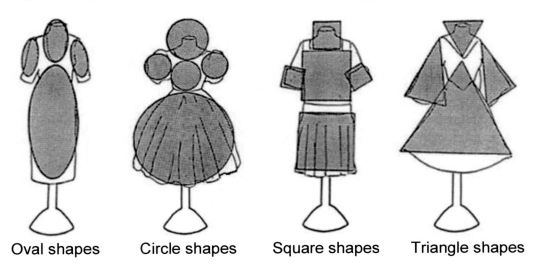

| Oval shapes | Circle shapes | Square shapes | Triangle shapes |

SILHOUETTE LINES

There are two kinds of clothing lines—the "outside" shape and the "inside" detail lines. A clothing silhouette is the actual outline clothing makes after one is dressed. The inside lines are the detail lines like buttons, pleats, pockets, collars etc.

Full Dress

Dress Silhouette
(outside lines)

Dress Details
(inside lines)

NEW CONCEPT FOR MEASURING BODY AND CLOTHING LINES

The concept now presented, impacts the feeling of well being more than any other aspect relating to appearance. The torso area dictates what lines fit the body shape. We are not concerned about large or small bones or conventional body measurements. All we care about is how clothes are going to fit the middle of the body. And this is important because this area affects 80% of all clothing choices and problems therein. Circles and squares do not match! The shape of this area determines the type of belts, waistbands and straight or fitted clothing lines. Below, note the 4 basic torso types and the lines they require. The black bathing suits highlight the different body shapes, and show how each fit into their own unique line.

GUIDING RULE FOR WAIST LINES

OVAL BODY
Needs fitted body lines - a skimming (but not skimpy) outside line.

CIRCLE BODY
Needs a fitted top and a slightly eased outside line below the waistline.

SQUARE BODY
Needs a straighter line - a more straight up and down outside line.

TRIANGLE BODY
Needs an angled outside line - a line that goes in or out below the bustline.

SENSUALITY EXPRESSED THROUGH "OUTSIDE" SILHOUETTE

The silhouette line, the outline shape of clothing, makes all the difference in feeling attractive and appealing. This applies to any stage of weight gain or loss—the outside line for a body type or shape will always remain constant. Sensuality is part of life and should not to be overlooked, but certainly not made so obvious that it makes an uncomfortable scene. Femininity in a classic mode of beauty is a delight. Remember, curves express the "0" part of the Perfect-10 representing the blending of male/female aspects "to completion." Men benefit from touches of beauty in their dress as well. But In her dress, a woman needs to express curves somewhere: either the <u>neck, breasts, waist, legs, ankles or wrists</u>. For example: fitted set-in sleeves add to femininity, small oval shoulder pads can add a curve, sleeves short enough to show a curve above the hand at the wrist, body stockings cover yet show leg or body curves, tight tops under over-clothing suggest there are curves underneath. Each body type has special areas which can be emphasized and become more attractive:

Oval Body Femininity — best displayed through the waist, breasts and shoulders.

Circle Body Femininity— best displayed through the waist, breasts, wrists and ankles.

Square or Rectangle Body Femininity — best through the legs, arms and trim thighs.

Triangular Body Femininity — Type 1 displayed through the breast and small waist
Type 2 through the breast, trim thighs, "the Lioness."

"BIG TOP, LITTLE BOTTOM – BIG BOTTOM, LITTLE TOP" RULE

This is for all body types. When wearing a large silhouette on top (like a large sweater or T-shirt) then balance with a tight silhouette line on the bottom (like leggings, slim skirt or tight jeans.) With a large bottom (baggy pants or full skirt) then wear a small silhouette line on the top (a fitted top such as a body-hugging sweater or a leotard.)

This prevents an unflattering boxlike silhouette because it adds curves either from the waist and breasts or from the ankle and leg curves—if both the top and the bottom are big, there are no feminine curves to the silhouette.

Big Top
Little Bottom

Little Top
Big Bottom

BASIC OVAL LINES THAT ARE FOR EVERYONE

Everyone can wear the classic basic oval lines albeit modified for a sure fit. This is because of the medium non-extreme properties of classic lines. Oval body shapes <u>must</u> stay within the oval clothing lines because other lines do not fit or flatter their shapes. However, the circle, square and triangle can wear modified oval lines as well as their own clothing lines. The following oval lines are applicable to all body shapes:

set-in sleeves	**hidden pockets**	**underarm side panels**
jewel necklines	**self buttons**	**long sleeves**
mock turtlenecks	**medium size lapels**	**classic medium heel boots**
A-line skirts	**classic blazers**	**classic pumps**

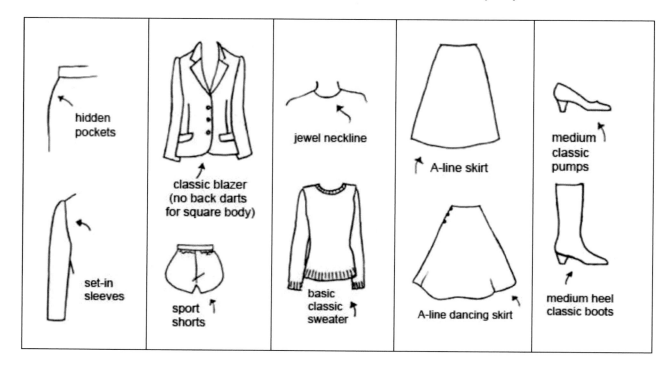

Important Comment Regarding Oval Silhouette Lines for Hairstyles

Hairstyles depend on framing the face within an oval silhouette for balance. Notice that circle and square faces are wider, therefore are better without fullness on the sides and need to be higher on the crown. Fill in areas around face to create an oval outline.

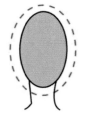  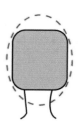  

SCIENTIFIC CLOTHING LINES ITEMIZED AND DETAILED

The following descriptions are the basic lines for each body type. Lines are first illustrated and then summarized according to the lines corresponding to each body shape—the discussion which follows is point by point specific so that one can learn not only the details, but the reasoning behind these valid concepts.

 ## OVERVIEW OF OVAL LINES

Blouses, Tops, Dresses
Fitted blouses that fall gently over the waistband. Easy leotard blouse looks. Fine-ribbed, lightly body-hugging sweaters. Body-fitting vests to "hip-dip" length. Light ovular ruffle effects. One piece or fitted dresses. Diagonal darts in bodice.

Sleeves
Always, set-in sleeves. Small oval shoulder pads. Short sleeves to above elbow. Fitted long sleeves. Flowing Bishop lines. Strapless (not sleeveless.)

Skirts and Pants
No pleats at waistband;. simple sewn down darts. 1- 1 ½" waistbands; low slung waistlines preferred. Medium and long A-line skirts. Short straight skirts under jackets. Low slung pants; legs slightly tapered. Bathing suit, angled leg up to "dip".

Jackets and Coats
Fitted, body forming. Keep coat and jacket waistlines at the waist. Jacket, vests, tops, sweaters need to hit at or just below dip in hip. Contoured underarm gore panel. Gore running from shoulder down over breast. A-line long coats, 3/4 short length. Simple coachman.

Waistband and Belts
1- 1 ½" band width can fit oval curve of body if body is thin, but low belts give more stability over the stomach. Flexible belts that mold into waistline and below are excellent. Skirts, dresses and pants with drop oval waistlines. Also, 1" keysize or 1-1/2" belt is all right.

Shoes
Classic pumps with medium heels. Oval longer vamp is better with simple closed-in toe sandals with strap around heel. Classic boots with medium heels.

DETAILED DISCUSSION OF OVAL CLOTHING LINES

 <u>Oval Body Basic Line</u>

This body shape needs a skimming fitted look. It can be body-hugging but not clinging or skimpy. It is a fact that oval body types have a hard time finding this silhouette line in both ready to wear and patterns for sewing, but it is vital to creatively adapt an oval slimming outside line wherever possible. Keep sides fitted; can have fullness in the middle of the body, but no blouson on the sides; keep fullness off sides for a sleek classic look. For thin types a leotard provides an easy sleek silhouette.

The natural slope of the oval body shoulder line is an asset, and necklines that expose the shoulders are especially good. Use fabrics and stitching of finest quality because details are noticeable on simple classic lines and materials (textured fabrics and pattern designs conceal irregular stitching.) Avoid stiff materials — fabrics should flow.

 Sleeves

Set-in fitted sleeves are a must because they give definition to the shoulder angle. Long narrow sleeves are best—even thin-fabric long sleeves in the summertime. Make sure that long sleeves do not completely cover wrists hiding the curve of the wrist; some classic sweaters do have longer sleeves onto the hand but are purposefully narrowed at the wrist for femininity. Can wear a small oval shoulder pad which suggests a puff, but absolutely no large shoulder pads unless looking for a "costume" look. No dolman or raglan sleeves because they exaggerate the slope of the shoulders. Cap or short sleeves cut the arm wrong, however longer short sleeves to the elbow are fine. Sleeveless dresses and styles are the worst, leaving an awkward line; actually, strapless dresses which do not draw attention to the arms are much more flattering. A great jacket sleeve is a narrow long sleeve with five button closures. A long bishop sleeve that is gathered at the wristband provides a long oval curve. A medium puff sleeve hitting above the elbow gives contrast and emphasizes a narrow waistline.

 Blouses, Tops and Dresses

The idea is to reveal the waist; even though the oval body waist is not extremely small, it appears to be small because of the oval body curves above and below it. Slim-fitted blouses that fall gently over the waist-band are especially good on oval body types. Diagonal side and center darts give a nice slim bodice fit.

Leotard looks are necessary even though they tend to be skimpy, however they do provide a slim top for baggy pant looks. The advantage is that leotards stay tucked in and smooth and do not blouson out; the disadvantage is that they can be too tight unless one is trim. Avoid blouses with front plackets, top-stitching, front buttons or broad set-in yokes (these are all busy distracting lines.)

Keep necklines simple; use oval, jewel or plain mock-turtlenecks to achieve classic looks. Wear fine-ribbed body-slinking sweaters with simple lines. No drop-shoulder cardigan sweaters because they produce awkward looking sloped-down shoulders. Graceful simple ovular-ruffle effects add feminine lines. One piece dresses are classic.

Avoid two-piece busy lines and overlays such as sweaters or over-blouses because they add bulk and take away from a slim line. Body-fitting vests that flow over the oval curve gracefully is one overlay clothing article that can work; another exception would be sheer overtops or see-through tops that reveal a slim body line underneath. No not wear heavy fabrics which add bulk; rather fine elelgant fabrics.

O Skirts and Pants

No darts are best, but can have simple sewn-down contour darts. Avoid pleats and gathers which add fullness (unless fabric is silk or soft enough for pleats to fall sleekly down over the oval body form.) Medium and long A-line skirts and dresses are best because they extend the hip-line and cover hip-dip curve; however, avoid bias-cut A-lines that tend to hug in-and-out curves and thigh bumps. Long straight skirts make the silhouette too straight and are awkward over hips and thighs. Shorter, above-the-knee straight skirts (with opaque hose) are good with 3/4 length A-line coat jackets.

Skirts, dresses and pants with drop-oval waist-lines fit the oval figure. Levi's with low-slung waists resting on the hipbone are better than high waist styles; in pants, a high waist accentuates the stomach and hips too much, whereas the lower waistline cuts across the middle and secures it like a girdle. No cuffs or bulky pockets on slacks (no pockets even better) and strive to keep the uncluttered simple classic look.

Pant legs are best slightly tapered to about 8 or 9" across; extreme tapered legs give a hippy look and straight pant legs actually look baggy on an oval body type. A soft A-line pant leg works here with the fuller flowing A-lines for dressy occasions. Be sure pants are not "high-water" because it would break up the long flowing line. Shorts are better if they are the high-cut sports style, and bathing suits are best in one piece with high cut legs—it is better to expose the complete thigh rather than have a lower line that cuts the thigh area in two, drawing unflattering attention to the indent between hipbone and leg.

O Jackets and Coats

Always form fitting jackets; avoid straight box styles because they cover the curve of the oval waist. Avoid peplums because they exaggerate the oval hip curves. Contoured underarm gore panels are good because they help give a fitted look. IMPORTANT: Jacket length must come down to the natural body indent between the hip bone and the leg so that the jacket hemline hits and just covers the concave dip curve. Longer 3/4 A-line jackets are excellent if worn with a short straight skirt. Avoid short-waisted princess styles because the princess-gore line allows too much fullness in the breast area and causes a short-waisted "little girl" look on oval body shapes. A gore line running from the shoulder straight down over the breast point is all right. This is the best category for fitted A-line coats and longer coachman length sophisticated coats. Be sure to keep waistlines <u>at the waist</u> in jackets, coats, sweaters and even bathrobes.

O Belts and Waistbands

On a thin oval figure, the 1½" belt and band width keeps a graceful curve whereas a 1" belt pinches in and causes the tummy to push out. Stiff 3" belts cover-up the oval curve and are uncomfortable because the belt presses against the oval rib cage on top and the prominent hipbone underneath—however, wide belts that are flexible and soft enough to mold into the waistline are good. Contoured belts are stiff but can work if they sit down on the hips and create an oval drop-waist line.

O Accessories

Accessories which are simple, genuine, singular and of fine quality are important in this category. Avoid plastic or cheap materials. Long shoulder straps on purses and bags keep sliding off sloping shoulders and become uncomfortable (usually falling down and hitting the wrist.) It is helpful to shorten straps so that one can hold the purse close. Medium size purses with elongated oval shapes are best. Avoid top-stitching, buckles, flaps and overly ornamented or square bulky styles.

O Shoes

Classic pumps with medium heels are a must for this category. Sandals are more classic with a closed-in toe and simple strap around the heel. Simple medium heeled boots are best if the line has a curved-in slimmer ankle line—straight-leg boots cover up the curve of the ankle and disturb the graceful curve of the oval line.

OVERVIEW OF CIRCLE LINES

Blouses, Tops, Dresses
Fitted blouses that create small bodice effect. Leotard tucked-in blouse good for thinner bodies. Princess line gores with shorter waists. Empire waistlines. Can have shirring above waist (avoid heavy blouson and wide set-in yokes.) Keep simple classic line, but can have more fine-detail lines, ruffle touches (but not busy flaps.) Keep lines smooth.

Sleeves
Set-in sleeves, carefully fitted at top pivot bone. Classic puff at top of sleeve. No drop-shoulder or dolman sleeves. Short sleeves that cover fleshy part of arm, cupped cap and 3/4 long sleeves with slight fullness at top. Tapered long sleeves (no baggy large or box-like sleeves.) Small oval-shaped shoulder pads to give puff effect.

Waistbands and Belts
Accommodates ¾ -1" bands and belts.

Skirts and Pants
No bulky pleats, rather light shirring or gathering. Soft A-line skirt or slight dirndl short skirt. Elastic or drawstring pants. Soft high-waisted pant line. Tapered pant legs slimming to thin ankles. Soft A-line pant legs for thinner types. Avoid boxy cuffed pant legs.

Jackets and Coats
Smaller, shorter fitting jackets. Jacket length is best 1" to 1 ½" below waistline. This is the natural body type for Princess lines flowing into medium A-line gores. Also Empire waistlines. Contoured, underarm gore helps fitted line. Be sure set-in sleeves fit properly. Avoid straight boxy styles.

Shoes
This is the natural home of the T-strap shoe and baby-doll look because circle foot has a shorter vamp. Closed-in toes with heel straps.

DETAILED DISCUSSION OF CIRCLE CLOTHING LINES

Circle Body Basic Line

This body shape needs a fitted top with an eased bottom outside line, or slight shirring at the waist. Whether weighing 100 pounds or two-hundred pounds, this is the most flattering outside line. The idea is to create a small bodice look and can even wear higher waistlines and set-in sleeves (this line will not look little-girlish on a circle body type.) The circle shoulders are sloped which set off pretty flowing necklines and off-shoulder lines. The bodice can be eased above the waist-band or belt. Lightly shirred to softly gathered waistlines fit the round curves of the circle body. Use fabrics that are soft enough to flow over the *Reubenesque* body shape; avoid stiff, bulky thick materials.

Sleeves

Set-in sleeves properly fitted at the top pivot-bone of the arm are very important in this category because this line keeps the bodice looking small. An eased-in puff at the top of the sleeve is excellent. Avoid baggy or large sleeves such as raglan, drop shoulder or dolman sleeve lines which give an extreme "Winnie-the-Pooh" sloping shoulder look. Cupped cap-sleeves, short sleeves, puff sleeves and slim long sleeves are all good. Three-quarter slim-fitting sleeves are flattering because they don't cover so much of the arm which gives a lighter feeling. Big shoulder pads do not flatter the circle body, however a small oval pad or puffed look gives balance. Sleeve lines can be more tapered to accentuate circle small wrists. Thin circle body types can wear moderate bishop puff sleeves, but not for heavier types because puff sleeves down by the hip line is not flattering. (If the body is exaggerated by weight, then lines need to be diminished.)

Blouses, Tops and Dresses

Fitted blouses that create small bodice effects are best. Leotard tucked-in blouse looks are good for thinner circle body types. Peasant or princess-line gores with shorter waists are natural for this body shape. Avoid heavy blouson silhouettes and wide set-in yokes—we are trying to emphasize a smaller feminine look rather than a muscular broad look. Keep lines simple similar to oval category; can have more ruffles and detail lines, but no complicated boxy flaps that would detract from a smoother silhouette. Soft, slightly fitted sweaters with slightly puffed sleeves are excellent. Keep sweater lengths on the short side, about 2" below the waistline (this shorter type sweater looks little-girlish on an oval body shape, but looks right at home on circle bodies without detracting from their womanly look.)

○ **Skirts and Pants**

No bulky pleats at waistline, rather use slight gathers or shirring. Soft A-line skirts and slight dirndl skirts are good. Elastic gathered or drawstring pants are natural for this category. Tapered legs on pants accentuate the slim ankle but has to be done carefully because that could emphasize larger hips of a *Reubenesque* voluptuous body shape. For thinner types a soft A-line flair to the pant leg works, but keep away from boxy, cuffed silhouettes and pockets.

A soft high-waisted pant line gives a flattering empire silhouette—the idea is to create spaces that keep bodice areas small. Circle bodies generally prefer skirts to shorts, but the short sport-style is best. A shirred, camisole-type bathing suit top with slightly shirred skirt is flattering. Avoid culottes and 2-piece styles that make the top and bottom proportions equal; circle silhouette lines highlight a small bodice which honors the balance of the Golden Mean proportions (1:3 or 2:3 ratios.) Also avoid stirrup pants which pull straight down and cover the important curve of the circle leg; tights are better.

○ **Jackets and Coats**

Smaller, shorter fitted jackets 1" to 2" below the waistline. Short straight skirts are fine under longer fitted, slightly A-line jackets or long line sweaters. This is the natural category for shawl collars and princess gores in coat bodices which flow into classic A-line silhouettes. Contoured underarm gore panels help give a fitted look.

Empire waistlines are excellent (gives a small bodice effect.) Princess-style fitted coats and jackets—be sure set-in sleeves fit properly and are set right at the top pivot-bone of shoulder. Avoid peplums, straight, boxy or double-breasted coats and jackets. *See below for heavy circle body type variations.

○ **Belts and Waistbands**

Belts and waistbands are ¾ to 1" because wider belts would bump up against the round rib cage above and the curve of the hip bone below. All measurements mentioned are to be considered proportionately—a larger person can, of course, wear a larger belt than a smaller person. Circle bodies do have small waistlines, but if they gain weight their waist gets covered over.

◯ **Accessories**

Fine or lacy soft effects in jewelry and scarves. This is the natural home for pearls, especially variegated which offer a monochromatic blended feeling.

◯ **Shoes**

This is the natural home of the T-strap shoe because it contours to the round foot; because the circle foot vamp is shorter, the T-strap helps hold the high heel shoe in place. A close-toe sling pump is also recommended. Round-toed shoes are more natural in this category but will still be "baby-doll" looking so has to be worn carefully and not overdone if one wants to achieve a poised classic look.

*Heavier Circle Body Types

Heavier circle types often make the mistake of thinking they are a square body shape and start wearing over-size shirts which take away any indication that a waist ever existed. Do not wear too-baggy looks, especially oversized T-shirts with drop shoulders. The 1/3:2/3 ratio is vitally important here; never cut the body in half by making the top and bottom equal in length (utilize big-top;little bottom and reverse rule.) Regardless of size or weight, a circle body can create a small bodice look. There are many ways to use lines to define a smaller bodice which will retain a feminine look. The first thing to check is to see where the shoulder seams are on the garment—a circle does not have broad shoulders, and yet incorrect lines made by shoulder pads and wide shoulder seams dropping down the arm will appear that way. The circle silhouette line is achieved by making sure that the shoulder seams come in closer toward the neck which forms a smaller bodice line by reducing the space. Re-set sleeves and move shoulder pads in and make sure skirts are not too draggy and long. As soon as this is demonstrated on a heavier circle person they never settle for the large box-look again.

Do not wear thick stiff fabrics; keep fabrics soft but with enough body for the fabric to flow easily over the shape. Sleeves and pant legs need to be more slim and classic. Add touches of feminine soft ruffle lines at neck to highlight the face, also can have ruffle effect at sleeves but be careful not to cover everything up.

When wearing an over-jacket or coat, wear something form-fitting underneath for femininity. Slim ankle boots are especially flattering because they are narrow at the ankle and show femininity. NOTE: Because added weight over-exaggerates circle body lines; heavier types may need to move toward straighter square lines in clothing to regain line-balance—this is because the circle quota has been used up in extra roundness of weight.

OVERVIEW OF SQUARE LINES

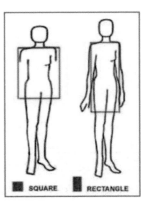

Blouses, Tops, Dresses
Blouson lines fall over waist area and rest on hips. Tank tops, shirts, polo, cowl, sweat- shirts, turtlenecks, plackets, flaps, set-in shoulder yokes, epaulets and pleats. Natural category for cardigans and bulky sweaters. Layered clothing effects. Straight shift dresses, shirtwaist, tunic, drop-waist, raglan, chemise styles.

Sleeves
All sleeve lengths are good; set-in sleeves plus drop shoulder, raglan, cap, short elbow, 3/4 push-ups, short sleeves and classic-shirt long sleeves, especially sleeveless. Square shoulders do not require shoulder pads unless shoulders are narrow.

Belts and Waistband
Belt width is 1" to 2½". Blouson tops with band gives the illusion of smaller waist.

Jackets and Coats
Can add straighter lines. Underarm contour gore for moderate fit. Bomber, safari, jean and detail jackets with blouson lines. Long straight coats, dusters, trench, 7/8 and classic long walking coats. Double-breasted jackets and coats. Avoid short bolero type lines that expose waist area.

Skirts and Pants
Classic two-pleat pants. Box pleats (no angled pleats.) Straight legs, cuffs optional, fuller pockets, sweats, overalls, tights, stirrups, Levi's, little boy legs on shorts/bathing suits. Straight line pleated skirts and straight skirts of all lengths.

Shoes
Classic pump and pumps with V cut-out-toes, spectators, sandals, moccasin toes, stacked heels, knee sock, leggings. All boots.

DETAILED DISCUSSION OF SQUARE CLOTHING LINES

 **Square Body Basic Line**

While this body shape may have somewhat of a waist indent, the rib cage is actually more square and adapts beautifully to straighter up and down silhouette lines which ride naturally on this form. Feminine points of interest are more apparent at the wrists, arms, slim thighs and legs. Because these lines are straighter, apply the concept of "big top with slim bottom, or slimmer top with bigger bottom" to achieve feminine look. Fabrics can be from medium soft flowing materials to fabrics that are more firm and textured. The thin square rectangle types (i.e. professional models) look very sensual even in straighter styles because straight clothing glides over the body without hitting bumps and curves. This is the natural category for overlays of clothing because busy, complicated, comfortable lines do not add so much bulk to a straighter body shape (round and oval types are curvier and show extra "padding.") See* below for heavy square body type variations and extra details for the rectangle body shape.

Sleeves

Set in sleeves are again good, however in this category the raglan or drop shoulder lines can be added. Since the shoulder line is already square, do not use large shoulder pads (but soft contoured shoulder pads can give a slight lift to the shoulder creating a set-in sleeve look.) If the shoulders are narrow to medium, then the drop shoulder seams are fine; if the shoulders are broader, then it makes sense to cut the line with set-in sleeves or raglan sleeve lines. All sleeve lengths are good including sleeveless, cap sleeves, short sleeves, elbow length, 3/4 push-up sleeves and long sleeves. Avoid puff sleeves or peasant looks unless a thinner rectangle.

Blouses, Tops and Dresses

This is the natural home of the blouson silhouette line because it blouses out covering the waist and then falls on slim hips which is very flattering. The tank top, shirt styles, camisoles and shirtwaist-dress are also most at home in this category. Straight-line shifts, straight skirts, jumpers and dresses of any length from very short to long are good. Square body types wear two-piece combinations but be sure to retain 1/3:2/3 ratio. Oversize T shirts with tighter or shorter skirt lines work well. Necklines are a focus point and this body shape can handle complicated effects such as cowl, polo shirt collars, collar stands, turtlenecks, plackets, flaps, epaulets, pleats and yokes. Most sweaters are for square bodies. The cardigan sweater is "classic" for this category.

☐ **Skirts and Pants**

Because of this straighter body shape, box pleats add dimension and lay straight on trim hips—there are no round bulges that open unsightly pleats. Avoid pleats that are set at an angle (this is not an angled body.) Two pleats on each side of the pant is the usual square body pant line. Gathered elastic waists are not as flattering, but sometimes softer gathers flatten down and adapt a flat-pleated look. The classic slightly tapered pant leg is good, but this category can also wear straight legs that are more boxy as well as cuffs and fuller pockets. This body type also handles overalls, sweats, tights, Levis and jeans because of their slimmer hips and less defined waist. The bonus here is that square bodies can wear all shorts and pants of any length. Bathing suits can be two piece, tank top or blouson styles with short boy-pant legs.

☐ **Jackets and Coats**

Straighter box lines on jackets and coats. Can also have underarm gore panels but less contoured or fitted than for oval bodies. Straighter up and down coats such as trench coats, pea coats, safari, dusters, long walking coats or 7/8 jackets. Jean jackets, bomber or Eisenhower type jackets that have a shorter line and blouson with a wide bottom band work well. Yokes, cuffs, flaps and button-downs add more lines and details. Double breasted coats and jackets are most at home in this category. Extra pockets, patch pockets, plackets, belt carriers and hoods give extra outside line details. Add ethnic looks, blankets, ponchos and shawls. Avoid very short jackets and boleros that expose the waist area. Furs are most at home in this category.

☐ **Belts and Waistbands**

Belt widths are from 1" to 2½." In this category, belts are primarily worn as part of outfits rather than spotlighted as ornamental to show off waistines. Belts resting on the hips are good. Belts are often inset or incorporated into the garment with belt carriers, blouson tops, in overalls or jumpsuits. Suspenders are definitely in this category.

☐ **Accessories**

Shoulder straps on purses and bags are good in this category because straps can naturally rest on square shoulders without falling off. Can wear more jewelry (multiple strands,) scarves, shawls, fringes, overlays and complex necklines. In a word, this category can wear more accessories than the other categories.

☐ **Shoes**

Casual shoes such as Birkenstocks, sandals, moccasins, 2-tone saddle, tennis shoes and boots are natural for squared feet and bodies. Two-tone spectator shoes. Special mention is a classic pump with a cut-out toe which communicates the "casual" feeling of this category. Also, important are leggings, textured hose and knee socks.

☐ ***Heavier Squared Body Types**

Fabrics must be softer and less bulky—fabric needs to flow gracefully over the body. Sleeves and pant legs need to be more slim and classic to avoid over-baggy looks. Push up jacket sleeves for a smaller-space bodice look. Straight shift one-piece dresses are not as good; rather use two and three piece combinations. Wear tank tops and camisoles under jackets to give a suggestion of curves underneath. No drop shoulders or cap sleeves, rather use set-in sleeves, raglan or diagonal cap sleeves to create a more narrow shoulder line. Be impeccable about making sure clothing fits the body properly. Avoid skimpy, tight-fitting clothing as well as too many layered bulky looks. Cleverly add bits of femininity to enhance the look because the square quota has been used up by overweight bulk. Further femininity is expressed by paying attention to the 1/3:2/3 ratio.

☐ ***Thin Rectangle Types**

Many models are tall rectangles. The fact that they have straight across shoulders and are so trim without curves and bulging spots enables them to display clothing to advantage. Especially in sleek clothing and straight lines. A plus for the thin rectangle is they can add more graceful classic oval lines and even circle lines for feminine balance.

The rectangle body can wear shifts and straight lines better than all the other categories. Their arms and legs are nicely shaped so sleeveless dresses and blouses are very good, along with most other sleeves including puff or peasant looks for variety.

Slacks and pants are natural for this category. Pleats stay pleats without bulging out over round places on this trim figure so the classic pleated pant is good; however, angled small-waisted styles are not for the rectangle waistline. Straight legs are easily worn and slightly flared-legged will work but will depend on the treatment of the waistline. This is the best category for wearing shorts because thighs are slim. Pants, tops, skirts, shorts, sleeves, sweaters and coats can be any length in the silhouette.

OVERVIEW OF TRIANGLE LINES

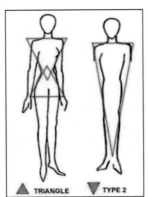

Blouses, Dresses and Tops Type 1 can wear styles that emphasize waist; corset leotard, bustier, peplum, vests. Type 1 and 2 both can wear halter, peasant, boat, under-bust A-line, bell, trapeze, cropped tie-fronts, boleros. Extreme novelty yokes, flanges, tucks, cut-out, flounces. Sleeveless, strapless dresses, kaftans, extreme styles.

Sleeves
Great variety of sleeves including set-in sleeves, dolman, raglan, flared, cap, bell, sleeveless, bishop, lantern, leg-o-mutton, batwing. Shoulder pads can be featured because they exaggerate and produce angles. Sleeveless, strapless dresses.

Belts and Waistband
Type 1 - Contour styles. Type 1 and 2 - All style creative belts plus wider 3" cinch belts. Unusual and decorative belts.

Jackets and Coats
Classic styles and all extreme styles: cocoon, trapeze, cropped tie-fronts. Extreme novelty yokes, flanges, tucks, cut-outs, insets, flounces, and decorated costume effects.

Skirts and Pants
Type 1 - Diagonal darts and pleats, inset yokes and waist- bands, bell bottom, harem, jodhpur, palazzo and wrap pants. Classic and A-lines to all the extreme lines. Full circular skirts, tulip. Type 1 and 2: Skirts with high slits and kick pleats, wrap pants, bias cuts and skirts that angle down to ankles. Slim-hip stretch pants and Capris. Trumpet and diagonal styles.

Shoes

Thongs, wedge heels pumps with angled sides or a vamp with a separated front and back. Boots with decorations and trendy effects. Leggings and all decorative hose.

DETAILED DISCUSSION OF TRIANGLE LINES

 Triangle Body Basic Lines

This body shape has more latitude and has more flexibility and possible variations than the other three body types. The actual triangle basic silhouette line angles in somewhere below the bustline and can angle out below the bustline.

Type 1: Because this body form has a triangular rib cage which angles in at the waist, the look is always slightly sexy even in business clothes. Even though their body lines are more straight, they still go in and out similar to the oval body. Taller professional Type 1 models have sleek lines and also wear oval lines easily, but if not very thin their thighs limit them from wearing straight clothing styles. Shorter, and especially heavier triangle shapes have fuller thighs and pyramid-shaped derriere. (Jennifer Lopez)

Type 2: This "Lioness" body form is more of an inverted triangle which adds to the dramatic flair in dress. Their larger shoulder and bust area give opportunity for exciting powerful dress statements and can be very striking—especially elaborate necklines, collars and sleeves. Because of their trim thighs and flatter derriere they are good in pants and styles that angle in below the bust and waist line. (Bette Midler)

 Sleeves

Again, this shape can wear a great variety of sleeve lines beginning with classic set-in sleeves. Even though the shoulders are fairly straight across (not quite as straight as square shoulders,) if desired this is the natural category for shoulder pads because the angles that pads produce are compatible with angled body lines. This is the best category for wearing more variety in sleeves: dolman, raglan, batwings, leg-of-mutton, kimono, lantern, bishop, triangle-flared, cap, bell, halters, sleeveless, strapless, with added ornamentation such as flounces, trims, flanges, tucks, tassels and beading.

 Blouses, Tops and Dresses

Blouses that emphasize the waistline are especially good in this category for Type 1: leotard corset, bustier, peplum, vests, diagonally angled darts and low-cut V necklines. Type 1 and 2 both can wear halter, peasant, boat, under-bust A-line, bell, trapeze, cropped tie-fronts, boleros. Extreme novelty yokes, flanges, tucks, cut-out, flounces, unusual ruffles and gores. Sleeveless and strapless dresses, kaftans and all extreme styles.

Skirts and Pants

Type 1: This body shape is angled from waist straight out to thighs—diagonal darts and pleats in pants and skirts repeat this line. The triangle body takes inset yokes, set-in waistbands and pants that fit without waistbands. Besides the classical oval styles there are bell bottom, harem, jodhpur, palazzo and wrap pants. Skirts can be anywhere from A-lines to full circular skirts, tulip and trumpet lines. Skirts with high slits and kick pleats are typically triangular. The triangle body handles extreme bathing suit lines such as thong styles, french cut legs and deep V necklines. If the person is on the thin side then full thighs will not be a problem but larger thighs will limit pant and skirts lines which emphasize that area. Again, if the quota for angled lines becomes exaggerated then one has to honor this and balance back toward oval lines to compensate.

Type 2: This body shape is fuller through the chest and shoulders and straighter down to the hips, therefore bigger tops with slim pant and skirts follow this vertical angled body shape. Batwing sleeves are good. Jumpsuits, Capri, bell bottom and stretch pants. Softly-draped harem, jodhpur and wrap pants. Diagonal draped dresses and skirts with slits up the sides, straight skirts and even a sleek sarong or trumpet skirt. Interesting neckline treatments and ornamentation highlight the breast focal point rather than the waistline—the advantages far outweigh disadvantages if lines are carefully selected.

 Jackets and Coats

Revved up classic styles and all extremes fit in this category. The contrast from very long coat styles to short jackets above the waist including boleros and vests. Cocoon, trapeze, fitted cut-away styles, gored, inset yokes and novelty collars and cuffs. Extended shoulders and shoulder pads. Angled line can come in anywhere below the bust line or angle out into A-lines and extreme flared styles with exaggerated sleeves. Type 2 is especially good in scarves, capes and wraps with flared dramatic lines.

 Belts and Waistlines

This body shape can wear all belts plus wider 3" belts because there are no round rib-cages or prominent hip bones to bump against. Contour belts lay nicely on Type 1 shapes. Ornamental belts of every variety are natural for this body type. All the above accessories plus beading, gemstones, feathers and plastic. Bags and purses with shoulder straps rest well on this straight shoulder type. Hats are best worn by triangle heads because of the angled contours of the triangular head type that can hold on hats.

 **Shoes**

Thongs were made for triangular feet. Triangle shaped wedge heels belong with this group as well as pumps with angled sides or a vamp that has a separated front and back. Boots and shoes of all shapes with decorations of every variety including gemstones and colorful embroidery with stud patterns, sparkly metals and exotice leathers. Leggings and all decorative hose. Costume and trendy effects are excellent.

REVIEW OF CLOTHING LINES TO STUDY FOR COMPARISON

Do Not Waste Time Trying On Wrong Clothing Lines...

A person needs to become conscious of what and why certain lines work and do not work. For example, short Square body types should not waste time trying on fitted jackets or triangular lines. For the Oval body type, trying on shirtwaist dresses is a waste of time—those lines will look and feel dumpy. A high waistline on an Oval will look girlish. Square shoulders are comfortable with shoulder strap purses and sloping down Oval and Circle shoulders are not. Circle bodies will feel frustrated and limited if they keep trying on box jackets and pleated pants that are for Squares, or peplums and dramatic Triangle lines. Knowing this will save guessing and wasted time in shopping.

EXAMPLES OF BASIC COAT LINES

◯ Classic Fitted Coat

Best for Oval body. This coat has a waistline right at the waist with classic A-line gores. A Triangle can also wear this coat. A Rectangle body would modify the fitted waist to fit. Overwhelms a Circle body.

◯ Classic Princess Coat

Best for Circle shape. Looks little girlish on Oval body but is perfect for a Circle. A Triangle body could wear it. A Square body cannot take this much fitting, however a thin Rectangle can add this feminine touch.

▢ Classic Straight Coat

This coat line is best for Square body shapes. It is the worst style for Oval and Circle body types because drop shoulders give a broad unflattering muscle look. The Triangle can wear this style but has better choices.

△ Extreme Angled Coat

Example of extreme angled line. Excellent for Triangle shapes. Type 1 wears nearly all styles. Oval bodies are better in fitted coats even though they can fit into this coat.

EXAMPLES OF THE FOUR BASIC PANT LINES

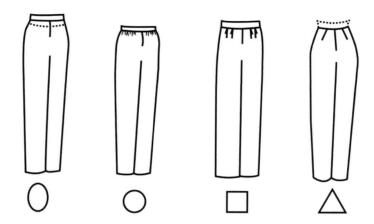

◯ Classic Oval Pant Line

No pleats. One small sewn dart is all right. If Oval body is thin, 1½" band feels secure and easy to wear; if not then drop waist is far better because it goes over the tummy for a secure girdle effect. Classic pant legs are moderately tapered to avoid a baggy look; no straight legs. Most body types can wear this classic pant.

◯ Circle Body Pant Line

Light shirring at the waistline eases gently over the curve of the round body frame. The 1" wide band fits the waist. A Rectangle or Square could wear this line because they are straighter and the shirring can substitute for full pleats. Not good for Ovals. Circles can also wear high-waisted styles as well (creates a small bodice effect.)

☐ Square Body Pleated Pant Line

Pants are natural for Square bodies. The 2" band is fine. Classic double pleats are good for Rectangle and Square bodies. Slight fullness under band gives illusion of smaller waist. Straight or slim thighs allow pants to fall straight in a relaxed straight line. This pant is not good for Ovals because they need to be flat and firm across the middle.

△ Triangle and Variety Pants

Any variety of styles with or without bands fit the Triangle body. Contour inset yokes particularly are compatible with Type 1. High or low waist styles are also included. These lines cannot be worn by Square body types for obvious miss-match-line reasons.

CLOTHING "INSIDE" DETAIL LINES

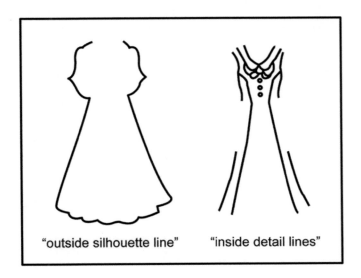

"outside silhouette line"   "inside detail lines"

INSIDE CLOTHING LINES ACCORDING TO KEYSIZE

After understanding outside silhouette lines, the next step is to determine what size "inside" detail lines are best. Are they small, medium-small, medium, large or extra large? A personal "Keysize" can be measured and serves as an important *key* for determining the best size lines and designs to balance with the body.

Correct Keysize is not a concept—it is a principle of fine dress! Few people realize the impact that face features have on a person's overall appearance. The size, shape, spacing and positioning of a person's eyebrows, eyes, nose, mouth and chin form a *design* right on the face.

Another dimension of awareness opens up when one perceives features on the face as a design which dictates the size and width of lapels, belts, cuffs, pleats, straps, bands, buttons, buckles, watches, rings, bracelets, earrings, eye glasses, purses, accessories.

FEATURES CREATE DESIGNS

Using a bow for example, the area of the bow should be no larger than the design on the face. If the bow is too large it will overwhelm the face and distract the eye from really seeing the person.   It is interesting to see how features can come into focus simply by adjusting the size of a bow.

DESIGN

Features which are widely spaced over the entire face relate differently to lines of clothing than features which are closely-set grouped in a little pattern in the middle of the face. This concept is immensely important to fine dress and when addressed answers why some garments just do not work, no matter the color. A person's features preset what size lines are best—lines are lines, whether they are expressed in the form of top-stitching and buttons or in the curves and shapes of facial features.

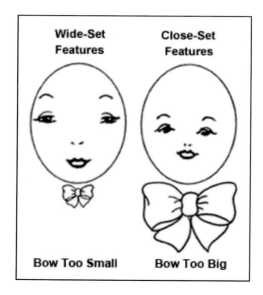
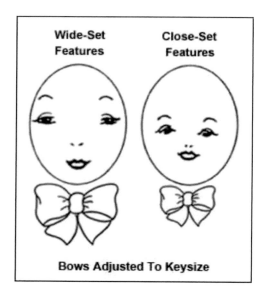

FACE FEATURES DESIGNED WITH LINES

First, here is a line review for application to facial features. Lines are energy and definitely communicate feelings which are felt both objectively (what you see) and subjectively (what you feel.)

A vertical line gives a feeling of balance, symmetry, centeredness, evenness, and a state of focused attention. (masculine)

A horizontal line gives a feeling of peace, rest, stillness and of being set or level. (androgynous)

A line tilted on an angle gives a feeling of excitement, tension, off-centeredness, asymmetry, movement and action. (androgynous)

A circle line always gives a feeling of flowing, soft, grace, ease and even dimples, fun and laughter. (feminine)

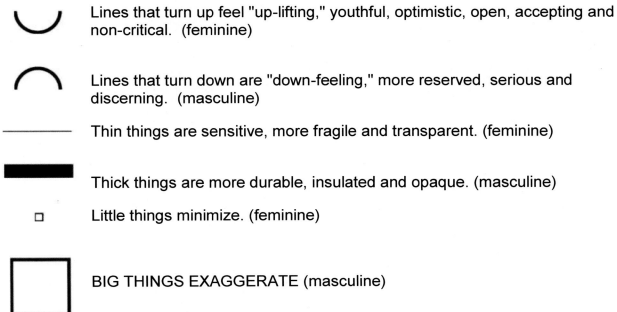

Lines that turn up feel "up-lifting," youthful, optimistic, open, accepting and non-critical. (feminine)

Lines that turn down are "down-feeling," more reserved, serious and discerning. (masculine)

Thin things are sensitive, more fragile and transparent. (feminine)

Thick things are more durable, insulated and opaque. (masculine)

Little things minimize. (feminine)

BIG THINGS EXAGGERATE (masculine)

EXAMPLES OF HOW LINES CREATE FEATURES

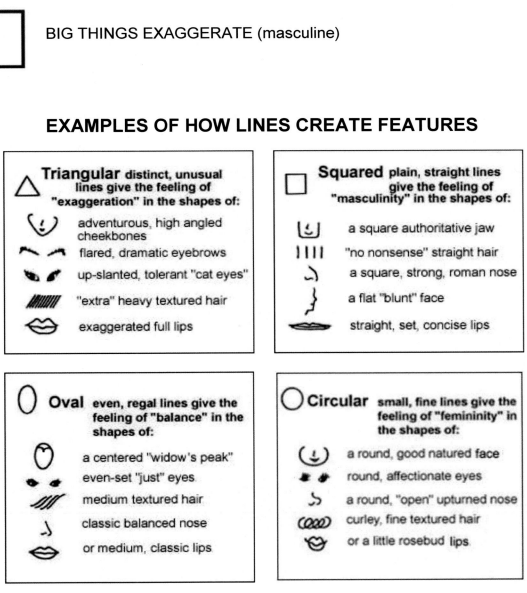

Triangular distinct, unusual lines give the feeling of "exaggeration" in the shapes of:

- adventurous, high angled cheekbones
- flared, dramatic eyebrows
- up-slanted, tolerant "cat eyes"
- "extra" heavy textured hair
- exaggerated full lips

Squared plain, straight lines give the feeling of "masculinity" in the shapes of:

- a square authoritative jaw
- "no nonsense" straight hair
- a square, strong, roman nose
- a flat "blunt" face
- straight, set, concise lips

Oval even, regal lines give the feeling of "balance" in the shapes of:

- a centered "widow's peak"
- even-set "just" eyes
- medium textured hair
- classic balanced nose
- or medium, classic lips

Circular small, fine lines give the feeling of "femininity" in the shapes of:

- a round, good natured face
- round, affectionate eyes
- a round, "open" upturned nose
- curley, fine textured hair
- or a little rosebud lips

189

FACE FEATURES FOLLOW THE 4 SEASON ARCHETYPE LINES

Seeing the impact face features have on clothing lines leads to the study of lines and shapes of features. Once again they align to the 4 archetype energies of the seasons. These same energies express through our features just as they express everywhere—they project definite feelings and indicate corresponding expressions and functions.

 WINTER FEATURE LINES (oval)

Any feature that is balanced - classic - symmetrical - even - sophisticated - has medium balance - good proportion — medium spaces

 SUMMER FEATURE LINES (circle)

Any feature that is feminine - small - petite - gentle - fine - round - curly - cute - soft - sweet - kind - shapely - curves — circles - small spaces

 AUTUMN FEATURE LINES (square)

Any feature that is masculine - straight - squared - plain - asymmetric - flat - indistinct - large spaces

 SPRING FEATURE LINES (triangle)

Any feature that is exaggerated - animated - accented - outlined - bold - unique - any feature which could be "cartooned" to show individuality - extra large spaces

THE STUDY OF FEATURE LINES

 OVAL FEATURE LINES

Any feature that is balanced, even, classic, medium size, and symmetrical fall into this category.

1. Oval shaped faces; looked at as classic; wears simple hairstyle because there are no unusual lines to compensate for; good balance.

2. Classic eyebrow has a natural arch and falls exactly like the brow line explained later in this chapter under "eyebrow guidelines."

3. Full bodied medium textured hair; medium length hairstyles are best; simple hairstyles that are free of extra lines; classic.

4. Classic well-shaped eyes; the width of one eye equals the distance between the eyes.

5. Eyes are even-set; lined up straight and even across.

6. Classic nose; easy straight lines; medium in shape and size.

7. Classic lips; medium in size and shape; rather on the feminine side but nicely formed even on a male.

8. Oval hair line and slight Widow's peak automatically divides the hair into even balance; peak at nape of neck.

9. Suggestion of cleft in chin which can indicate even balance.

10. High classic cheekbones, the look that models try to achieve; gives a refined chiseled look.

11. The overall features are evenly shaped and well balanced; they are in good proportion to each other and to the whole face.

12. Stature; balanced and well-proportioned.

CIRCLE FEATURE LINES

Any feature that is round, softened, curved, fine or small falls into this category.

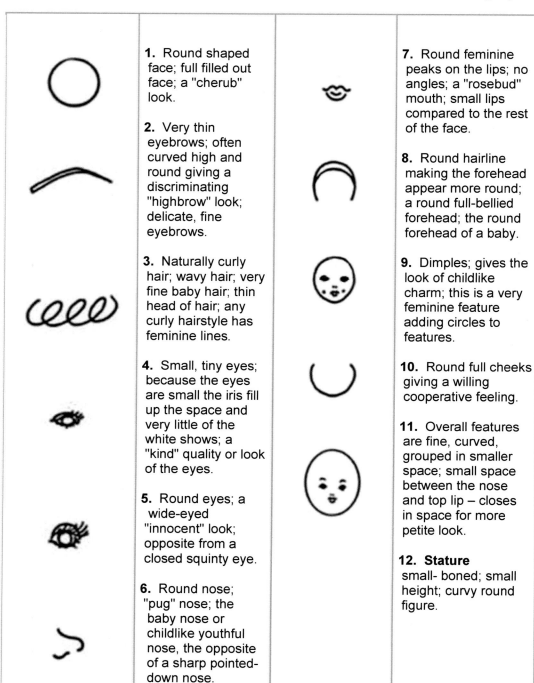

1. Round shaped face; full filled out face; a "cherub" look.

2. Very thin eyebrows; often curved high and round giving a discriminating "highbrow" look; delicate, fine eyebrows.

3. Naturally curly hair; wavy hair; very fine baby hair; thin head of hair; any curly hairstyle has feminine lines.

4. Small, tiny eyes; because the eyes are small the iris fill up the space and very little of the white shows; a "kind" quality or look of the eyes.

5. Round eyes; a wide-eyed "innocent" look; opposite from a closed squinty eye.

6. Round nose; "pug" nose; the baby nose or childlike youthful nose, the opposite of a sharp pointed-down nose.

7. Round feminine peaks on the lips; no angles; a "rosebud" mouth; small lips compared to the rest of the face.

8. Round hairline making the forehead appear more round; a round full-bellied forehead; the round forehead of a baby.

9. Dimples; gives the look of childlike charm; this is a very feminine feature adding circles to features.

10. Round full cheeks giving a willing cooperative feeling.

11. Overall features are fine, curved, grouped in smaller space; small space between the nose and top lip – closes in space for more petite look.

12. Stature small- boned; small height; curvy round figure.

☐ SQUARE FEATURE LINES

Any feature that is straight, plain, square-angled or somewhat asymmetrical falls into this category.

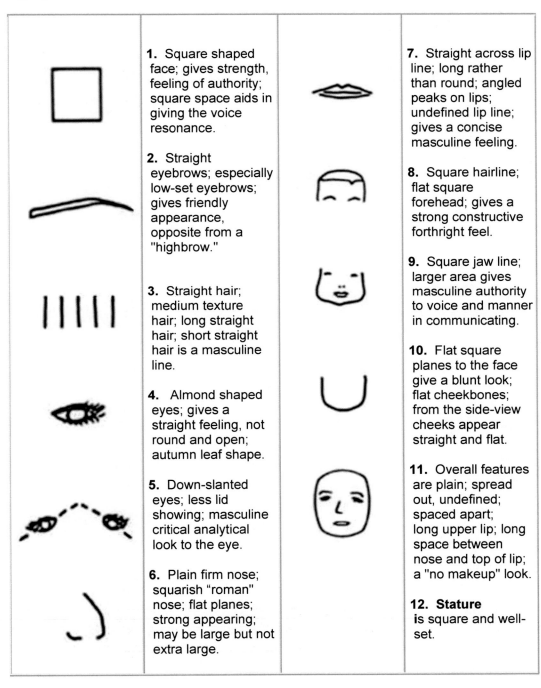

1. Square shaped face; gives strength, feeling of authority; square space aids in giving the voice resonance.

2. Straight eyebrows; especially low-set eyebrows; gives friendly appearance, opposite from a "highbrow."

3. Straight hair; medium texture hair; long straight hair; short straight hair is a masculine line.

4. Almond shaped eyes; gives a straight feeling, not round and open; autumn leaf shape.

5. Down-slanted eyes; less lid showing; masculine critical analytical look to the eye.

6. Plain firm nose; squarish "roman" nose; flat planes; strong appearing; may be large but not extra large.

7. Straight across lip line; long rather than round; angled peaks on lips; undefined lip line; gives a concise masculine feeling.

8. Square hairline; flat square forehead; gives a strong constructive forthright feel.

9. Square jaw line; larger area gives masculine authority to voice and manner in communicating.

10. Flat square planes to the face give a blunt look; flat cheekbones; from the side-view cheeks appear straight and flat.

11. Overall features are plain; spread out, undefined; spaced apart; long upper lip; long space between nose and top of lip; a "no makeup" look.

12. **Stature** is square and well-set.

TRIANGLE FEATURE LINES

Any feature that is accentuated, distinctive, exaggerated or unique would fall into this category.

1. Triangular or diamond shaped face; especially wide at the top with pointed chin.

2. Bushy eyebrows; grows out like a ledge; very coarse eyebrow hair; eyebrows with a dramatic arched flair.

3. Very thick "mane" of hair; extremely coarse hair; off-angled, extreme long or extreme short hair; faddish or trendy hairstyles.

4. Very large eyes; bold or outstanding eyes; unusual in animated fashion.

5. Cat eyes; eyes that slant upward; noticeable because of their unusual angle.

6. Distinctive nose; unique in character and form; chiseled effect; unusual.

7. Large lips; full; generous; well defined; natural outline accent around lip edge; large accent dip on upper lip running perpendicular to nose; extreme peaks on lips.

8. An exaggerated, definite, well-defined Widow's peak.

9. Very large cleft in chin; an over exaggerated dimple.

10. Wide-angled cheekbones; cheeks angled in giving a sharper look rather than full one.

11. Overall features appear bold, animated or have a distinctive quality; features stand out in some way.

12. Stature has angled or unusual lines.

EVERYONE'S FEATURES ARE BALANCED

Nature demonstrates her wisdom by giving our faces the exact balance we need—a unique arrangement of different proportions of nicely balanced features (Winter) beautiful features (Summer) strong features (Autumn) or distinctive features (Spring.) Just as a complete year has all four season energies, people have been created with all four energies expressed in balance though their hair, skin, eyes and body.

A Touch of "Beauty" for Each Man

A man may have a nice mouth which gives him a touch of beauty; or a man may have wavy or curly hair which gives a graceful soft expression; or a man may have beautiful energy apparent in light blue eyes and delicate Summer coloring which balances a strong large masculine stature.

A Touch of "Strength" for Each Woman

A woman may have a more masculine mouth giving her face just the strength it needs; and a woman who has quite a few masculine straight features will naturally be balanced with other feminine characteristics—either curly hair, a circle body, blue eyes or perhaps soft Summer coloring.

INTRODUCING "KEY" KEYSIZES RELATED TO SEASONS

KEYSIZE EXTRA LARGE   Since Spring is exaggerated it relates to extra large animated features and stature as well as extra large animated patterns. It even expresses in bright "extra large" colors. If there is extra-large energy expressing through one of these avenues, adding a zing of bright color or exaggerated line in accessories or trims will connect the person in a special way.

KEYSIZE LARGE   Since Autumn is masculine it relates to large strong, square features and stature and large strong natural patterns. It even expresses in muted earthy "large" colors. This energy allows a bit more strength somewhere in the expression. This is the person that can wear that large sweater or large shoulder bag with *panache.*

KEYSIZE MEDIUM   Since Winter is balanced it relates to medium classic balanced features and stature lines as well as balanced medium-set patterns. It even expresses as basic "medium" colors (like basic box of crayon colors.) Just understanding this medium energy will give the tools needed to wear things outside of the normal realm—colors can be modified and lines simplified to make medium, classic, reserved energy. The motto here is "not too large, not too small.....just right"

KEYSIZE SMALL Since Summer is feminine it relates to small, soft, curved features and stature lines as well as soft blended patterns. It even expresses as delicate "small" colors. Touches of this energy are found around the edgings on collars, in fine chains, slim lines and delicate variegated blended designs. This Keysize is used to give the finishing touch of refinement which gives a pleasing look.

IMPORTANCE OF KNOWING KEYSIZE

Determining the best size of inside detail lines on clothing can save mistake after mistake. For one thing it makes an enormous difference to the appearance if the lapel on a jacket is out of balance with one's features. It also makes a difference with ruffles around the neckline on a blouse; if it is too large, a person may not know why they feel uncomfortable and decide they don't like ruffles…period—and sadly miss the beauty of wearing a ruffle in a keysize they would love. Just knowing enough to question this will open up many possibilities and considerations that may have not been thought about before.

There is a big difference between a 1" face on a watch and a 2" face if the person's true measure is a 1" Keysize. Regardless of fads, once one becomes aware and conscious of the difference they begin to see the distinction and feel uncomfortable in a wrong Keysize.

Everyone can wear Medium Keysize and perhaps smaller (small button closures sewn in a decorative line) but not larger unless they test Large or Extra-large.

THE KEYSIZE TESTER

In addition to The Personal Color Tester tool is an actual Keysize Tester which gives a whole new perspective to dress. This extremely helpful tool has 20 comparative testers that reveal this important aspect of dress. This concept is immediately seen by comparing different size patterns held up under the features of the face. Can be ordered on www.thescienceofpersonaldress.com under products.

RELATIVE COMPARISON OF THE KEYSIZES

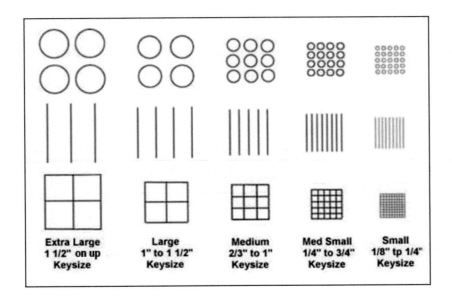

| Extra Large 1 1/2" on up Keysize | Large 1" to 1 1/2" Keysize | Medium 2/3" to 1" Keysize | Med Small 1/4" to 3/4" Keysize | Small 1/8" tp 1/4" Keysize |

"INSIDE" LINES CONNECT TO CLOTHING

A strong square chin communicates the same energy as a square neckline. The feminine lacy patterning in a blouse repeats the same energy as the patterning in curly hair. Lines are subjectively expressing and It is pleasing to see a line repeated even if it is subtle.

But don't overdo it. Picture this ridiculous exaggeration.
A lady with *round* eyes, *round* rosebud lips, *round* button nose, *round* face, and *round* curly hair, doesn't need to add *round* puff sleeves, a *round* peter-pan collar, *round* ruffles, a *round* full-gathered skirt with a *round* polka dot pattern.

LINES CAN BE READ LIKE A BOOK

It is empowering to identify things and know what energy is being expressed.

- A rubber sole on a shoe makes it masculine, not feminine.

- A stacked or cube heel immediately becomes practical, comfortable and easy, and is certainly more masculine (Autumn) than a curved French heel would be.

- Pearl buttons are delicate (Summer,) if the button is flat and round without button holes (still Summer,) if there are two thread holes (less Summer,) if it has a border around the edge (less Summer but more practical Autumn,) with four button holes creating a little square design (even more masculine Autumn.)

- Cowboy boots made of exotic leathers are costume (Spring,) if that same boot is in a black leather with fine stitching (more Winter,) but in a brown leather with top-stitching it becomes decidedly more casual and practical (Autumn.)

- Sweaters are basically casual (Autumn,) but become more classic if the lines are in fine wool or cashmere without ribbing (Winter,) added jewel beading would add more flair and color (Spring.)

- A man's blue fine-cotton dress shirt (Summer,) becomes less dressy in a woven oxford fabric (more casual (Autumn,) change color to beige (very Autumn,) change fabric to silk and it becomes dressy, now change color back to pure classic blue silk (Summer/Winter.) Each effect molds distinctive differences.

GOLDEN MEAN RATIO

The Golden Mean also referred to as the Golden Ratio, the Fibonacci Ratio or Phi (1.168.) Known since antiquity, this magical number is perplexing and enchanting—a phenomenon relating to the universal recognition of good proportion running throughout the beauty in all of nature and art. This is the rule that artists and architects use to achieve proportional balance in their creations, so much so it is called the Divine Proportion and the most beautiful number in the universe.

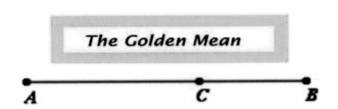

The Golden Mean

A   C   B

The rule says that a ratio of 2:3 or 3:5 is more interesting than something that is just divided in half or 1:1 ratio

The Golden Mean proportions are found everywhere and in everything from planets to the growth sequence in plants to the very body proportions that make up the human body. The Phi ratio is all over the human body in the ratios between the bones, the length of the arms and legs, in the distance from the navel to the toe and the distance from the navel to the top of the head.

These ratios correspond with the frequencies of the notes produced by the white keys of the piano when attuned in the Diatonic scale. If the octaves are extended 49 more octaves, the notes in the last two highest octaves will correspond with the frequencies of the colors of 7 light—the colors of the rainbow!

Comment On Beauty: The eye likes to rest upon points of good proportion. The relationship between two line segments can add-to or take-away from beauty. The eye may become disquieted if something is equally divided, or conversely if the parts are too far apart the relationship is obscured. The idea is to keep the smaller part large enough to be interesting and the largest part small enough to entice the eye to compare them. Again, the eye wants to connect things and at least try for a match to keep things exciting. Inside detail lines of beautiful clothing require conscious spacing of areas.

Boring

1:1 proportions are pretictable, unexciting and boring.

No Connection

If one space over-powers another the imbalance makes the eye lose interest.

Interesting

2:3 or 3:5 ratio gives the eye a comfortable point to rest upon, with just enough imbalance for interest.

APPLYING CLOTHING RATIOS IN COLOR COMBINATIONS

The "big-top little-bottom, little-top big-bottom" rule is an easy guideline which can be applied here. Often one will feel awkward in a blouse and short skirt (50/50 ratio) whereas with slacks the *Golden Mean* is achieved (1:2 or 2:3 ratio.) It is assumed that slacks are just more comfortable to wear, but more likely the reason is that proportion-wise they simply look better than a fifty-fifty-cut-in-half line.

Skirts can be connected with shoes creating a nice line by wearing the same color in opaque hose. This "mock boot" treatment also serves to lengthen the "big bottom-little top" balance, and again, it just feels better not to have one's legs hanging out. A longer line A-line jacket worn with a short skirt and opaque hose gives a sleek nicely balanced look.

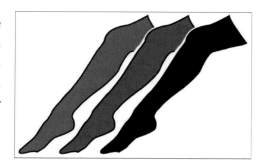

For a classic, smooth, sophisticated look a full one color-statement is best and matching hose completes this look. It is better to avoid styles that cut across and break sleek lines in half; a violet sweater and black skirt combination is not as striking as a violet sweater and skirt or dress all one smooth color. Even at that, it is more flattering to wear a violet sweater with black slacks (1:2) than with a short skirt (50/50 ratio.)

Comment On Bright Colors: It is natural for a Winter person with Spring influence to be drawn to bright jewel colors. To avoid an overdone costume effect, a simple one-color statement is more striking (remember, one color is classic, two are casual, and three begin to be costume.) The point here is that a combination of black with a very bright color is harsh even on a dark haired person (especially for daytime wear.) Except for sports and play, bright colors for fine dress require rich materials such as cashmere, fine woolens and knits (for daytime) and silks and blends for evening.

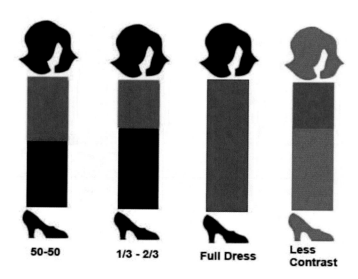

50-50   **1/3 - 2/3**   **Full Dress**   **Less Contrast**

All hair-color neutrals tone-down bright colors. Notice how Autumn can wear brown with a brighter purple which serves to tone down the brightness, thus giving a feeling of casual flexibility. For a light-haired person, cream or camel would tone down bright colors as well. This is a good example of how neutrals qualify bright and outside colors.

THE RULE FOR NECKLINES

People often wonder about necklines and necklaces. How long should a necklace be and what about necklines? They know it makes a big difference but have not had a guideline. Necklines are dictated by the length and width of one's face. Optimal balance is achieved when the neckline or necklace repeats the length of the face which gives the eye a comfortable point upon which to rest.

If a neckline, pendant or scarf-knot goes lower onto the chest, simply repeat the same face-measurement again (the length from the hairline to the chin) to give the eye another resting point. This attention to spacing is magical.

Measure the length of the open-face area (depending on the hairstyle) to determine the best length for the neckline. When necklines and collars are in balance attention is drawn to the person's eyes and face. For example, if the neckline or necklace is too long it can make the face appear drawn down, whereas the correct length would nicely frame the face. If a string of pearls doesn't look right, check the length—it possibly could go with many things if the proportion was corrected. If one is not comfortable wearing jewelry, recognizing the proper keysize may change that. Necklaces and chains come in different lengths and one should be measured and be aware of the size along with ring and glove sizes.

The length of your face determines the length (depth) of your neckline, shirt opening, collar, necklace, bow, pin, flower etc.	If you have bangs or hair down on your forehead, measure by the amount of face that shows and repeat that length in your neckline.	The width of your face determines the width of your necklines and collars. The eye likes this width repeated.	If your neckline is less than the length of your face, then a wider neckline will balance out the area–this makes up the difference in volume and is comfortable to the eye.	Can repeat the line of your jaw line for high necklaces or neckline treatments. The eye likes things that match.

HOW LINES COMMUNICATE

WINTER

A classic high back-centered bun says, "I am regal and poised and I think I am beautiful enough on my own to allow this severe hairdo. It has a striking look and makes me feel Queenly."

SUMMER

An upswing ponytail says, "I think I'm pretty and I go to special trouble to arrange these darling little tendrils to fall just so. Curls are my specialty. I wish I was a Princess."

AUTUMN

Two straight braids say, "I am more practical and have work to do. But I do have lovely hair even though I like to keep it neat and out of the way at times. I dare to be natural."

SPRING

One large braid high on the side says, "I dare to be different. it's fun to be original and who wants to do the same old boring things over and over. I know it's only noon, but do you know where there's a party?"

EVERYDAY EXAMPLES OF HOW LINES "SPEAK"

The Universal Language can be applied to anything from choosing curtains to carving a pumpkin. Looking at things from line awareness makes life exceptionally interesting.

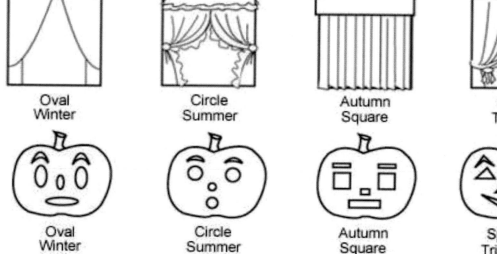

Oval
Winter

Circle
Summer

Autumn
Square

Spring
Triangle

Oval
Winter

Circle
Summer

Autumn
Square

Spring
Triangle

Oval Winter lines are always more classic sophisticated, a "standard" in the sense that their medium non-extreme quality lasts forever.	Circle Summer lines are always more youthful and delicate, "baroque" in the sense that they are refined down to subtle elegance.	Square Autumn lines are always more plain, sturdy, rough hewn "frontier" sturdy quality that is durable, practical and unpretentious.	Triangle Spring lines always have a more dramatic, trendy, arty "Picasso" quality of breaking through into the new, modern and untried.

Cartoonists certainly understand this language. Scrooge is drawn with sharp angled features giving a feeling of pinched, steely-eyed non-emotional hardness. Dear old Santa Claus just has to be full of round, friendly good-natured jolly lines.

STUDENT'S WORK: Students at the Academy of Art in San Francisco were instructed to use colors and lines from each season template to express and communicate the exact <u>feeling</u> of each category. If a color or a line was off, it was immediately apparent that the intention was not clearly known and stated. These were excellent examples.

A wonderful student from The Academy of Art, Jeanette Bakkemd from Norway, created these four comparison drawings based strictly on the lines, colors and feelings of the Four Seasons. Each drawing had to be accompanied by a written explanation of the feelings expressed. (This earned her the highest grade!)

WINTER SUMMER AUTUMN SPRING

An entirely different subject can still express the contrast between the four season energies. Lance Lone designed the following Tarot cards using the same four energy lines, colors and expressions. An impressive testimony for the creative use of colors and lines.

TEXTURES AND PATTERNS

THE SAME 4 ENERGIES EXIST IN TEXTURES AND PATTERNS

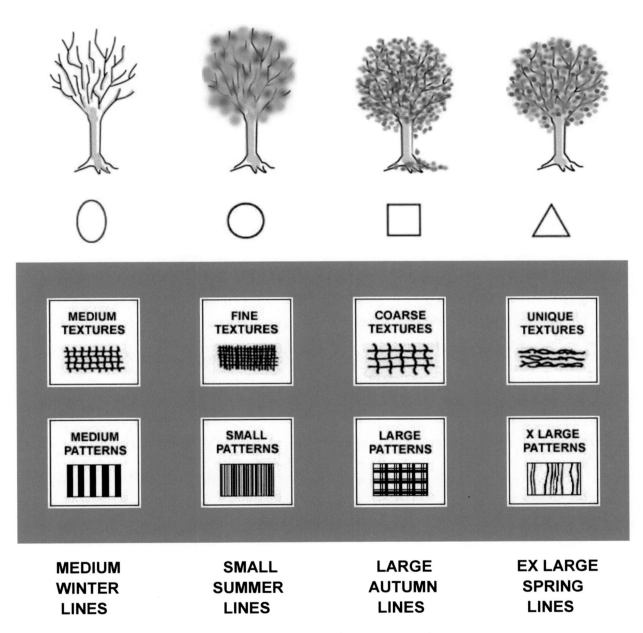

| MEDIUM WINTER LINES | SMALL SUMMER LINES | LARGE AUTUMN LINES | EX LARGE SPRING LINES |

The very same 4 energies in colors continue into texture and pattern lines. A person's best textures and patterns will follow the Homebase colors and lines. However, it is possible for everyone to wear medium textures and patterns. The "Keysize" is a big factor and can be adjusted or chosen to be in larger or smaller patterns according to how the design of face features are spaced.

THE 4 ENERGIES IN PATTERNS

O **Winter Oval Patterns**

Energy is still and set (no movement.) Stripes are equally spaced and evenly repeated. Oval designs are even, definite, striking and symmetric. Includes equally spaced stripes, checks, polka dots, geometric and patterns that are set, repeated and balanced. Avoid off-center, faded, uneven, busy, paisley or wandering patterns. Use contrasting dark and light colors together for definition.

O **Summer Circle Patterns**

Energy becomes softer. Lines subtly blend into one another and become small or curved. Designs suggest softness, blended tones and understated subtle effects. Soft marbled patterns, blended stripes, small polka dots, full bloom flowers, small geometrics and checks. Use blended colors, tone-on-tone, watercolor, monochromatic schemes with three to five values of one color.

▢ **Autumn Square Patterns**

Energy begins to move. Lines cross over and become busy, detailed and more complex. Designs suggest multifaceted, busy, enriched, practical or natural patterns. Plaids, textures, random dots, paisleys, all-over effects, true-to-life motifs, tie-dye, batik, tapestry, complex ethnic patterns. Additional overlays of braid, fringe, rick-rack and cross stitching. Use multiple warm-medium-value colors.

△ **Spring Triangle Patterns**

Energy moves into excited action. Lines undulate, become any size, are exaggerated, set apart and unique. Designs are exaggerated and accented with bright colors. Animated geometrics, border prints, undulating random stripes, colorful embroidery, obscure backgrounds with outstanding characters, diagonal designs and exaggerated random dots. Can use patterns outlined with black or white accents.

THE 4 ENERGIES IN LACE

 ALENCON LACE

WINTER This sophisticated lace is an example of a French needlepoint distinctive for classic design. Its texture has raised, defined lines achieved by padded design outlines. This lace texture falls gracefully into harmony with oval lines.

NEEDLEPOINT LACE

SUMMER Fine needlepoint lace is delicate and expresses the essence of the circle energy. Fragile and dainty lace with little flowers and dots and scallops are included. Fine tatting and bobbin lace are other examples of feminine lace.

CROCHETED LACE

AUTUMN This lace is equated with chain lace and is worked with a crochet hook. Thickness of lace depends on gage of thread. Filet lace is also autumn because it is made from a net background that is knotted in a square shaped mesh.

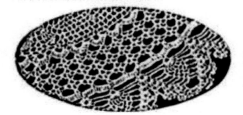

CUT WORK LACE

SPRING This lace represents unusual lace. Cut work consists of holes cut in linen and grows elaborate as more foundation cloth is cut away. Any lace that is dramatic, exaggerated, brightly colored, large design, animated, stiff or bold has this energy.

LINES ARE EXPRESSED IN FABRICS

The very yarn or thread used greatly impacts how clothing appears. Colors are affected by the textures of the material or fabric on which they are expressed. The color RED in a shiny satin material reflects light giving a very different effect from the same RED in fine wool.

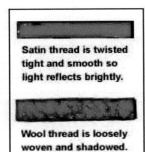

Satin thread is twisted tight and smooth so light reflects brightly.

Wool thread is loosely woven and shadowed.

Here are magnified examples to show the variance of diverse fibers:

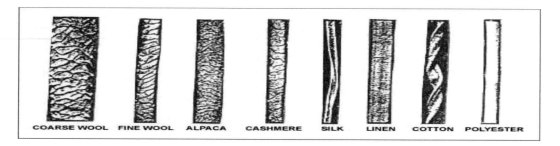

COARSE WOOL   FINE WOOL   ALPACA   CASHMERE   SILK   LINEN   COTTON   POLYESTER

(a) Variances arise from how thick, thin, shiny or dull the thread.

Natural fibers—from animals (sheep, camel, goat) and plants (cotton, flax, jute) make a short staple yarn that is spun into strands for weaving, knitting or making thread. The short fibers (or cut filaments) spun together tend to form shadows between filaments. Because of shadows these yarns are naturally more muted (Autumn) and dark (Winter.)

Manufactured filaments—made from petrochemicals, are heated and forced into long continuous fibers such as nylon, acrylic, polyester and spandex. Because these filaments are a continuous thread, they have less shadowing and reflect more light. These filament yarns are more shiny and bright (Spring) and light (Summer.)

Silk fibers—made from silkworms (animal) but spin long reflective filaments. Notice that light silk fabrics have a silvery light reflection and dark silks have a black dark shadow reflection.

(b) Variances arise from how loosely or tightly the threads are twisted.

Obviously a tightly twisted thread or yarn is going to have less space for shadows and will be more reflective. A coarse yarn made of many strands will show shadows.

(c) Variances arise from how dense or open the weave.

Woven fabrics can be tightly woven (small,) less tight (medium) or loosely woven (large.) Tightly woven fabric is more reflective than coarsely woven fabrics.

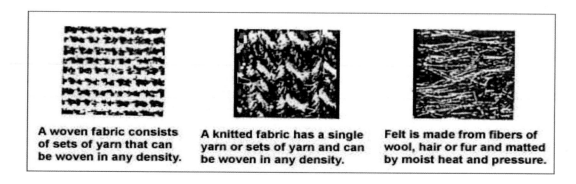

A woven fabric consists of sets of yarn that can be woven in any density.   A knitted fabric has a single yarn or sets of yarn and can be woven in any density.   Felt is made from fibers of wool, hair or fur and matted by moist heat and pressure.

THE 4 ENERGIES IN FABRIC TEXTURES

MEDIUM TEXTURES	◯ **Winter Oval** *Quality Fabrics* **Fine cotton, silks, fine woolens, smooth knits, fine gabardine, wool crepe, velvet**
FINE TEXTURES	◯ **Summer Circle** *Thin Fabrics* **Very fine cotton, fine silk, velveteen, chiffon, voile, batiste, crepe de Chine, lace, eyelet, dotted Swiss, transparent fabrics**
COARSE TEXTURES	▢ **Autumn Square** *Textured Fabrics* **Cotton, raw silk, woolens, nubby weaves, corduroy, denim, twill, suede, kettle cloth, woven fabrics**
UNIQUE TEXTURES	△ **Spring Triangle** *Crisp Fabrics* **Polished cotton, embossed silk, linen, satin, taffeta, organdy, sailcloth, chintz, faille, lame', straw weaves**

VARIOUS FACTORS AFFECT THE APPEARANCE OF FABRICS

Even though Homebase colors are your best colors, there are other factors which impact dress; the elements of line, keysize, texture and pattern can change the picture dramatically. You may like something that you know goes against the rules but you still feel good in it. This is not confusing when you understand the reason behind the apparent contradiction and can see exactly why—some other element is making it work.

The eye takes in all the colors, and subjectively a feeling is received. Shadows from textured or heavy knitted garments read "charcoal gray" and will actually connect with the gray shadows in a person's hair. A purple-colored satin is too shiny and bright for an Autumn person, however the same purple when muted by a shadowed fabric will look earthy and connected. The color of skin showing through open weave fabrics such as lace or net will serve as a connection making the repeated skin-color part of the fabric color. All these elements give great creative options.

DARK FORMAL APPEARANCE IN TEXTURE

 Colors will appear darker on fabrics that absorb fully saturated color—such as fine woolens, fine cotton, silk and velvet. These fine natural fabrics take dye readily. Dark colored silks and plush velvet show black highlights when they are draped or in movement on a person. Black shadows add dark contrast. Very finely finished leathers appear more formal and are best for this category.

LIGHT DRESSY APPEARANCE IN TEXTURE

 Colors will appear lighter in thin, transparent or delicate materials—such as voile, chiffon, lace, sheers and dotted Swiss. Even if the color is dark, it will appear lighter on thin or lace materials, especially if a light skin color shows through. The feeling of lightness is doubled by silver reflections from light colored silks and silver lame'. Cashmere, mohair, and very soft lacy knits diffuse and soften color. Lightly colored ultra-suede or micro suede reflects light highlights. Very soft, gray-highlighted leathers seem "lighter."

MUTED CASUAL APPEARANCE IN TEXTURE

 Colors will appear duller on fabrics which are textured or coarsely woven —such as terry cloth, corduroy, kettle cloth, gauze, tweeds, denim, knits and nubby weaves. The reason these materials look dull is because the textures create gray shadows which diffuse the light (if the threads themselves are not tightly twisted, they are also shadowed.) Leathers which are untreated, rough-edged or in their natural state appear duller. Textured materials diffuse light because they do not reflect light.

BRIGHT COSTUME APPEARANCE IN TEXTURE

 Colors will appear brighter on shiny flat materials—such as satin, polished cotton, embossed silk and taffeta. Anything that shines will appear brighter, exaggerated and lively. Tightly twisted thread such as silk thread will reflect brighter in color. Warm gold lame' will seem brighter than cool silver lame'. Unusual shiny leather materials such as simulated snakeskin, lizard, and alligator appear brighter. Also, sparkly jewelry and especially shiny patent leathers. These elements add dramatic, fun and flourish to ensembles.

CONNECTING COLORS WITH DOT-TO-DOT BUTTONS

One quick and clever way to customize clothing items is through buttons. The power of a button is amazing. For one thing, buttons can easily be changed. A sweater or a coat of any color can be dramatically altered by the impact of different buttons— the feeling of a charcoal jacket with wooden buttons would be dramatically changed if the buttons were cut off and replaced with sparkly rhinestone buttons. Because a button has both color and shape, they can be used to creative advantage. Just apply the same color/line associations that have been learned. For example:

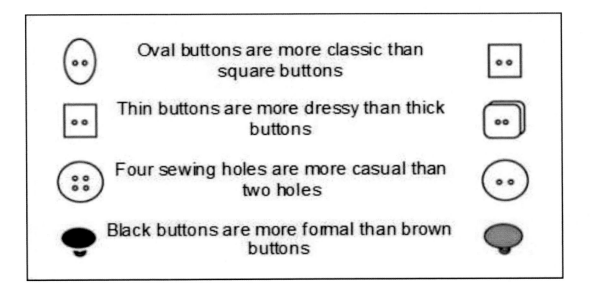

An "outside" color can be connected by repeating the hair color through buttons; kind of like a trail of dots making a bridge of color tying the person into the picture. Pay attention to *value* matches—the colors do not have to be exact matches. For example:

- Apply the same Homebase keyword to button choices – light, dark, muted or bright
- If the hair is light, all light colored buttons will mimic the hair color
- The eye sees all dark buttons as a repeat of dark hair
- Warm bright buttons pick up the highlights in red hair
- Muted medium-value buttons repeat medium brown hair

Example: If a warm rust-colored garment appears too warm it can be balanced by adding silver or pewter buttons.

Example: If a cool navy-color garment appears too cool balance it by adding bronze or gold buttons.

Important Point for Brown-haired People: The magic of adding warm brown or wooden appearing buttons to repeat brown hair deserves special mention. Regardless of a person's Homebase, the subtle mixtures of brown, taupe, charcoal, sand and beige in warm buttons are often just the touch needed to connect and repeat brown hair. Buttons add character and finishing touches besides providing the necessary function for openings on clothing. This special section on buttons underlines the importance of the effect buttons make on garments, accessories and clothing items. They can make something have a personality all its own…magically.

BUTTONS ARRANGED IN HARMONIC SEQUENCE

gold buttons
brass buttons
colorful buttons
bright copper

warm colored buttons
muted buttons
wooden buttons
leather buttons

bright colored
shiny brass
satin buttons
different shaped
gemstone buttons
rhinestone buttons
frog buttons
triangle shapes
star buttons
velvet buttons
large buttons

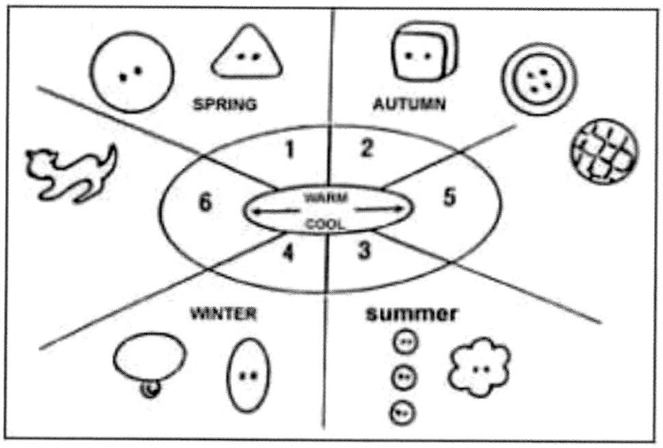

thick buttons
four hole buttons
bronze buttons
antique brass
basket weave
knitted buttons
earth colored
square buttons
textured buttons
woven buttons
copper buttons

silver buttons
dark colored
pewter buttons
medium classic

no thread holes
black buttons
oval buttons
shank buttons
silver antique
no buttons

pastel buttons
tiny buttons
thin buttons
round buttons
scalloped buttons
mother-of-pearl

soft silver
light colored

ILLUSTRATED CLOTHING LINES

This is not a fashion study! The purpose of the following illustrations is to provide templates showing the contrast between the four different energies when applied to dress lines. These paper-doll silhouettes do not limit a body type to one specific line, but they do provide information which will assist in deliberately creating what is wanted to express. However, the fact remains that the appointed lines do flow more naturally over the body type indicated. Keep in mind Oval lines are adaptable to most body types.

Coats

Triangle Coats – The illustrations are merely to suggest variety and the fact that angled or unusual lines with flourish or exaggeration fall into this category. Costume influences often intertwine in designs and styles.

Square Coats – Straighter up and down lines, such as trench, long walking coats, double-breasted, capes, drop shoulder, duster styles. Underarm panels but less fitted. Extra pockets, patch, flaps, plackets buttons and belts.

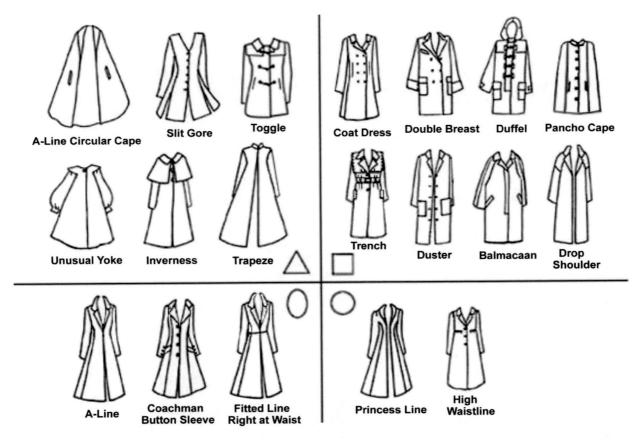

A-Line Circular Cape   Slit Gore   Toggle

Unusual Yoke   Inverness   Trapeze

Coat Dress   Double Breast   Duffel   Pancho Cape

Trench   Duster   Balmacaan   Drop Shoulder

A-Line   Coachman Button Sleeve   Fitted Line Right at Waist

Princess Line   High Waistline

Oval Coats – The waistline needs to be right at the waistline; very important because higher waistlines will look little girlish. Long fitted A-line with sleek gores running whole length.

Circle Coats – Higher waist Princess gores in bodices which flow into classic A-line coats; contoured underarm gores help fitting. Empire waistlines. Also for thin Rectangle shapes.

213

Jackets

Triangle Jackets – All possible styles, classic to extreme; from very long to short jackets above the waistline, cocoon, fitted cut-away, trapeze, gored, inset yokes, novelty collars and cuffs. Extended shoulders and pads. Angled line can be anywhere below bust line or angle out into A-lines and extreme flared styles with exaggerated sleeves.

Square Jackets – Straighter box lines; trench coat style, pea coats, safari, underarm gore panel but less contoured or fitted are fine here and the extra detailing, pockets and plackets. Extra details do not detract from the person, but these lines are more casual. Avoid very short jackets and boleros that expose the waist area.

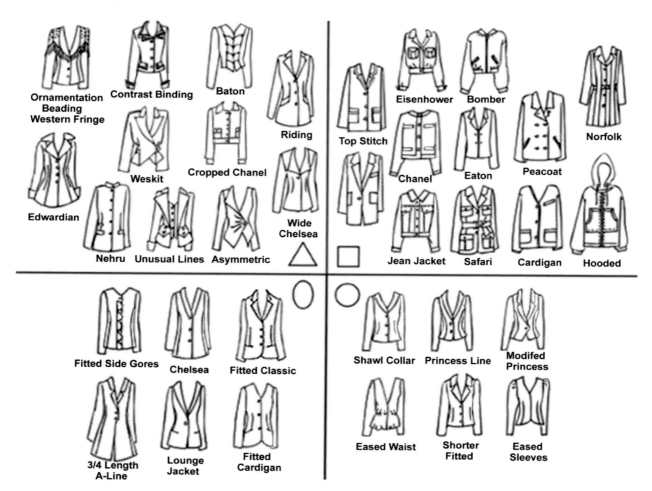

Oval Jackets – Form fitting and underarm gore panels. Important: Jacket length at concave-dip between hip bone and thigh. Keep waistlines right at the waist (avoid full breasted or short-waisted Princess styles.) Longer fitted A-line jacket with short straight skirt. Sleeves set-in right at top of pivot bone of shoulder – no drop shoulders. Self-buttons best avoid plackets, flaps or complicated lines.

Circle Jackets – Smaller, shorter fitted jackets 1" to 2" below waistline. Contoured underarm gore panel helps give a fitted look. Be sure set-in sleeves fit properly and are set right at top of pivot bone of shoulder. Slight puff is excellent. Avoid peplums, double breasted, straight and boxy or drop-shoulder coats and jackets. Best category for the combination of jackets worn with dresses.

Vests

Bolero **Fitted Weskit** **Grommets** **Halter Vest**

Border Effects **Jerky** **Tie Vest** **Angled Line**

Zipper Vest **Sweater Vest** **Straight**

Unfitted   **Tabard** **Tunic** **Sleeveless Pullover**

Formal Vest **Fitted Vest**

Princess Line

Keep in mind that overlays of clothing are best for Triangles and Squares, but fine quality elegant fabric can be adapted for Ovals and Circles.

Sweaters

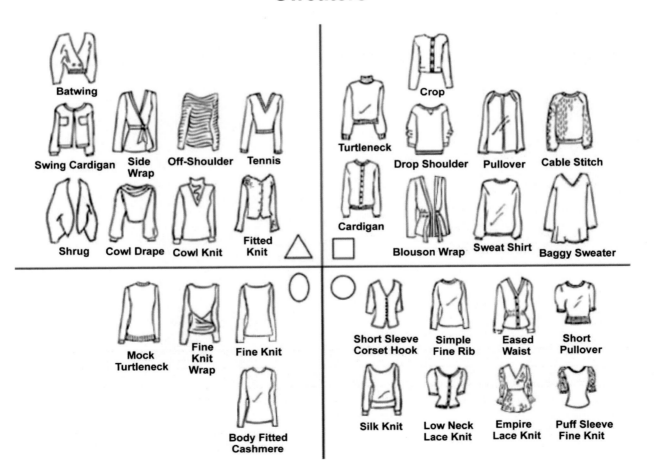

Batwing

Swing Cardigan **Side Wrap** **Off-Shoulder** **Tennis**

Shrug **Cowl Drape** **Cowl Knit** **Fitted Knit**

Mock Turtleneck **Fine Knit Wrap** **Fine Knit**

Body Fitted Cashmere

Turtleneck **Crop** **Drop Shoulder** **Pullover** **Cable Stitch**

Cardigan **Blouson Wrap** **Sweat Shirt** **Baggy Sweater**

Short Sleeve Corset Hook **Simple Fine Rib** **Eased Waist** **Short Pullover**

Silk Knit **Low Neck Lace Knit** **Empire Lace Knit** **Puff Sleeve Fine Knit**

Dresses

Triangle Dresses – This body shape has more latitude, flexibility and possible variations than the other three body types. Dresses with peplums are most comfortable in this category and oval classic lines are worn easily by this shape. Because <u>Type 1</u> rib cage angles in at waist; the look is slightly sexy even in business clothes. <u>Type 2</u> broad shoulders angles down from shoulders to slim hips and flatter derriere (does not angle in and out as much.)

Square Dresses – Straight lines such as shifts, shirtwaist, tunic, jumpers and dresses of any length from very short to long are meant for this shape because of slim thighs. Thin square <u>Rectangle</u> shapes look sensual even in straighter styles because straight clothing glides over the body without hitting curvy bumps; also wears the oval classic lines and high waisted feminine lines as well.

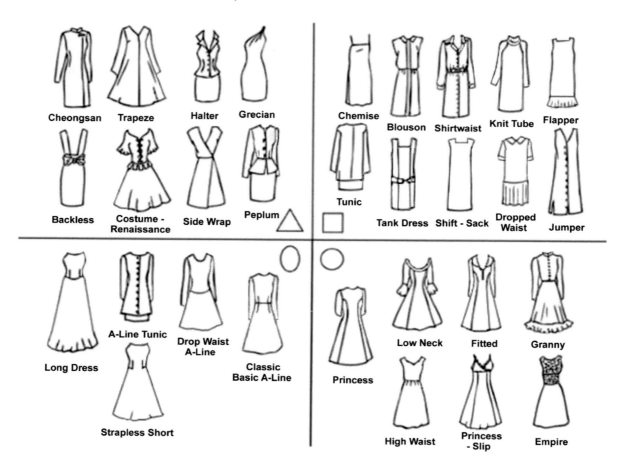

Triangle: Cheongsan, Trapeze, Halter, Grecian, Backless, Costume - Renaissance, Side Wrap, Peplum

Square: Chemise, Blouson, Shirtwaist, Knit Tube, Flapper, Tunic, Tank Dress, Shift - Sack, Dropped Waist, Jumper

Oval: Long Dress, A-Line Tunic, Drop Waist A-Line, Classic Basic A-Line, Strapless Short

Circle: Princess, Low Neck, Fitted, Granny, High Waist, Princess - Slip, Empire

Oval Dresses – One piece dresses are classic and simple. The idea is to reveal the waist even though the oval waist is not extremely small (it appears small because of oval curve above and below it.) Skimming lines are preferred to skimpy tight lines. Graceful oval ruffle effects add feminine lines. Avoid bulky fabrics. Drop-waistline minimizes tummy and adds girdle-like comfort.

Circle Dresses – Fitted top with eased bottom outside line, slight gathers or shirring at waist (regardless of weight) fit the round curves of the circle shape. The idea is to create a small bodice look by using higher waistlines and set-in sleeves. Princess lines are basic to this category. Use soft fabrics that flow over Reubenesque round body lines – avoid stiff, hard materials.

Blouses and Tops

Triangle Blouses – Blouses that emphasize the waistline are especially good in this category: leotard, bustier, halter, peasant, flared, under-bust A-line, peplum, bell and trapeze shapes. Extreme styles with novelty yokes, gores, flanges, cutouts, tucks, unusual ruffles and darts – especially diagonal (angled) darts. Type 2 broad shoulders angling down to slim hips and flatter derriere will naturally reverse the lines and angle down past waist to hipline. All sleeve styles are good.

Square Blouses – This is the natural home of the blouson silhouette line because it blouses out covering the waist and then falls flatteringly on slim hips. Feminine points of interest are at the wrists, arms, slim thighs and legs (not at the waist) therefore sleeveless, cap sleeves and all sleeve lengths in blouses are good. Apply "big top, little bottom and reverse" rule to avoid boxy silhouette. Square body has naturally squared shoulders; so drop sleeves are good; <u>Rectangles</u> have more variety.

Oval Blouses – The idea is the line needs to be skimming, not skimpy; fitted blouses that fall gently over the waistband to reveal the waist curve. Set-in sleeves, no drop shoulders. Diagonal bodice side and center darts give nice fit. Leotards stay tucked in and smooth.

Circle Blouses – Fitted tops that create small bodice effects are best. Set-in sleeves, eased puff, short sleeves and 3/4 length. Avoid baggy sleeves, large sleeves, raglan, drop shoulders and big shoulder pads. Bodice can be eased above the waistband.

Straight Skirts

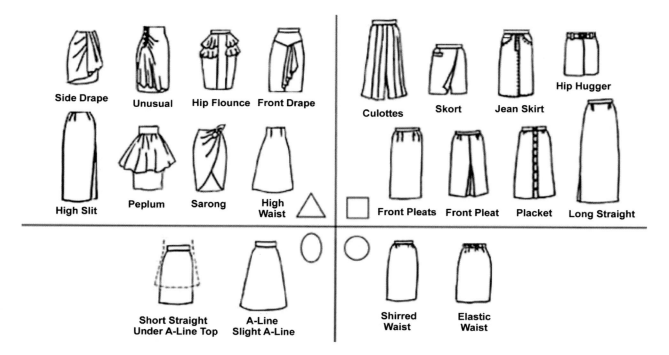

Side Drape Unusual Hip Flounce Front Drape

Culottes Skort Jean Skirt Hip Hugger

High Slit Peplum Sarong High Waist

Front Pleats Front Pleat Placket Long Straight

Short Straight Under A-Line Top A-Line Slight A-Line

Shirred Waist Elastic Waist

Flared Skirts

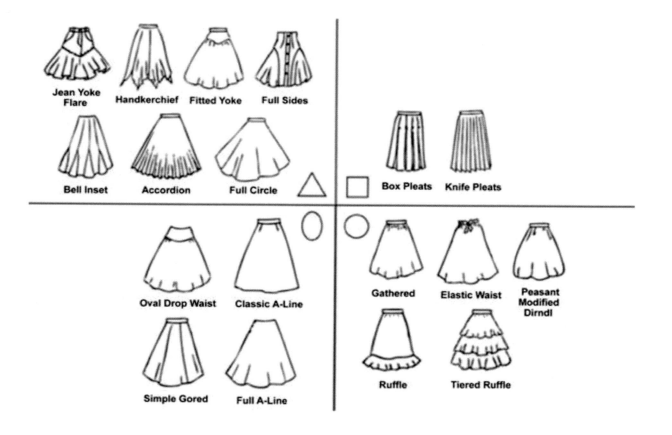

Jean Yoke Flare Handkerchief Fitted Yoke Full Sides

Bell Inset Accordion Full Circle

Box Pleats Knife Pleats

Oval Drop Waist Classic A-Line

Gathered Elastic Waist Peasant Modified Dirndl

Simple Gored Full A-Line

Ruffle Tiered Ruffle

218

Pants

Triangle Pants and Shorts – Type 1 body is angled out from waist to fuller thighs so angled out diagonal darts and pleats in pants and skirts repeat this line; bell bottom, Palazzo, A-lines, wrap, high and low waist, inset yokes, pants with and without waistbands in exaggerated angled lines. High French-cut legs in swimwear de-emphasize thighs. Type 2 body angles in from shoulders to slim hips and thighs, so bigger tops and slim pant and skirts which follow vertical angled-in body shape are best; capris, stretch pants and leggings.

Square Pants and Shorts – Best category for pants, skirts and shorts because straighter body shape allows classic two pleats to lay straight on trim hips (no round bulges that open up pleats.) Gathered elastic not as good but softer gathers can flatten down and adapt a flat-pleated look. All straight leg styles of all lengths from boxy to leggings as well as stirrups, cuffs and fuller pockets. This is the best category for shorts in all lengths and styles. This is the only category for boy-leg bathing suits.

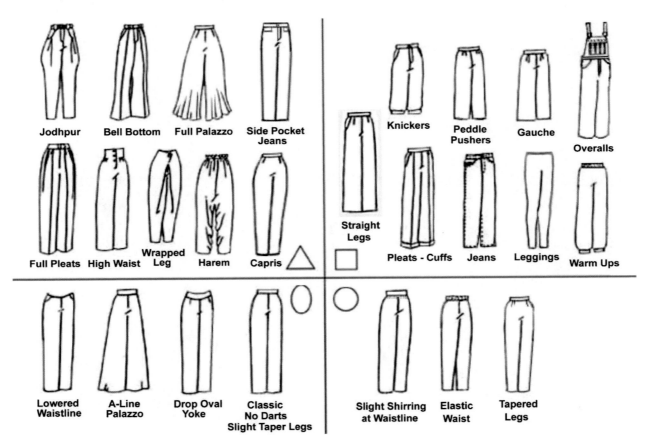

Jodhpur   Bell Bottom   Full Palazzo   Side Pocket Jeans

Full Pleats   High Waist   Wrapped Leg   Harem   Capris

Knickers   Peddle Pushers   Gauche   Overalls

Straight Legs   Pleats - Cuffs   Jeans   Leggings   Warm Ups

Lowered Waistline   A-Line Palazzo   Drop Oval Yoke   Classic No Darts Slight Taper Legs

Slight Shirring at Waistline   Elastic Waist   Tapered Legs

Oval Pants and Shorts – Waistbands that girdle across the stomach are best. No pleats except sewn down for fit. No straight full-leg slacks, rather a classic slight taper or can wear reverse A-line but not cut on bias. Inset yokes, fuller A-line Palazzo pants. High-cut sports-shorts and swimwear deemphasize thighs and are classic for all body types.

Circle Pants and Shorts – This is the least comfortable category for circle shapes. Small ankles are accentuated by tapered pant legs (no stirrups) but have to be done carefully not to emphasize larger hips. High-waist highlights small bodice. Shirred or elastic bands in pants, shorts and shirred over-skirts in swimwear.

Shorts

Shorts and swimwear basically follow the same parameters as pants, slacks and skirts. What is important is the fit over the stomach and thigh areas. Keep in mind that Oval classic lines are easily adapted and worn by all body types—but not the other way around. Flowing lightweight materials allow more flexibility than stiff, heavy fabrics.

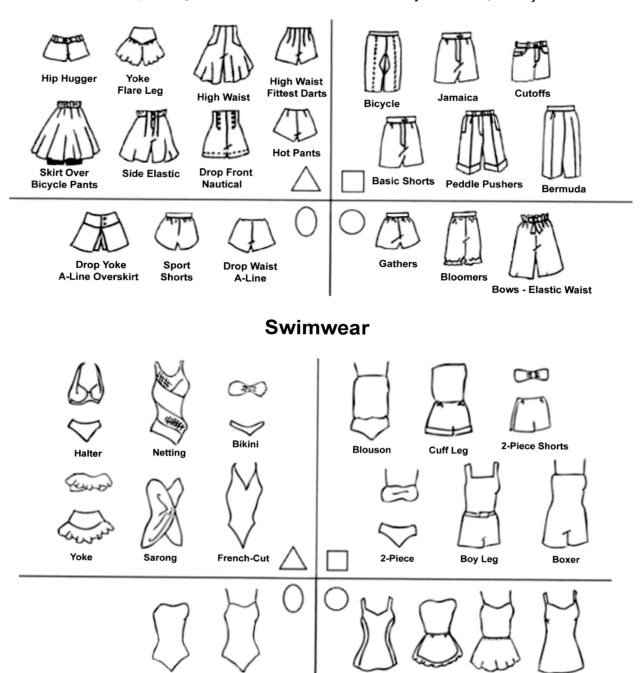

Swimwear

Loungewear

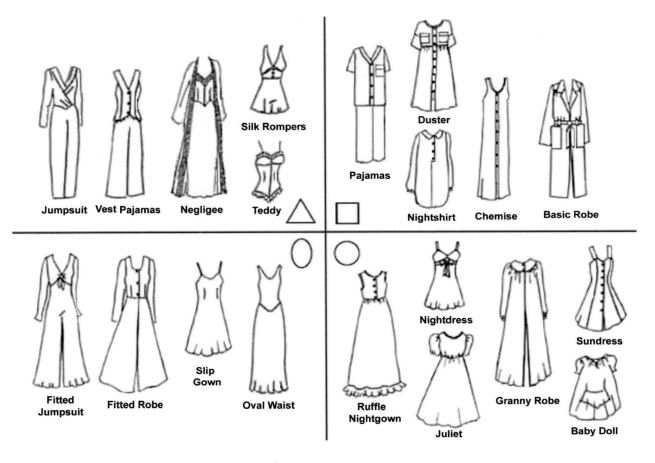

Jumpsuit Vest Pajamas Negligee Silk Rompers Teddy

Pajamas Duster Nightshirt Chemise Basic Robe

Fitted Jumpsuit Fitted Robe Slip Gown Oval Waist Ruffle Nightgown Nightdress Juliet Granny Robe Sundress Baby Doll

Pockets

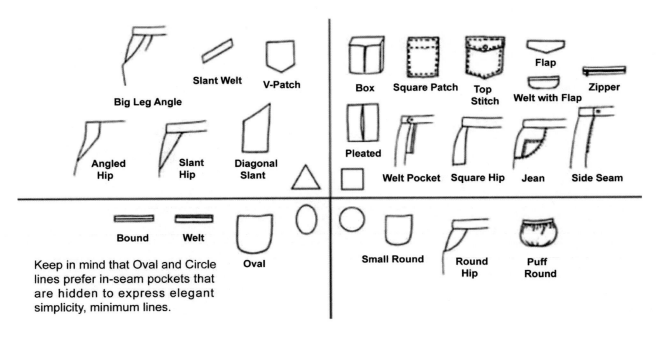

Big Leg Angle Slant Welt V-Patch Box Square Patch Top Stitch Flap Welt with Flap Zipper

Angled Hip Slant Hip Diagonal Slant Pleated Welt Pocket Square Hip Jean Side Seam

Bound Welt Oval Small Round Round Hip Puff Round

Keep in mind that Oval and Circle lines prefer in-seam pockets that are hidden to express elegant simplicity, minimum lines.

Sleeves

Triangle Sleeves – Again, this body shape can wear a great variety of sleeve lines beginning with classic sleeves. This is the homebase for shoulder pads because the angles they produce are compatible with their angled body lines and give drama. Sleeves with flounces, beading, trims, flanges tassels and tucks add costume fashion-trendy looks.

Square Sleeves – Classic set-in sleeves are good on everyone, but the squared-off shoulder gives a good line for raglan or drop-shoulder styles. The straighter line of the arm allows for sleeveless shirts and blouses. In fact sleeves of all lengths; cap sleeves, short, long, 3/4 length. More detail in this category such as buttons, top-stitching and patches.

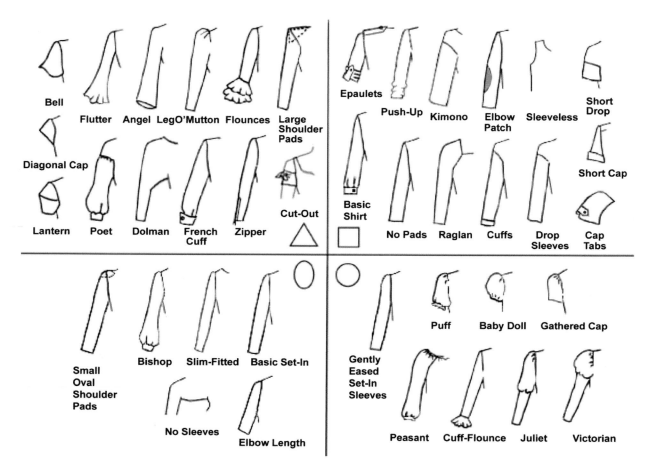

Oval Sleeves – Set-in sleeves right at the top pivot line of shoulder are most important in this category. Because the shoulders slope, there has to be a line definition; a small contoured pad can give a nice turn to silhouette as well a slight puff line. Completely sleeveless is flattering but short sleeves cut the arm line and look awkward. No drop shoulder or extra flaps or buttons. Keep sleeves slim at wrists.

Circle Sleeves – Set-in sleeves fitted at top pivot bone of arm are important because this line keeps bodice looking small and less muscular. Eased puff is excellent giving a lift to the round slope of shoulders. Shorter shaped sleeves good; no large shoulder pads. Long sleeves need to be tapered to show off small wrists. Be careful not to completely cover the wrists because that curve is attractive.

Necklines

Necklines are best determined by the shape of the face, the shoulder line and the chest. (concave chest shows more cleavage; convex shows less.) Circles and Ovals show cleavage easily; Triangles and Square chests do not. Triangle necklines can plunge modestly. The Circle is the only body shape that is flattered by the Sweetheart neckline.

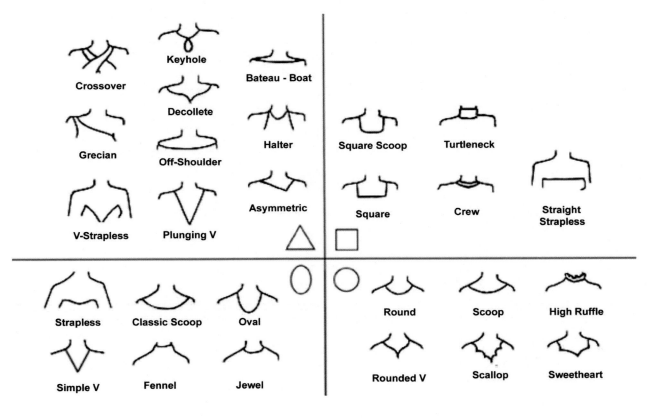

Collars

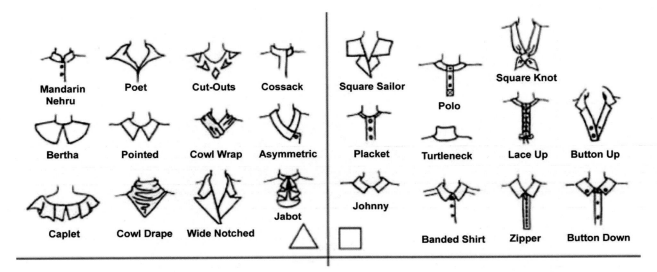

223

Collars continued…

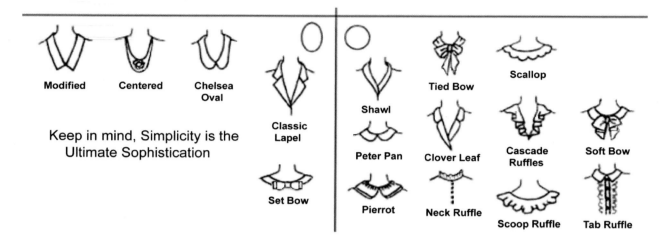

Modified Centered Chelsea Oval

Keep in mind, Simplicity is the Ultimate Sophistication

Classic Lapel

Set Bow

Shawl

Peter Pan

Pierrot

Tied Bow

Clover Leaf

Neck Ruffle

Scallop

Cascade Ruffles

Scoop Ruffle

Soft Bow

Tab Ruffle

Belts

All belts add interest and color accent. The following suggestions are grouped according to the space provided by waist and hips. Best fitting belts are determined by what will flatter the waist and flatten the stomach. The Oval body is most comfortable with belts which help girdle the stomach. If Oval and Circle shapes wear hard belts right at the waist it tends to make the stomach protrude underneath. <u>Type 1</u> Triangle does very well with most belts and wears them with flourish. For Square shapes, belts are practical and necessary to hold up pants and add touches of interesting leather work and color. Circles are better with soft ties. Hard belts need to rest comfortably in the space allowed without cutting into the ribcage or hips.

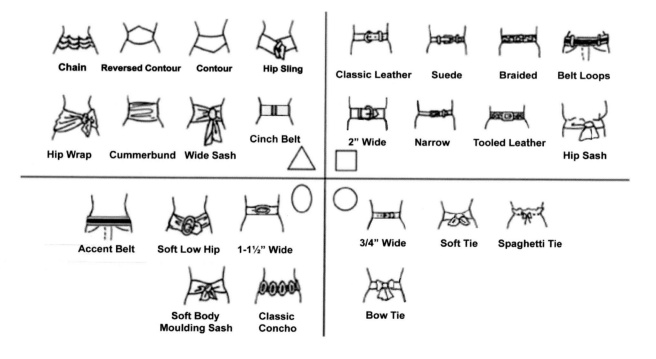

Chain Reversed Contour Contour Hip Sling

Hip Wrap Cummerbund Wide Sash Cinch Belt

Classic Leather Suede Braided Belt Loops

2" Wide Narrow Tooled Leather Hip Sash

Accent Belt Soft Low Hip 1-1½" Wide

Soft Body Moulding Sash Classic Concho

3/4" Wide Soft Tie Spaghetti Tie

Bow Tie

Shoes

Triangle Shoes and Boots – Triangle feet have a high instep. The shoes styles that express this energy are compatible with the angled foot. Dramatic expression is more trendy than practical; more decorative than classic. The word *temporary* applies to ankle straps, slings and fun shoes. Thongs were made for triangle feet. Can wear everything from decorative pointed cowboy boots, high-top or high-heeled boots to flat ballerinas. The unique triangle-heeled Espadrille is classic in this category.

Square Shoe and Boots – Casual shoes of every description are natural to this category; Birkenstocks, sandals, moccasins, rope effects tennis shoes and boots are natural for squared feet and bodies. Special mention is a classic pump with a cut-out toe which communicates this "casual" feeling. Two-tone spectator shoes. Also, leggings, stirrup, textured hose and knee socks. Straight leg boots and straps, buckles and top-stitching. Shoe laces add practical touch and serve useful need.

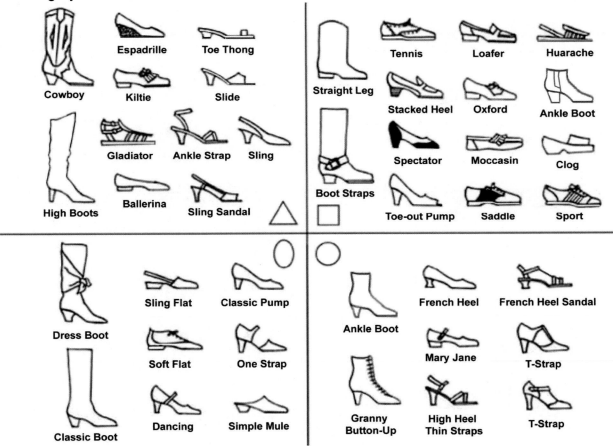

Oval Shoes and Boots – Simple classic shoes are a must in this category. The Oval foot has a longer vamp. Avoid exposed toes in shoes (detracts from classic look.) No bulky sport shoes; choose simple classic Keds or European style leather casual shoes. Invest in medium non-extreme lines that last. Simple one-strap styles. Fine boots, beautifully made.

Circle Shoes and Boots – The Circle foot has a shorter vamp and therefore T-straps are most comfortable. French heels are a classic in this category. No bulky sport shoes. Button-up or ankle boots are especially good and express feminine energy; because circle feet tend to be small, these boots provide an attractive balanced foundation.

Handbags

Handbags, totes and carry-alls are very descriptive of the individual and communicate much about the owner. It is important to keep what is carried in good repair and careful attention to details on this subject will give the perfect purse, wallet, briefcase and dressy handbag. A longer narrow shoulder bag adds height to a person's stature. Note the handle on the square brief case. An important detail is that the angle and slope of one's shoulders determine in large part the comfort of one's handbag selection.

Triangle Handbags – The Triangle body has straighter across shoulders and because of this, shoulder-strap bags sit comfortably in place and remain there. Unusual, highly decorated and creatively fashioned bags reflect the *joie de vie* of life. Articles are more changeable and temporary in fabrics and materials. They add fun and excitement.

Square Handbags – Square handbag lines express casual, practical, secure, comfortable earthy energy. The Square body shape is endowed with straight across shoulders which make shoulder straps easy to wear. Extra size, flaps, compartments, straps, buckles, stitching and leather goods give easy access. Earthy materials express this category.

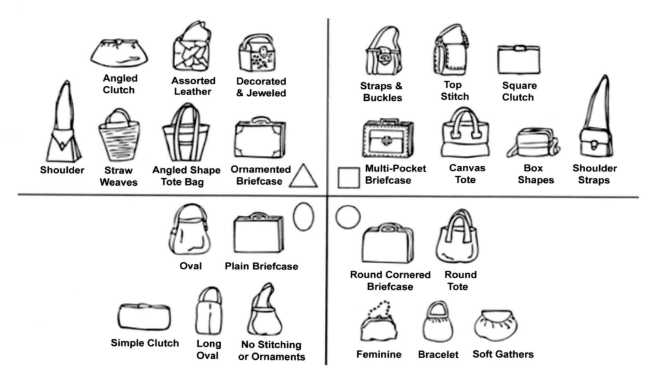

Angled Clutch	Assorted Leather	Decorated & Jeweled

Shoulder	Straw Weaves	Angled Shape Tote Bag	Ornamented Briefcase

Straps & Buckles	Top Stitch	Square Clutch

Multi-Pocket Briefcase	Canvas Tote	Box Shapes	Shoulder Straps

Oval	Plain Briefcase

Round Cornered Briefcase	Round Tote

Simple Clutch	Long Oval	No Stitching or Ornaments

Feminine	Bracelet	Soft Gathers

Oval Handbags – Because the Oval body shape has down-sloped shoulders, purses with shoulder-straps constantly slip off; better to shorten strap so bag hits at waist. Classic bags need to be made of the finest materials and workmanship. Choose long lines rather than square wide bulky styles. No top-stitching, flaps, obvious ornamentation. Simple and long-lasting is best investment.

Circle Handbags – Round, feminine lines portray femininity and express a delicate touch. The Circle body has sloping shoulders so shoulder-straps on purses and bags are not very comfortable; shorten the straps which helps secure the bag under arm at waist. Fine leathers or fabrics allow soft gathered lines throughout designs and styles. Patterning and subtle textures give lacy effect.

Jewelry

Jewelry is a powerful balancing tool and can adjust wardrobe combinations into perfect balance. Silver jewelry draws forth cool-blue-tones in warm fabrics; whereas gold jewelry doubles the warm yellow tones. This is the most important aspect for adjusting colors "outside" of the Homebase. Study and compare these lines carefully.

Triangle (Spring) Jewelry
Yellow gold, bright gold, polished copper and brass. Use special effect or ornamental pieces such as brass lion-head on belts, jeweled designs on glasses, watches set in original bracelets, unique rings, bangles, beads and large earrings. Animated designs. Triangular and unusual or fancy shapes.

Stones — artificial or real clear jewels that sparkle, vibrant hues such as rhinestones, diamonds, emeralds and very blue turquoise.

Square (Autumn) Jewelry
Yellow gold, copper, bronze and brushed gold. Use natural wooden, ceramic, macramé, earthy chunky effects and stones. Square or rectangular cuts, crisscross and complicated designs are good. Bracelets, rings and necklace strands in multiples are congruent with these lines.

Stones — coral, topaz, green turquoise, yellow diamonds, creamy pearls, citrine and petrified wood.

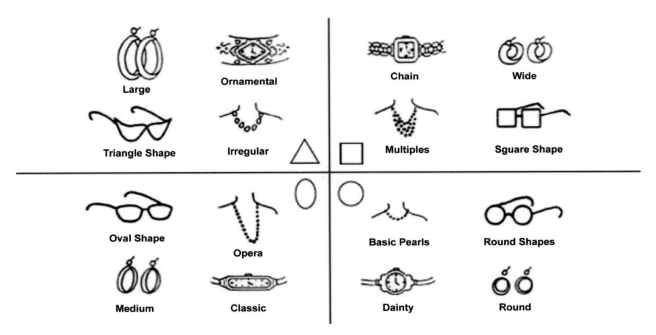

Large	Ornamental	Chain	Wide
Triangle Shape	Irregular	Multiples	Square Shape
Oval Shape	Opera	Basic Pearls	Round Shapes
Medium	Classic	Dainty	Round

Oval (Winter) Jewelry
White gold, platinum, silver, pewter and grayed metals. Keep lines even, balanced, centered, simple, single and of good quality. Oval cuts and lines such as opera pearls. No fussy dangle earrings...rather one medium loop. Do not overdo.

Stones — precious jewels, rubies, diamonds, garnets, opal, amethyst, white quartz, onyx.

Circle (Summer) Jewelry
White gold, rose gold, silver platinum and "Black Hills" gold. Use cameos, dainty settings, round lines, chokers, ribbons, delicate bracelets, lockets, filigree, fine chains. This is the natural Homebase for pearls.

Stones — soft luster stones, mother-of-pearl, pink pearls, diamonds, aquamarine, rose quartz, amethyst.

Hairstyles

These suggestions are just showing the energy expressed by certain lines in hairstyles. A Winter Inter-season influence can bend toward the classic Oval. If there is Summer Inter-season influence then add tendrils and ringlet touches. Short hairstyles are automatically going to add practical strength. And for something different, innovate with unusual off-centered exciting lines. Oval classic hairstyles tend to be best with features which are classically medium in size and centered. Unusual facial-features coincide with creative, exciting unusual hairstyle lines which can and will balance them—just be sure that the overall outside silhouette still maintains a balanced oval in combination with the shape of face.

Triangle (Spring) Hairstyles

Unique and original styles. Full side flips, long upsweeps, artistic braids, angled, asymmetric, exaggerated or trendy lines. One streak of warm vibrant hair color is a natural accent. No busy frostings.

Square (Autumn) Hairstyles

Asymmetric, casual, long and straight, short efficient styles, wedge or feather cuts. Extra lines: scarves, braids, twists, combs, barrettes. Streaking hair with warm tones gives a natural pattern effect; no platinum or silver.

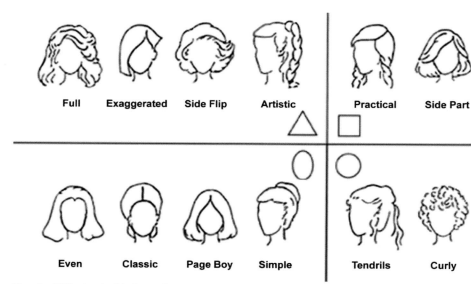

| Full | Exaggerated | Side Flip | Artistic | Practical | Side Part | Short | Straight |

| Even | Classic | Page Boy | Simple | Tendrils | Curly | Bangs | Long Curls |

Oval (Winter) Hairstyles

Symmetric, even, classic lines. Simple, center part, page boy, oval-curved waves. Classic, medium length and natural dark hair color is best. If gray, keep gray hair in the silver family—no blonde, busy streaks or frostings. Winter/Summer influence can add curls and tendrils and even ringlets that fall down in soft extended graceful S shapes.

Circle (Summer) Hairstyles

Adding circle lines to hairstyles communicate dressy, feminine, soft, curved and romantic lines. High-crowned styles or bows tied around hair for Princess look. Symmetric pony tails, light bangs, soft flips, short curls, long hair with tendrils. These lines are refreshing. Ash or platinum frosting highlights. No gold, red or black.

IN A NUTSHELL – THE UNIVERSAL LANGUAGE OF COLOR AND LINE

Yes, in a nutshell—from this point on is a summary of all the principles, concepts and cumulated information giving vital tools for a complete educated color and body analysis study. These rules will not change because they are based upon the science of a universal language. If something becomes vague there is a reason, and there is a gift in the discovery. This gives a solid, proven foundation of expanding awareness.

THE FOUR CATEGORIES OF DRESS

○ **CLASSIC "POISE" – Classic long lasting clothing, formal in the conventional standard, appropriate, proper, customary fashion.**

○ **DRESSY "BEAUTY" – Daytime and nighttime, lighter more refined materials (not as practical); a negligee is dressier than a flannel nightgown.**

□ **CASUAL "STRENGTH" – Informal clothing, practical in warmth and comfort; flannel pajamas are more comfortable than a negligee.**

△ **COSTUME "LIFE" – Any dress that expresses fun, variety and drama, is trendy or out of the ordinary, temporary, changeable clothing.**

THE 3 ELEMENTS OF A DESIGNER'S BOX OF TOOLS

This is the most important information in the whole teaching. Each season has 3 elements with their own unique function. This will provide a designer's box of tools for everything one wishes to create. The definitions for these 3 Elements are:

1. **Imagery** — These descriptive words are listed to stimulate the imagery of how each energy group expresses. Nothing can be created until pictured in your mind. Do not underestimate the value of these word images—take the time to focus and <u>feel</u> each word and they will become second nature in your creative toolbox cache.

2. **Color Modifications** — This information shows how to take <u>any</u> color and modify its energy by degrees and change its meaning. For example an olive green can be darkened into a formal color, or lightened into a delicate feminine color.

3. **Detail Lines** — For your use, the lines listed here have been sorted into the 4 season groups which become powerful creative tools. With this knowledge you can create any feeling desired in clothing, makeup, accessories and hairstyles as well as apply to all creative arts and endeavors.

TOOLS TO CREATE THE BALANCED FEELING OF "POISE"

1. IMAGERY — words that describe the balanced feeling of "poise":

classic	balanced	distant	perfection	sophisticated
still	even	set	endless	dark
stark	regal	quiet	contrast	striking
simple	stately	frozen	dignified	serene
proper	poised	formal	refined	equal
serene	impeccable	aloof	finished	etching
complete	royal	calm	ideal	quality
symmetrical	elegant	absolute	complete	aristocratic

2. COLOR MODIFICATIONS — technique used to express the feeling of "poise":

Any color that has been darkened or becomes richly deep with fully saturated color moves toward this feeling. The "darkening" in this sense remains clear, more the blue-black dark than the brown muddy darkening of duller colors. However, darkening any color still adds poise and the reserve of the mature. The extra blue in dark colors adds formality and sophistication. In fully saturated colors, the bluer colors are more regal (blood-red seems more formal than bright yellow-red; hunter green is more formal than bright lime green, royal blue is more regal than powder blue.) Stark white is called "stark" because it has the same impact as black. It can create wonderful contrasts and even doubles for "bright" in its extreme whiteness. If black is too dark for the person, white will create contrast coming from the other end of the spectrum. Extremely cool-icy colors act as white and also create contrast.

TOOL — Create with dark colors when a reserved sophisticated or dignified feeling is desired, such as for classic dress, formal attire and mature clothing.

3. DETAIL LINES — technique used to illustrate the balanced feeling of "poise":

Any line that balances, is even, uncomplicated, definite, stately or regal suggests the simple flow of the classic line. The word "balanced" indicates medium or middle ground. There is a classic feeling or basic medium expression here because the lines are not too feminine, too masculine or too exaggerated. These lines endure because their simplicity is timeless. Most of these feelings can be derived from oval figures and straight lines.

Itemized detailed examples of these lines are as follows:

O
Oval necklines, opera length pearls, oval or longer rectangular faces on watches, oval shaped toes on shoes and insteps, oval and longer soft rectangular lines on purses, oval page-boy hairstyles, hair parted in the middle or centered balanced hairstyles.

"NO"
No fussiness or extra complicated lines. Just as the tree in winter is without leaves, the corresponding feeling in dress in its purest sense would be "less" —fewer buttons and cuffs, no flaps, no loops, no fussiness, no tailored busyness, no top-stitching, no extra darts, pleats or ornamentation. Everything beautifully formed without clutter. The quality has to be good because there are no busy lines and ornaments to hide poorly constructed work.

SIMPLICITY
The simplicity of plain sweaters, plain sleeves, classic slightly tapered slacks and long sleeves, hidden pockets, self belts and buttons, A-line skirts, one-piece outfits, one color rather than two, secured bows, leotard simplicity and classic shoes such as pumps with medium-shaped heels.

MEDIUM KEYSIZE
There is a basic medium expression in this category—medium waistlines, skirt lengths and jacket lengths. Medium length hair styles. Jewelry is of moderate size; not too tiny, heavy or asymmetrically ornamental; rather one piece and of finest quality.

PATTERNS
Medium size patterns that are set, repeated and balanced—such as evenly spaced stripes, polka dots, checks and geometrics (when patterns are equally spaced they remain frozen and still; irregular patterns move.) No busy, fussy, complicated patterns unless they are set in even blocks. Contrast light colors against dark colors for a simple uncluttered "pattern."

WARDROBE ADVICE: When working with a person's wardrobe, simplicity is the strategic key. The strategy is to consider Oval (Winter) lines first regardless of the actual Homebase. Begin with minimum lines (picture a winter tree without leaves) and if that is understated then add a feminine touch (lacy soft summer tree,) if that weakens the picture change and add more lines (strengthening multifaceted effect of the autumn tree) and if this doesn't do it pull out all the stops and go for more (accents and flourish of the tree in full spring regalia.) But in your mind's eye go for the striking simple classic lines and colors first. This is the reason hair and eye color repeats are so effective; keeping the look simple and more striking yet immediately connecting the ensemble to the person. However when more is called for it is pure magic to see what can happen when incorporating their own Inter-season colors and lines. The quickest surest way to buy clothes for children and family is to simply match the colors you see in their hair and eyes. Think about it, teal eyes are not the same as powder-blue eyes, indicating a whole different take. In every outfit at least repeat something—connect the dots so to speak.

TOOLS TO CREATE FEMININE FEELING OF "BEAUTY"

NOTICE FOR MEN: Every man has a touch of beauty expressed in beautiful
hair and features; this energy plays out in men as "genteel elegance."

1. IMAGERY — words that describe the feminine feeling of "beauty":

delicate	curved	small	romantic	youthful
subtle	languid	tiny	blended	beautiful
gentle	softened	fine	darling	circular
soothing	graceful	fragile	sweet	lovely
soft	sensual	dainty	shy	pleasing
dressy	innocent	thin	pastel	precious
pretty	frilly	allure	watercolor	charming

2. COLOR MODIFICATIONS — technique used to express the feeling of "beauty":

Any color that has been lightened, thinned or diluted <u>moves toward this feeling</u>. The lighter the color, the more delicate and fragile (especially in terms of being less practical) the more feminine it appears.

Stark white is not included because it appears as overly bright, but off-white is soft and feminine. Light color lifts the feeling and acts as light-accent relief. Shining more light on the subject relieves tension in the eyes. Lightness is pleasing and commonly associated with youth. Its softness is part of monochromatic color schemes. Even though beauty is a feminine characteristic, men need this genteel expression—just as women need to express parts of masculine strength.

TOOL — Create with light colors when youth or a dressy light-touch is desired; use in blouses and shirts to lighten the face, feminize clothing for women, give a genteel lift for men and in children's clothing.

3. DETAIL LINES — technique used to illustrate the feminine feeling of "beauty":

Any line that softens, circles, curves, is fine, delicate, thin, tiny, small, subtle or suggests youth and beauty. These feelings can be derived from the circle, curved graceful lines, blended lines and effects like variegated lines and sizes.

<u>**Itemized detailed examples of these lines are as follows:**</u>

Round necklines, scoop necklines, puff sleeves, round toes on shoes (baby doll,) round shaped in-step on shoes, round pockets, round lines on purses, round buttons and buckles, round faces on watches, scalloped edgings and short curly hairstyles.

Any softly gathered effect, gathered skirts, soft drape effects, bows, soft belts, open delicate knits, lace edgings and insets, soft gathers at waistline on pants (rather than pleats,) ribbons, filigree, shirring, long wavy or curly hair with tendrils, medium long curly hair on men.

THIN

Thin straps on dresses or shoes, T-straps on shoes (associated with youth,) thin belts, extra thin buckles and buttons, delicate rings and bracelets, slim-line watches and thin bands.

TINY

Tiny buttons and buckles, tiny eyelets, fine cut-out detail, tatting, tiny pleated pin-tucking and laces, fine chains on jewelry.

SMALL SPACES

Whenever a space is made smaller, femininity and youth are suggested—small bodice, high waists, empire waists, short skirts, short curved French heels on shoes, short lengths on jackets and even "high-water" pants all decrease space area and give a young look. Low necklines, strapless dresses, sleeveless blouses and tight-fitting clothes are small in the sense that the clothing area is cut down.

SLIM LINES

Even in men's clothing, the European slim-line cut in jackets, pants, tapered shirts and finely finished shoes and thin soles have the feeling of refinement because of this touch. Women often wear their suit jackets too large through the shoulder area giving a "big-armed" masculine look; smaller fitting jackets are more becoming on women.

Even pushing up long sleeves on a sweater will make a wide-shouldered woman appear more feminine. Note that baby-dresses have small bodices, and youth is implied by the high waist on Princess-line dresses.

SMALL PATTERNS

Anytime a pattern is made smaller, it leans toward a more delicate, beautiful feeling. Soft marbled lacy patterns, blended stripes, small polka dots, soft full bloom flowers, tiny geometrics, small checks, dotted Swiss, monochromatic color schemes, tone-on-tone patterns and effects. White-on-white for men and small stripes and patterns for ties.

NOTICE FOR WOMEN: Rather than a wholly masculine feeling, interpret this energy as adding an expression of "genuine stability and strength."

---

1. IMAGERY — words that describe the masculine feeling of "strength":

natural	enriched	realistic	casual	structured
earthy	dependable	practical	neutral	tailored
mature	masculine	sporty	true-to-life	powerful
warm	textured	cozy	rustic	aged
mellow	genuine	secured	heavy	country
multifaceted	rugged	solid	comfortable	unfinished
informal	oil paint	complex	tapestry	efficient

2. COLOR MODIFICATIONS — technique used to express the feeling of "strength":

Any color that has been enriched by warmth or muted by brown-gray-black tones, or that grounds the color by giving it strength <u>moves toward this feeling</u>. To mellow and "dusty" a color, or making the color duller in a rich way expresses subtlety and good taste (i.e. burgundy colored velvet with cream-colored lace conveys a richer feeling of quality than burgundy velvet with stark-white lace.) The enriched creamy background in a kettle-cloth print gives rich depth and character to the texture; whereas a stark white background would look less rich. Neutral colors are more practical, adding a degree of background comfort—the warm thread which connects things. The rich wood in home decor grounds and furnishes a rich feeling of hominess.

TOOL — Create with muted colors when good taste, practicality and more obscurity is desired; for uniforms, business clothes, casual sportswear and neutral colors used as backgrounds to tie in and connect other colors.

3. DETAIL LINES — technique used to illustrate the feeling of "strength":

Any line that is straight, square, square-angled, enriches or underlines another line, top-stitching or any element that tacks down other lines, stabilizes, textures that add depth, heaviness or thickness—<u>all lean toward a masculine feeling</u>. These lines are large (enriched) in contrast to small tiny lines, but not extra large, even though boxlike lines do tend to appear quite large. These feelings can be derived from straight or squared lines.

<u>**Itemized detailed examples of these lines are as follows:**</u>

Square necklines, boat necks, square collars, flat square sleeves, cuffs on sleeves and pants form boxlike shapes, busy pants and jackets, shirtwaist dresses, square practical heels on shoes and boots, square toes and square insteps on shoes, square chain links, square faces on watches, short squared-off efficient hairstyles including straight bangs and hair parted on the side. Zippers, side openings on clothing, doubled breasted openings.

TWO PIECE

Two-piece outfits immediately say "more casual" even if the outfit is dressy. The more equal in space the two pieces are the more boxy and casual they look, especially in contrast to one-piece classic lines. Therefore, low waistlines, mid-calf dress lengths, pedal-pushers and wide shoulders all create squarish lines. Regular shoulder pads and especially inset yokes at the shoulders always make clothing appear more masculine and strong because of the squaring effect.

BUSY

Busy lines are indicated by zigzag as well as by extra lines used to tack-down, stabilize and strengthen things. This feeling even flows over into home-like qualities; being secure, natural and comfortable. A masculine heavy or thick feeling comes from materials in their raw, unrefined state such as thick natural leathers, wood buttons and buckles, rubber, stone, ceramic and petrified natural stones. The zigzag line used in cross-stitching or lace-ups on shoes, zippers, laced vests and clothing and even the crisscross lines of braided hair are all part of this energy.

It is interesting to see how many forms of being grounded, tacked down, secured or stabilized are used in clothing. Buttons certainly secure things, as do belts, belt carriers, button-down flaps, collars and cuffs. Suspenders are the epitome of "security." Casualness and stability, as well as multiplicity of lines is conveyed by top-stitching on slacks, shirts, dresses, pants, coats, jackets, gloves, wallets, purses and sportswear. Military effects are extremely casual and masculine in feeling.

TACKED DOWN

This strong casual look is felt from top-stitching on leather goods in purses, wallets, luggage and shoes, especially when the stitching is made visible by a lighter or darker color. The all-time loafer shoe with its top-stitching and squared moccasin toe is a prime example of this casual feeling.

BUSY PATTERNS

Medium size patterns, busy plaids (i.e., crossed lines stabilize and tack each other down,) random dots, paisleys, random stripes of different widths, "true-to-life" scenes of nature, complex Persian effects, country designs, braid, rick-rack and "homey" cross-stitching.

TOOLS TO CREATE EXCITEMENT FEELING OF "LIFE"

1. IMAGERY — words that describe the excitement feeling of "life":

colorful	animated	changeable	dramatic	vibrant
bright	caricature	temporary	original	sexy
vivid	unusual	surprised	dynamic	accent
budding	unreal	acrylic paint	flamboyant	energize
vital	abstract	spontaneous	flair	artificial
sparkle	crisp	charismatic	trendy	magnify
zippy	starched	diagonal	expand	Avant-garde

2. COLOR MODIFICATIONS — technique used express the feeling of "life":

Any color that has been brightened <u>moves toward this feeling</u>. The brighter the color, the more life (even a dull olive green can be brightened, thereby giving it more of this feeling.) Brightness accentuates and exaggerates color making it even "bigger than life" which also tends to make it more unreal. Bright colors spontaneously excite the eye and tend to invite other colors along for the "party."   However, just as too many parties are tiring, so the eye tires of bright colors.

Nature only uses bright colors for accents and then changes them often. Therefore, these colors have a temporary feeling; they are not used for long lasting classic looks. Black and white (Winter colors) often substitute for bright colors: black out-lining to set off colors and black background in patterns; stark-white serves as a lifting bright accent similar to black.

TOOL — Create with bright colors when attention and drama are desired, such as for party clothes, accent blouses and shirts, playwear, team sportswear and costumes.

3. DETAIL LINES —technique used to illustrate the excitement feeling of "life":
Any line which accents, animates, exaggerates, is different, unusual or original, has a bold or flamboyant flair, or has a surprise action which is crisp or startling gives this impression. The exaggerated line tends to turn other medium lines into costumes—from western outfits and ballerina dresses to sailor suits. Most of these feelings can be derived from the triangle figure, the asymmetric lightning bolt or pyramid pointed lines.

<u>**Itemized detailed examples of these lines are as follows:**</u>

Bell shaped sleeves, bell bottom pants, inset angled yokes, raglan sleeves, extreme A-line skirts, peplums on dresses, triangular shaped purses, wedge heels on shoes, extreme wedge haircuts, triangular lines caused by extended shoulder pads, star shapes, diamond shapes, angled or diamond-shaped faces on watches.

 Angled waistlines, angled one-shoulder dresses, side ties on dresses and blouses, side angled draping, side-flip hairstyles, irregular asymmetric lines on jewelry. Wrap around dresses or sarong-tied clothing is temporary (not sewn-on and secured) therefore invites spontaneous variety and change.

 Pointed toes on shoes, V-insteps on shoes, extreme points on collars, points on yokes, uneven "costume" hemlines, unusual skirts or skirts and sleeves which drape in irregular points.

BOLD Bold accent lines, contrast color piping, border effects, unusual straps, fancy straps, angled straps on shoes or dresses, unusual exaggerated cuts of clothing, out-lining in any way.

ACCENT LINES Rhinestones, beading and ornamentation give accent. Decorated clothing is more fun and trendy and can even be faddish because change is an inevitable part of the feeling.

EXTRA LARGE Dramatic large collars, extremely large puffed sleeves, large pleats, full circular skirts, very large buttons and bows, faddy hosiery, very high-heeled shoes or the other extreme of completely flat. Pants tucked into boots. Extra long hairstyles, exaggerated upsweeps and hair lines. Extra dramatic long fingernails; bright nail polish doubles the feeling.

UNIQUE PATTERNS Anytime a pattern is outstanding or different it is leaning toward this feeling. Undulating random stripes, star and diamond patterns, border patterns, border prints, animated geometrics, appliqué, colorful embroidery (especially crewel,) obscure backgrounds with out-standing characters, V-pointed mitered designs, exaggerated random or large dots, zebra, leopard or tiger patterns (from furs to underwear.)

Comment: The person that is easily and naturally drawn to more "interesting" lines and colors is going to be just as interesting—they will have a body shape or features which balance with more colors and lines. Consequently all these effects make life fun and interesting for everyone and can be enjoyed by all Homebase seasons on occasion. Men love things that sparkle, move and have color…we all do. So feel free to dip into all the creative tools and add your dashes—just tie them in and connect them to some of the basics. Once recognized and understood, these powerful tools will consciously serve one throughout life in all endeavors.

ADAPTING PERSONAL COLORS TO CHANGES OF LIGHT

Lighting changes throughout the day and different times of the year. Lighting impacts whatever feeling is being expressed. Most of it is felt subjectively, but it is still *there*. Morning light is clear, bright and fresh so the colors are brought up a bit; play-clothes and freshly applied makeup. Noontime light is more white, and with the over exposure of light, makeup colors are softened and fabrics of clothing give a more subtle lighter feeling. Afternoon light gives greater realism revealing texture, enriched color and natural-looking makeup. Evening light then prevails with the mystery of dark colors, and because artificial light replaces natural light we introduce more exaggerated colors in clothing and makeup.

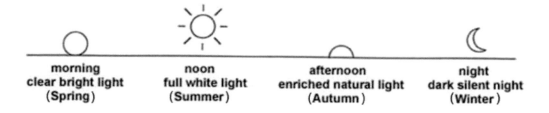

morning	noon	afternoon	night
clear bright light	full white light	enriched natural light	dark silent night
(Spring)	(Summer)	(Autumn)	(Winter)

SEASONS AND WEATHER IMPACT COLOR CHOICES

People tend to wear brighter colors and more patterns in the spring season; lightweight clothing in lighter colors to reflect the heat in the summertime; muted warm earthy colors and clothing in the autumn; and darker heat absorbing colors and materials in the winter season. Here are some tried, true and helpful suggestions:

IF YOUR BEST COLORS ARE DARK

Wintertime is your best season because your Homebase colors are primarily dark. It will be easier for you to dress in the wintertime when darker clear colors are available. However, in the summer season you will have to be more creative, wearing light colors while keeping a dark accent going. Even if the dark color is just in a dark accent blouse, belt, purse or shoes (or even the dark line on the soles of shoes) your own dark hair color will be repeated so that you are connected with your ensemble. Also in the summertime, wearing dark colors in thin materials or in a smaller-space (brief clothing like a dark halter top) is very striking and will add the needed touch of dark contrast.

COAT COLORS Although black is basic for this category, contrast is paramount (black coat over white evening dress.) One of the best suggestions is to wear light colored coats over your basic dark colors to create striking light and dark contrast; raincoats and 3/4 length coats in light taupe, white, pearl gray or icy colors are important items for this category. In the summertime, to maintain contrast, add a dark sweater or over-clothing in the summer evenings to contrast light-colored summer wear. Furs can be in white, taupe, pearl gray over dark clothing, and of course black or dark fur to repeat dark hair.

IF YOUR BEST COLORS ARE LIGHT

Summertime is your best season because your Homebase colors are light. In the wintertime you can still wear more light space than dark—simply wear lighter colors in *heavier* materials. Coordinate your light colors with medium to dark accents in blouses, shirts, sweaters and accessories. It looks a bit elegant, but then that's your specialty.

COAT COLORS Your best choice will be to wear medium-value colored coats such as taupe, blue, gray, cranberry, or soft-navy. Another suggestion is to wear monochromatic values of one color blended between your coat, clothing, scarves and accessories. Coats worn over clothing of the same color make an important classic statement for this category. Hair color repeats in coat colors are practical and can then easily be worn over medium and light shades of other Summer Homebase colors making nice coordinated ensembles. Furs are best in repeat colors of your hair color.

IF YOUR BEST COLORS ARE MUTED

Autumn time is your best season because your Homebase colors are warm. Casual clothing is associated with this season and there is a great variety to choose from—more than in any of the other categories. Layered clothing gives the opportunity to combine the multiplicity of color and values which can express through busy patterns and textures. Your basic colors are not extreme (notice that autumn leaf colors of orange, brown and green have multiple shades and tints but are close in value,) therefore you can easily adapt your colors to each season of the year. In the summertime wear creams, buff and lighter tints of basic colors in lightweight materials. You can even wear white and pastels if they are combined with medium brown and camel. In wintertime combine ecru, beige and camel to warm up black or dark colors.

COAT COLORS Hair color neutrals and multicolored tones in medium values (wine, teal, camel, brown) serve the very best here. Cream colored coats for contrast over medium dark colors are excellent. This is the best category for fur coats because it is easy to repeat Autumn hair-tone colors in natural fur colors.

 **IF YOUR BEST COLORS ARE BRIGHT**

Springtime is your best season because your Homebase colors are bright. You will feel at home in the springtime when all the new colors in clothing come out. You glow with rich color and wear fashion trends easily. In fact, in this category attention to what is currently fashionable can feel exhilarating. Summertime is also compatible with bright colors; just add more light space by using cream or very light neutrals in tones of your hair color. When the cooler season arrives you can give dark colors bright dashes of color in accent blouses, sweaters, scarves, shirts and ties.

COAT COLORS Bright colored coats is your specialty—wear it over tones of your hair neutral colors. A coat, jacket or over-sweater in your neutral hair-color is basic and solves coordinating problems. Leopard designs or multicolored furs are costumey and unique and fit into this category.

COMMONLY ASKED QUESTIONS COLORS AND LINES

Do I have to just wear the lines that go with my body type? What if I am a Circle body type but don't want to wear ruffles and little girl styles? What if I have an Oval body but I want to jazz up my look with a plunging neckline or relax in an oversized T-shirt? What if I have a Square body but I still want to express more femininity?

You now know how to adapt and modify creative effects to get the look you desire. Your Homebase merely gives you a place to start from, a solid platform from which to expand and express—and there are 5 different aspects of dress to be considered:

1. Lines expressed through your body and facial features.
2. Clothing lines that are naturally compatible with your body lines.
3. Lines that are appropriate for different occasions.
4. Lines which emotionally satisfy different moods.
5. And lines that connect with the overall desire for personal expression.

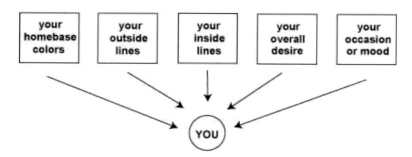

FITTING INSTRUCTIONS FOR ALL BODY TYPES

A word about fitting...the importance of precise correct fitting needs to be emphasized! These instructions are valid for all body types but they are a *must* for the Oval body shape and to some extent, for the Circle shape. The importance of following these mechanical detailed instructions cannot be overstated!

- For all body types, be sure sleeves do not end at the mid-point of the hand completely covering the curve of the lower wrist—if women cover the complete curve of the wrist with long sleeves they will appear matronly. Particularly watch out for this for Oval or Circle body shapes. Wrists are an important curve.

- Actually, without realizing it many sleeves are just too wide and bulky whereas slimmer sleeves add class and refinement. This is an important item to check.

- Set-in sleeves are classic for all body types. Oval and Circle body shapes have to be extremely careful about their sleeves because they have sloping shoulders and need to have a line which defines the arm seam. Shoulder seams or pads have to be precisely placed right at the joint where the arm attaches to avoid a broad football-shoulder on women. Larger jackets are for work, not dressing up.

- Shoulder pads actually broaden the shoulders on women so that is not helpful unless used for deliberate effect. However a small, contoured oval pad right at the top pivot bone of the arm will define the shoulder angle—this adds a graceful sleeve line especially for the Oval and Circle shapes.

- Oval and Circle bodies also have to avoid pleats in pants because fuller stomach curves tend to cause pleats to lay open, whereas Square/Rectangle bodies have flatter stomachs which allow pleats to hang down straight without bulging out.

- Ovals will find they look better in slightly low-cut jeans or pants that are positioned lower over the stomach which keeps it flat and snug. It also helps to have form-fitting belts which function like small girdles. Nothing is more tiring than having a belt right at the waist with the stomach pouching out underneath; there is no good reason to feel that way when pants and skirts can be changed to ride a little lower for comfort. Pockets may need stitching down to prevent bulging. Lower hip-slung belts or waistlines provide good balance for boots.

- There are individuals who have their colors right but their lines are completely wrong, and they don't feel good about their clothes. The whole closet can be upgraded merely by changing the lines. Lines are more important than colors (makeup can be adjusted for color balance.)

If it doesn't feel right, it isn't! Just keep changing things until you connect to your clothing and a feeling inside says, "Yes, that feels better!" When something is completely right we usually want to wear it to threads. And for good reason! All the elements align with you.

EASY ALTERATIONS WHICH MAKE ALL THE DIFFERENCE:

- For example, a sweater can be laid out, pinned, and sleeves re-set in closer to the pivot point of the shoulder. Also, try cutting away some of the sleeve bulk and slimming up the sides. A professional is not necessarily required because no matter how it goes it is going to be an improvement.

- Shorten skirts to show the contour curve of the leg. If the hemline is too far down covering the curve of the calf, the only thing left is sort of a straight uninteresting curveless line to the ankle. However, wearing an opaque hose connects to the shoe, giving a smooth curve, and the eye does not get disturbed by the interruption of bare leg.

- Boots magically provide the solution for many problems giving a feeling of connection, comfort and ease. All skirt lengths are good with opaque hose and medium-heel classic boots, western styles or any boot with a shaped-in ankle line. Straight-up-sides boots are casual and fun, but not for more classic dress.

- Remove or take out pleats in pants to flatten bulk and slim the figure.

- Oval and Circle body shapes actually have a nicely curved feminine line to their shoulders. High collars and buttons clutter up this area; by simply cutting down the neckline thereby eliminating complexity, the look is beautifully transformed.

- Slenderize lapels. It is very important to be in balance with the Keysize. There is nothing more awkward than large lapels worn by someone with fine features who is then overwhelmed by wide lapels and even large size bows and buttons.

- Change buttons to add contrast or repeat hair color. This is effective; for Autumn coloring or Influence, use beige or wooden-like buttons (never white) and it will completely enrich the whole garment. For Winter Influence then simply add contrast or dark buttons. So easy and so overlooked. Same goes for silver and gold buttons; change them to be in harmony with Homebase.

- Eliminating cuffs from pants immediately adds sleek length to the figure as well as creating a classic smooth look. Remember, a cuff is a horizontal line so the eye stops there and cuts off the length.

- Implement hair-color repeats by adding embroidery. A "picture" can be cleverly embellished by adding or replacing wrong colors for interesting connections.

- Re-dye wrong color shoes. This is huge and makes everything new and totally connected. **Important:** Have shoe-trees for all shoes and boots to keep original shape and toes from tipping up. The key here is the habit of inserting shoe trees immediately after wearing while shoes are still warm.

PROFESSIONAL METHOD FOR UPGRADING WARDROBE

People are amazing surprises. Even though they have been analyzed, dressing the whole person opens up more possibilities, bringing to light all the ramifications of the person's unique combination of color, line and design. Most of the client's special clothing can be worked with to harmonize with the individual. "Outside" colors can be brought into balance by adding or combining with their hair or eye colors. Do not make premature judgments until the whole perspective is apparent.

1. CLIENT IDENTIFIES ALL GARMENTS THAT ARE "FAVORITES"

Have the client or individual go through their wardrobe and eliminate clothing they dislike and put in a separate pile—later surprise the client by making many of those items work. Advise him/her to set aside three of their very favorite items for you to see. If a person has a favorite item of clothing there is a good reason and this gives the biggest clue to the person's individual color and style; they have spent time and money on these items and are usually wonderfully right on target. This also verifies if the Homebase and Inter-season category is correct. And, to be in agreement with the client right from the beginning is extremely helpful and puts everyone at ease.

2. HAVE THE CLIENT PREPARE AHEAD

The day before, have the client separate his/her wardrobe into these categories. This is the order you will work with as you proceed through the wardrobe.

- Coats
- Suits
- Dressy dresses
- Dressy slacks
- Dressy blouses or shirts
- Casual pants or slacks
- Casual skirts
- Casual blouses and sweaters
- Playthings and "around the house, fix the car" clothes
- Robes and sleepwear
- Jewelry pile
- Scarf pile
- Belts, purses and accessories pile
- Dressy shoes and then sport and play shoes

3. COLORIST IDENTIFIES ALL GARMENTS THAT ARE IN THE CLIENT'S PERSONAL FAMILY OF COLORS

- Be sure to have a full length mirror available...you will need it.
- Just quickly go through everything including prints, shoes, scarves, jewelry, belts and accessories and identify okay colors.
- In each category gather the Homebase colors in clothing to try on first—this is the quickest way to bring order.
- Set "outside" color garments aside to try on last.

4. HAVE CLIENT TRY ON CLOTHING

- Before digital cameras it was helpful to take a notebook and keep a list of combinations, repairs, alterations and new items to purchase for the client to refer to later. However, we found that it was much better merely to take a picture of the outfit on the person for reference, keeping a written list of what needed to be fixed, altered or purchased to fill in a "hole" to complete the outfit.
- Begin with the large items of clothing first, dressing from outer garments to smaller items and underclothes.
- Be checking shoes, belts, scarves and jewelry for hair and eye color repeats. Complete each ensemble before proceeding. Suggest client complete outfits when shopping before taking off the labels and not to "hope" they will find something to go with it later. Keep track of how many times a certain shoe color is needed. Be sure to have a shoe, belt, purse or wallet in client's hair color.

5. COLORIST IDENTIFIES ALL MARGINAL GARMENTS (USUALLY NOT WORN BY THE CLIENT) AND SUGGESTS ALTERATIONS TO SALVAGE IF POSSIBLE

- Dyeing leather goods into basic colors (shoes, belts, bags.)
- Removing extra wrong color adornments on blouses, skirts and dresses such as lace, buttons, ribbons and bows.
- Changing wrong color embroidery by over-embroidering in correct colors.
- Changing button type and color such as from gold to silver, pearl to wooden.
- Simplifying garment – removing cuffs, shortening skirts, streamlining extra bulk and jewelry (yes jewelry can be adjusted.)
- Coordinating "outside" colors with the client's hair or eye colors.
- Narrowing bulky sleeves and re-setting shoulder seams properly.
- Suggesting leotards in hair colors (to wear under suits) and opaque hose worn with pumps for a boot look, along with actual classic boots in hair colors as well.

SKETCHBOOK WARDROBE ORGANIZER

Using a paper-doll sketch in a notebook to catalogue all the outfits you coordinate is particularly useful because it is easy to forget what has been put together from your wardrobe planning times. Whenever you discover a new combination, make an easy drawing-note so you don't have to re-think shoes, jewelry etc. Planning trips from quick drawings is extremely helpful and you can keep summer clothes sketches together to remember what you did last year. Print the blank paper-dolls below, label with arrows and add touch of colored pencil. Great fun!

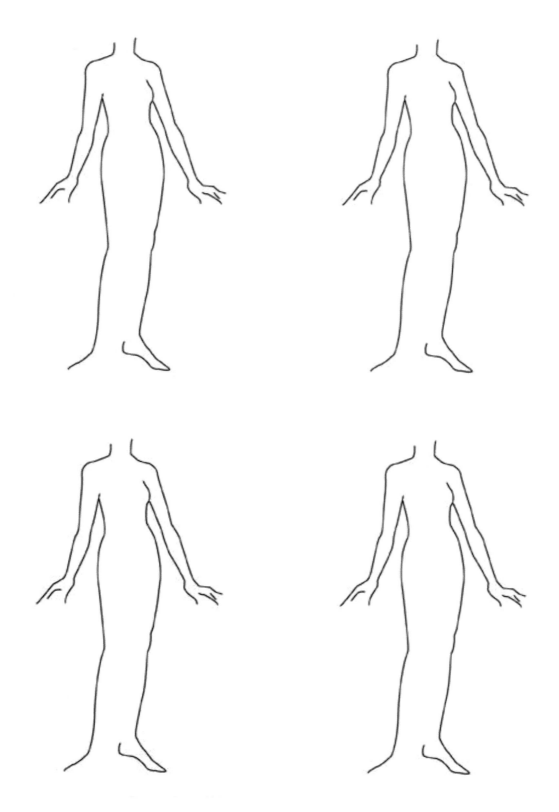

To copy for wardrobe organizer notebook, request free paperdoll sketch at
ireneeriter@comcast.net

QUESTIONNAIRE ~ COLOR AND BODY ANALYSIS
FOR WOMEN AND GIRLS

FIRST YOUR COLORS...THEN YOUR LINES

Question 1, 2, 3

Hair color to establish Homebase Season

Question 4, 5, 6

Eye color to establish Inter-season colors

Question 7

Skin color characteristics to validate Homebase and Inter-seasons

Question 8

Hair characteristics to further establish Inter-seasons

Question 9

Eyebrows and Lashes to finish fine-tuning.

Question 10 thru 21

Body Shape Analysis to establish correct clothing lines

On a separate piece of paper keep a running total of how many times you choose a color or a trait in each category.

QUESTION 1. HAIR COLOR CATEGORY

Everyone has one Homebase, either a Spring, Summer, Autumn or Winter. If you had to choose one of the following Homebases, choose the one that is closest to the color of your natural hair color in your prime or teenage years—otherwise, not gray or artificially colored. Add a point.

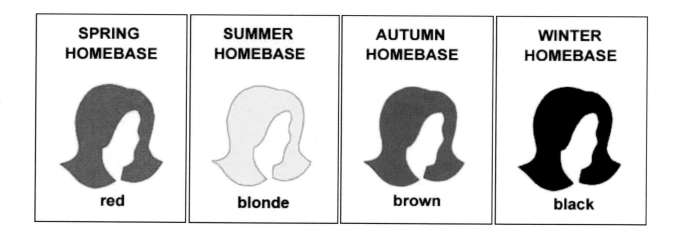

QUESTION 2. HAIR COLOR IN HARMONIC SEQUENCE

Into which season/section does your hair color fall? Count as another point.

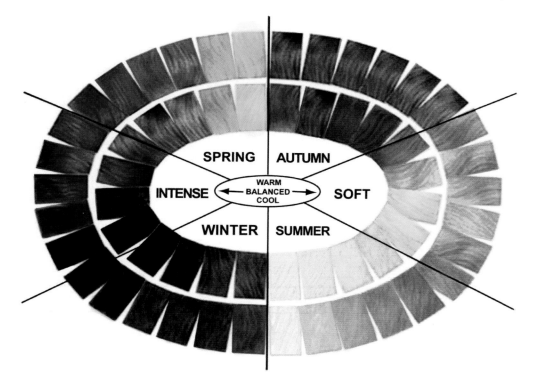

QUESTION 3. HAIR COLOR NAMES

There are 6 general categories of descriptive information. The white check-boxes represent the traits of each section. Add a point for <u>each item</u> that describes the color of your hair; if undecided add both.

Go by the hair color near the roots, not the sun-bleached ends.

1 BRIGHT SPRING	2 MUTED AUTUMN	3 LIGHT SUMMER	4 DARK WINTER	5 SOFT BALANCE	6 INTENSE BALANCE
☐ red hair ☐ strawberry blonde ☐ bright-gold blonde hair ☐ auburn hair ☐ reddish hair as a baby	☐ light brown hair ☐ warm-medium brown hair ☐ warm-dark brown hair ☐ golden-chestnut brown hair	☐ blonde hair ☐ taupe or "mousy" colored hair ☐ medium ash-brown hair ☐ towhead as a child*	☐ black hair ☐ soft-black or off-black hair ☐ very dark brown hair ☐ dark-ash brown hair	☐ honey-blonde hair ☐ sand-colored hair ☐ champagne colored hair	☐ very black-black hair ☐ dark auburn hair

*If a person was a "towhead" as a child (white-blonde) it always substantiates a Summer Homebase.

Trivia: Why are people with white-blond hair called "towheads?" In early times, flax fibers were combed through a bed of nails to separate the long thin fibers from the shorter coarser ones. This process was called towing, and the shorter fibers which were extricated were "tow." This led to the term "towheads" to describe people, particularly children, whose hair resembled the light flaxen strands.

QUESTION 4. EYE COLOR CATEGORY

Choose the colored eye section closest to your eye color. Add a point.

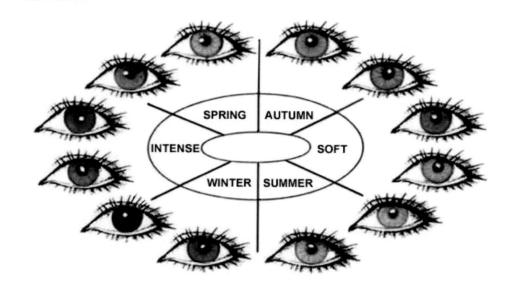

QUESTION 5. EYE COLOR IN HARMONIC SEQUENCE

In this eye-color display, choose the season/section or sections in which your eye colors are most represented. Add another point.

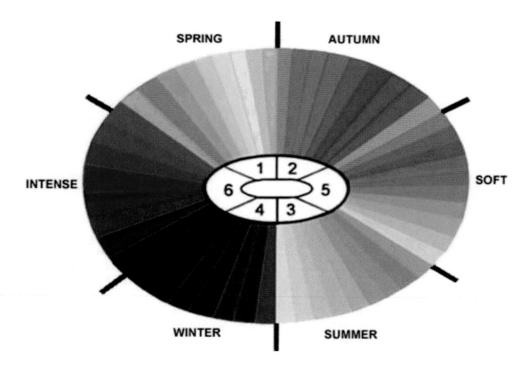

QUESTION 6. EYE COLOR NAMES

Fine-tune by adding one point for every trait which describes your eyes regardless of season or category.

1 BRIGHT SPRING	2 MUTED AUTUMN	3 LIGHT SUMMER	4 DARK WINTER	5 SOFT BALANCE	6 INTENSE BALANCE
☐ green eyes ☐ golden-colored eyes ☐ amber-colored eyes ☐ translucent "pool-like" window into the eye	☐ light brown eyes ☐ medium brown eyes ☐ golden-brown eyes ☐ muted-rust eyes ☐ dusty olive or khaki colored eyes ☐ hazel or autumn colors in eyes (no blue)	☐ blue eyes ☐ gray eyes ☐ very light colored eyes	☐ black eyes ☐ brown eyes ☐ dark brown eyes ☐ dark "appearing" eyes	☐ dusty teal-blue eyes ☐ bluish-green eyes ☐ greenish-blue eyes ☐ soft gray-green eyes ☐ matte-like appearing eye (more like an opaque "door" than a window)	☐ jet-black eyes ☐ dark amber-cast to eye color ☐ violet-cast to eye color

QUESTION 7. SKIN CHARACTERISTICS

Add one point for every trait that describes your skin characteristics regardless of season category.

1 BRIGHT SPRING	2 MUTED AUTUMN	3 LIGHT SUMMER	4 DARK WINTER	5 SOFT BALANCE	6 INTENSE BALANCE
☐ thin skin ☐ peaches and cream glowing skin ☐ blushes-flushes easily (shows red on neck and upper chest area when rubbed) ☐ freckles ☐ sunburns easily	☐ pale skin ☐ lacks red in skin	☐ light skin ☐ porcelain-like skin ☐ olive skin (lacks red)	☐ fair skin ☐ fair skin with sallow cast ☐ fair skin with olive cast ☐ black skin ☐ thick skin ☐ tans easily	☐ extremely freckled skin on face and arms ☐ skin, hair and eyes near the same color (less contrast) ☐ brown skin	☐ very black-black skin ☐ "Irish" rosy cheeks with light-skin ☐ Ethnic very warm skin ☐ "orangey" warm skin

NOTE: Skintone determines the correct Homebase. *The Law of Attraction* and the Color Tester always provides the proof. However, certain characteristics are distinctive to each category and provide short-cut information which validates and reveals Inter-season influences. The type of skin: thin, thick, oil content, blood circulation near the surface and even freckles are consistent, and every little aspect indicates something.

QUESTION 8. HAIR CHARACTERISTICS

Add a point for each characteristic of your hair.

1 BRIGHT SPRING	2 MUTED AUTUMN	3 LIGHT SUMMER	4 DARK WINTER	5 SOFT BALANCE	6 INTENSE BALANCE
☐ coarse-textured hair ☐ extremely defined widow's peak	☐ straight hair ☐ thick hair ☐ off-centered widow's peak	☐ fine hair ☐ curly hair ☐ wavy hair	☐ centered widow's peak ☐ slight widow's peak ☐ medium texture hair	☐ extremely fine-curly hair	☐ very coarse kinky-curly hair

QUESTION 9. EYEBROWS & LASHES

Add a point for each characteristic that applies to you.

1 BRIGHT SPRING	2 MUTED AUTUMN	3 LIGHT SUMMER	4 DARK WINTER	5 SOFT BALANCE	6 INTENSE BALANCE
☐ thick eyebrows ☐ bushy eyebrows	☐ medium eyebrows ☐ straight eyelashes	☐ light-color eyebrows ☐ blonde eyelashes ☐ curly eyelashes	☐ dark eyebrows ☐ dark "appearing" eyebrows and lashes	☐ sparse eyebrows (reduces contrast)	☐ extremely black eyebrows ☐ "wild" hairs in eyebrows

QUESTION 10. HEAD

On the following 12 part Questionnaire, symbols are used to indicate categories.

 Oval/Winter  Circle/Summer  Square/Autumn ▲Triangle/Spring

● **Oval head — is shaped more like an egg; oval on top.** **Neck — the oval neck is medium in length.**	● **Round head — is shaped more like a ball.** **Neck — the circle neck is shorter than the oval neck.**	■ **Square head — is shaped more like a box; flatter planes.** **Neck — the square neck is shorter and wider than the triangle neck.**	▲ **Triangle head — can be wide at top and narrow at jaw or vice-versa.** **Neck — the triangle neck is longer, or appears longer if jaw line is angled down to a V.**

QUESTION 11. SHOULDERS

● **Shoulders — are sloped down with smooth angle at base of neck and at shoulder points.**	● **Shoulders — have extra muscle at the base of neck and have rounder shoulder points.**	■ **Shoulders — more square and straight across; square angle at neck and shoulder points.**	▲ **Shoulders — straighter across and broad in proportion to small waist.** ▼ **Type 2 has very broad straight shoulders.**

QUESTION 12. BREASTS

Breasts — are oval shaped. **Chest** — is concave; dip in bone gives the appearance of more cleavage. **Collarbone** — area is moderately smooth.	**Breasts** — are circular shaped, fullness continues around under the arms. **Chest** — area has more cleavage from round shape of breasts. **Collarbone** — area is smoother because round flesh hides boniness.	**Breasts** — not as full, lines are not as curved. **Chest** — area is more flat across; less cleavage. **Rectangle collarbone** — is more prominent on the longer body shape than on the shorter Square body shape.	**Breasts** — are pyramid shaped, more perky and lifted. **Chest** — is convex, fullness across breast-plate; less cleavage. **Collarbone** — is distinctive and prominent.

QUESTION 13. RIBCAGE

   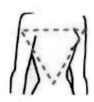

Ribcage — more oval than straight down.	**Ribcage** — round and somewhat thicker.	**Ribcage** — more straight up and down. Square boxy type ribcage is thicker. **Rectangular** body ribcage is longer and more narrow.	**Ribcage** — is V- shaped; the downward angle is easily seen from the back view. **Type 2** angles down into inverted triangle (so waist is not as small.)

QUESTION 14. WAIST

⬭ **Waist —** more medium with a smooth flowing oval curve.	⬤ **Waist —** shorter waisted because space between breast and waist is less; waist is definitely small, but becomes covered over with weight gain (like two balls being pressed together.)	⬛ **Waist — has** less indentation; the square boxy shape termed "short-waisted" is only because hipbone is right at waistline. ⬛ **The longer** rectangle body has hipbones right at waist also, but doesn't seem short-waisted because ribcage is longer.	▲ **Waist —** small in proportion to the hips and shoulders. ▼ **Type 2 Triangle shape** has fuller waist but more narrow thighs as body angles down to ankles.

QUESTION 15. BACK

⬭ **Back — is** slightly cylindrical from the side view.	⬤ **Back — is** fuller and more rounded.	⬛ **Back — is** flat and straight.	▲ **Back — is** straight; angles down to waistline. ▼ **Type 2 is** broader and thicker.

QUESTION 16. HIPBONES

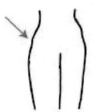 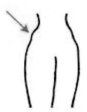 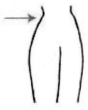

⬤ Hipbones — the key to the oval shape is low-set hipbones; the top of the hip is 2" lower than the waistline.	⬤ Hipbones — circle shapes also have lower hipbones; the top of hip is 1½"- 2" lower than the waistline.	◼ Hipbones — the square body shape has high-set hipbones right at the waistline.	▲ Hipbones — set high right at the waistline; therefore there is no hip-bone protrusion near the waist.

QUESTION 17. THIGHS

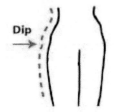  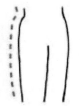 

⬤ Thighs — oval shape has oval line with a definite dip at side halfway between the hipbone and the thigh; the lower-set hipbones protrude.	⬤ Thighs — circle shape is rounder with a slight dip under hipbone as well, but this type is rounder in this area.	◼ Thighs — the square shape has less curve, more straight up and down lines with no dips; hipbone is right at waist so there is no lower hipbone to protrude and cause a curve.	▲ Thighs — Type 1 triangle thighs slant out. Since hipbone is right at waist there is no protrusion over the hip, so the line slants down to a full lower thigh. ▼ Type 2 triangle has a fuller waist with narrow thighs.

QUESTION 18. DERRIERE

  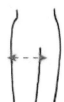 

Derriere — has overall oval shape.	Derriere — has round fuller shape; more Reubenesque.	Derriere — is flatter, more straight down.	Derriere — Type 1 has a fuller triangular shaped derriere. Type 2 "The Lioness," broad fuller chest and back which angles down to narrow tapered hips with flatter derriere.

QUESTION 19. ARMS

Fleshy spot on upper outer arm

 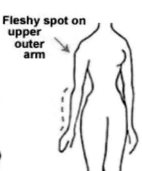  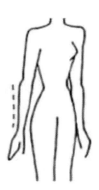

Arms — have gradual smooth oval line.	Arms — are curved; have a full fleshy spot at upper outer arm; the wrists are smaller.	Arms — lines are less curved and more straight; Square boxy type has fuller arms, but still not curvy.	Arms — a straight taper to the elbow, and again a straight tapering down to the wrist.

QUESTION 20. LEGS

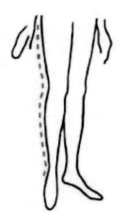   

| ⬭ Legs — have a gradual oval-shaped line to the ankle.

Knees — are medium in size.

Ankles — medium, but the graceful oval curve of leg makes the ankles appear smaller. | ⬤ Legs — rounder lines on legs are more curved; slight indent under knee with fuller calf curving down to ankle.

Knees — smaller and rounded with slight curve under kneecap.

Ankles — small. | ◼ Legs — square body type legs are more stocky.
Knees — medium.
Ankles — medium in size, less curve.
◼ Rectangle legs are longer. Rectangle ankles are more slim than the stockier square type. | ▲ Legs — have a straighter angled leg line which goes straight down to ankle with fullness through lower leg above ankle; no curve.
Knees — triangle legs and knees are fuller.
Ankles — larger; less curve indent. |

QUESTION 21. HANDS & FEET

⬤ Hands & Feet — fingers and toes more oval shaped and longer.

Hands — palm area more oval shaped; longer.

Feet — more oval with a longer vamp from toe to heel.

⬤ Hands & Feet — fingers and toes are bit more fleshy and round.

Hands — palm area more round.

Feet — ball of foot is rounder because of shorter vamp from toe to heel.

◼ Hands & Feet — fingers and toes more even across and square.

Hands — palm area more square than oval or round.

Feet — more square; shorter vamp from toe to heel.

◼ Rectangle body differs from square; has longer fingers, palms, feet and vamp.

▲ Hands & Feet — ends of fingers and toes taper down to form angles; fingers are more pointed.

Hands — palm area more tent-like, not as flat.

Feet — has an angled high-instep and overall triangular shapes.

COLOR AND BODY POINTS SUMMARY

(Fill in the points from your Questionnaire here.)

HOMEBASE COLORS:

Spring Points _____

Summer Points _____

Autumn Points _____

Winter Points _____

Balanced-Soft Points _____

Balanced-Intense Points _____

HOMEBASE BODY SHAPE:

0 □ O △ 0 □ O △ 0 □ O △ 0 □ O △ 0 □ O △

Oval Body Points _____

Circle Body Points _____

Square Body Points _____

Rectangle Points _____

Triangle Body Points _____

Triangle Type 2 _____

MALE BODY SHAPES AND CLOTHING LINES

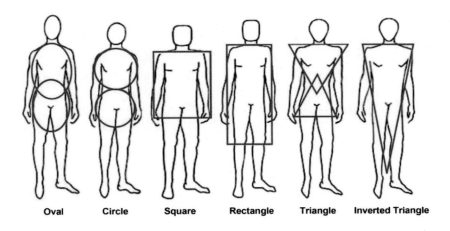

MALE BODY SHAPES

Men have the same general characteristics as women's body shapes. The shoulder lines, either straight or sloping are the same, the high or low hipbone has the same comparison, and men first put on weight in the same areas as their women counterparts.

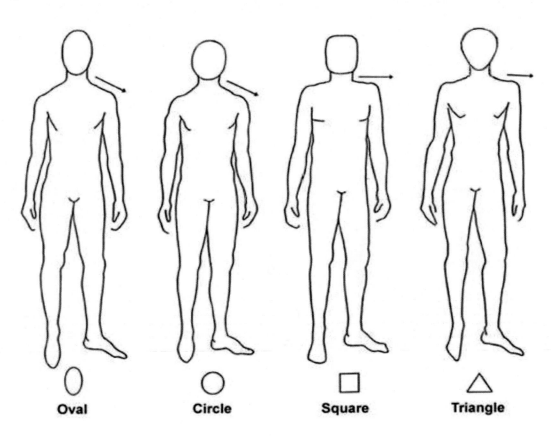

OVAL MEN — Body Shape

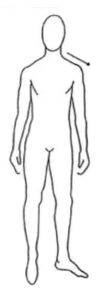

The man's oval body has many of the same characteristics as the oval female body. The shoulders slope down and the top of the hipbone is set lower than the waistline. The longer oval curve shows in calves of legs and arms and even in the longer vamp of the feet. Head shapes on oval bodies are usually oval.

Jimmy Stewart, Jerry Seinfeld and David Copperfield are good examples of classic oval body types. This body shape is generally taller than the other body types. If they put on weight, their torso areas become more ellipsoidal or egg-shaped.

Classic styles are a must in this category. Keep smooth lines on shoes and boots, no overhang or flange soles. No flaps or obvious top-stitching on clothing. Keep plackets, set-in yokes and complicated lines to a bare minimum. Important to wear fine quality fabrics that have a medium soft feel, very fine knits, silk ties and shirts. The oval lines are in effect sophisticated.

JACKETS Set-in sleeves at shoulder pivot bone No vents or one simple vent Welt pockets —– no flaps Sometimes has an angled pocket Medium lapel Smoking jacket and ascot look **PANTS** No pleats No cuffs Sansa-belt is good for this shape Straight, slightly tapered legs — no baggy styles Can have elastic in waistband **BELTS** 1-1½" wide belts Genuine leather, no vinyl	**SHIRTS** Custom or very fine quality shirts Mock-turtle neck V neck Silky knits **COLLARS** Close-set collar tips Collar pins that stay put Edge stitching (not top-stitching) **TIES** Silk and of fine quality

CIRCLE MEN — Body Shape

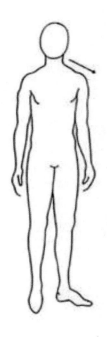

The man's circle body has many of the same characteristics as the woman's circle body. Rounder lines all around. The distinctive feature is sloping shoulders and extra muscle between neck and top of shoulder. The most obvious characteristic is the shoulder line which slopes down and there is a fleshy spot on the outer upper arm. The top of the hipbone is below the waistline and the derriere is fuller. Circle hands and feet tend to be smaller in proportion. Circles put on weight first below and above the immediate waist.

A geometric circle is not as tall an oval. Robert Redford is a circle but Pavarotti is a larger circle. Smaller circle types can wear sleek European lines. Circles wear softened, curved, subtle lines for genteel look. Be sure clothing is well fitted or tapered. No extra bulk. Can wear slightly fuller sleeves and simple round necklines. Fine edgings or fine-stitching on shirts. No busy military or heavy textured effects. Shoes, smooth European look.

JACKETS
Slimmer European cuts
Set-in sleeves
One vent (round body lines tend to
   open vents)
Rounder pockets if appropriate
 	
PANTS
No bulky pleats
Flat front pants
5 pocket jeans
Slight fullness from soft pleats
   or elastic waist
Legs tapered a bit more
Sansa-belt for casual look
 	
BELTS
1" wide belt with subtle buckle
	SHIRTS
	Set-in sleeves
	Classic dress shirts
	Slim-cut shirts
	No button-downs
	Simple no collar styles
	Casual T shirt with round neck
	Collarless 3 button styles
	Mock turtlenecks
	
	COLLARS
	Spread collar tips (rounder line for
	   rounder body)
	Fine edge stitching, not top-stitching
	
	TIES
	Silk and of fine quality

SQUARE MEN — Body Shape

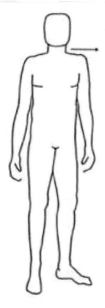

<u>Type 1</u> The man's Square body has squared-off shoulders and a very high-set hipbone and less waist indent. They have straight down thighs and are more straight up-and-down through the torso area. The hands and feet tend to be more evenly square. Square shaped men first put weight on through the waist. Robin Williams is a square body shape.

The chest and shoulder area is also thicker which calls for fuller-fitting sleeves such as raglan and full-cut shirts. Lines can be squared, off-centered, busy, tailored, casual or sporty. This is the natural home of the English country gentleman, patch elbows and all. Wing-tip and casual shoes with over-hanging soles fit into this category. Sweaters of every kind. Body can handle overlays of clothing because of straight body shape.

<u>Type 2</u> The Rectangle shape is simply taller and not as boxy and thick as the square but still has straight across shoulders and flatter straight lines. Paul Newman is an example. The distinction here is longer rectangular legs, arms, hands, feet and even neck.

JACKETS Straighter up and down cuts Can be double breasted One or 2 vents Flaps Country Englishman look Leather elbow patches Sporty layered epaulet styles Eisenhower, bomber style jackets **PANTS** Pleats in pants (no angled pleats) Can have cuffs **BELTS** 1"– 2" wide Natural leather (can be heavier thickness) Suspenders excellent for straighter body	**SHIRTS** Classic dress shirt, not fitted Button-down effects Top-stitching Extra flaps, plackets and buttons Polo shirts Drop shoulder styles Raglan **COLLARS** Button-down (square men have flat planes so collar needs to lay flat to body) **TIES** Wool or textured ties are appropriate and special mention for this category

TRIANGLE MEN — Body Shape

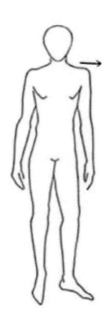

<u>Type 1</u> The man's Triangle body has straight across shoulders and angle down in a V silhouette toward a small waist and angles out again. Triangles have a high top-hipbone right at the waist. Puts weight on first through the thighs. This Triangle body wears high fashion better than any of the other body types. Can wear pants with pleats or fullness. Wears Oval lines. Clint Eastwood is a good examples of a Triangle body type.

<u>Type 2</u> Triangle has very straight broad shoulders and narrow hips, so the V silhouette goes from the shoulders to waist and angles down to the thighs to the ankles. They also have a high hipbone right at the waist. Has less defined waist. Puts weight on first through the chest area, thus, "Lion" king of the forest fame. This body type prefers to accentuate this look with trim narrow pants.

JACKETS
Athletic cut styles
Extended shoulders, narrow-angled body
Extra large lapels if Keysize allows
2 side pleats in jackets work well
Long A-line coats

PANTS
Type 1 wears pants with a flourish with
    pleats and either shaped to peg leg or
    fuller bell lines. No straight boxy legs.
Type 2 prefers no pleats. Minimize
    fullness at waist. No straight boxy legs;
    better in slim or more narrow pants

BELTS
All belts, and especially belts with unusual points of interest designs and gemstones

SHIRTS
Classic dress shirts, tapered Kaftans
Cowboy or costume style shirts
Full sleeve "swashbuckling" styles
Lace-up front shirts and classic open
 collars

COLLARS
Can handle extreme points
Mandarin collars

TIES
Triangle types go with trends or they
 tend to look out of fashion

ILLUSTRATED WARDROBE DETAILS

This is not a complete thesis on men's fashion, clothing styles, or details of fitting. It is designed to align a man's natural coloring and body type with scientific principle. Men's lines are best explained by comparison. FACT: All men can wear classic oval lines, but the Oval body <u>needs</u> to wear classic oval lines (Circle, Square and Triangle body shapes have more choices.) The illustrated clothing lines shown here fit naturally on the body type indicated. Remember, the following terms are used interchangeably because they express the same energy:

Oval/Winter Circle/Summer *Square/Autumn* Triangle/Spring

COMMENTS ON MEN'S JACKETS AND SHIRTS

O Oval Coats and Shirts (Winter Homebase) For Everyone.

This is a very sophisticated category. Follow the simple flow of the classic line; single breasted coats, stately, regal, dignified and strong. Invest in classic styles that last. Create striking contrast with simple two-tone color schemes—never combine more than two colors unless one of them is the hair color. Avoid fussiness or tailored busyness, western, military or extreme sporty looks. No cuffs, extra buttons, flaps or ornaments.

O Circle Coats and Shirts (Summer Homebase)

Use traditional lines adding refined genteel or "European" feeling. Wear softened, curved and blended lines for an elegant look. Be sure clothing is well-fitted and tapered, single breasted—no extra bulk. Smaller detailed work is excellent; white-on-white, fine edgings and stitching on shirts. May wear fuller sleeves and simple plain necklines. Keep away from heavy military lines, coarse looks or polo shirts unless fitted.

☐ **Square Coats and Shirts (Autumn Homebase)**

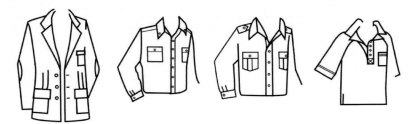

Think of the "English Country Gentleman" with a full range of flexibility into tailored, casual and sporty lines, single and double breasted. Lines can be asymmetric, busy and more complicated. Military pleats and button-down effects are good. Can use extra flaps, cuffs, overlays (sweater or vest over shirt,) top-stitching, buckles, cable stitching, leather buttons, leather patches on sleeves and pockets, even some ethnic looks. Combine different textures, such as suede and knit.

 Triangle Coats and Shirts (Spring Homebase)

High fashion, original style and strong accent of colors are very important. Good in dramatic lines such as A-line long coats, exaggerated (large or unusual) collars, cuffs, inset yokes and sleeves. Western styles, mandarin collars, Spanish, Indian or foreign lines and designs are fitting and give colorful accents. Use contrasting colors for piping, collars, cuffs, trims, accent linings, decorative stitching and buttons.

COMMENTS ON MEN'S ACCESSORIES AND SHOE LINES

History shows that symbols of lines, shapes and colors have always represented and distinguished men—in the form of emblems, seals, coat of arms, uniforms and all assortments of men's clothing and accessories.

Pay attention to lines and colors of shoes, wallets, belts, hats, key-holders, briefcases, gloves and luggage. It is an advantage and pleasing to see golf shoes, golf bags, boats and cars which reflect the individual man. All details count and if chosen thoughtfully according to the Homebase, the man will have an uncomplicated smooth overall look which serves him efficiently and economically.

Oval Shoes   (Winter Homebase)
Classic, smooth, well finished. Keep boots plain. No extra stitching, over-hanging soles, raised moccasin toes, saddle casual looks, extra buckles, straps, flip-flops, large eyelets or laces.
Accessory colors — black, navy, gray charcoal, dark brown, and maroon.

Circle Shoes (Summer Homebase)
Smooth "European" look. Fine stitching and nicely finished. No over-hanging soles, bold top-stitching, large eyelet holes, extra buckles or straps. Use soft leathers, mesh or perforated designs. Can wear light colored shoes that match hair color.
Accessory colors — taupe, bone, wine, grayed-brown, gray, charcoal, French blue, maroon, light gray, wine and bone.

Square Shoes (Autumn Homebase)
Any style is appropriate, but earthy looks are wing-tip, raised moccasin toes, saddle shoes, thick soles, top-stitching, laces, straps, flaps and buckles. Boots are excellent. Natural leathers.
Accessory colors — brown, tan, camel, cordovan, beige, orange-tan, teal blue, rust, gold, olive and cream.

Triangle Shoes (Spring Homebase)
Use unusual simulated leathers; lizard, snake and alligator. Multicolored leather patterns and patents. Western boots and belts, wedge soles, large shoe buckles and elaborate scandals.
Accessory colors — red brown, wine, cordovan, gold, teal blue, rust, green, brown, caramel and cream.

COMMENTS ON MEN'S HAIRSTYLE LINES

Men's hairstyles have become as interesting and varied as are women's. Presented below are guidelines for balancing lines through men's hairstyles. Medium length hairstyles are classic; wavy or curly hair is better worn a bit longer; straight hair contours are naturally aligned with masculine practical styles; and very full or extreme hairstyles are cuts which express lively, exaggerated and often dramatic flair.

Oval Hairstyle Lines (Winter) Symmetric, classic lines. Medium length is best — halfway over the ears and soft around the neck. Natural dark hair color.	
Circle Hairstyle Lines (Summer) Hair may be worn longer and allowed to curl softly. This category looks better without a definite side part. Naturally wavy or curly hair is typical.	
Square Hairstyle Lines (Autumn) Asymmetric or angled lines make a side part very appropriate in this category. Straight hair may be worn short or of moderate length. Clipped-to-the-head cuts suggest a down-to-earth business or efficient feeling.	
Triangle Hairstyle Lines (Spring) Unique and original styles. Full, asymmetric and exaggerated lines have full sway here. Long curly hair, pompadour or extreme comb-backs fit into this category. Dreadlocks or shaved heads are dramatic.	

COMMENTS ON MEN'S PATTERNS

Each of the 4 Homebase categories has special patterns most compatible with their lines and colors. Designs and patterns are important to pay attention to because they can overwhelm or understate a man's appearance if chosen out of balance with his features. Features make a composite design on the face and are "key" in determining if the individual should wear small, medium, large or extra large textures and patterns.

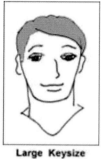 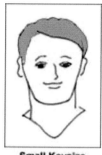

Large Keysize   Small Keysize

A Keysize is based on the line-design of the face—the spacing, size and positioning of the eyebrows, eyes, nose and mouth. A large Keysize has features which are spread out over the face—a small Keysize has features set in closer together.

A Keysize applies to everything: button sizes, belt widths, jewelry sizes, lapel widths, patterns on ties and shirts, large or fine stitching on edges, sunglasses, hats, rings, watches and buckles. The following examples of dots, stripes and checks measured in inches gives an idea of the size of extra large, large, medium, medium small and small. If unsure of the correct keysize, <u>medium</u> patterns are safe and good on everyone.

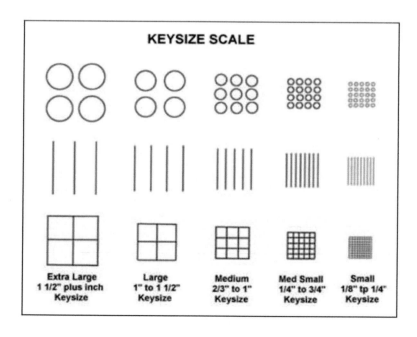

KEYSIZE SCALE

| Extra Large 1 1/2" plus inch Keysize | Large 1" to 1 1/2" Keysize | Medium 2/3" to 1" Keysize | Med Small 1/4" to 3/4" Keysize | Small 1/8" tp 1/4" Keysize |

O Oval Patterns   (Winter Homebase)

Designs are set, still, quiet, calm, even, definite, striking and symmetric.

Patterns include equal stripes, polka dots, geometric, check and patterns which are set, repeated and balanced. Avoid patterns which are off-center, paisleys, faded, obscure, busy, uneven and wandering. Contrast dark colors against light colors.

O Circle Patterns   (Summer Homebase)

Designs are smaller in detail, blended tones or the elegant understatement which says it all.

Patterns can be lightly marbled, blended stripes, small polka dots, full bloom flowers, small checks and small geometrics. Use blended colors, tone-on-tone, water color effects, or monochromatic schemes.

□ Square Patterns   (Autumn Homebase)

Designs are square and suggest multifaceted expressions of busyness, enrichment, practicality and naturalness.

Patterns can be plaids, random dots, paisleys, textured, chevron, random stripes, "true-to-life" scenes of nature, complex Persian effects and all-over busy designs. Patterns should reflect the warm multiple colors of Autumn.

△ Triangle Patterns   (Spring Homebase)

Designs are exaggerated and accented with bright colors.

Patterns include undulating random stripes, animated geometrics, border prints, colorful embroidery, obscure backgrounds with outstanding characters, mitered designs and exaggerated random dots. Patterns can be outlined with black or accented with white.

EYEBROWS FOR MEN...IMPORTANT

Men often have a problem with their eyebrows thinning or graying, which tends to make the person appear expressionless. The ends of the brows thin first, which takes away from the look of breadth through the forehead which is needed to project a strong masculine statement—to be a "LION" rather than a "deer" the whole natural brow line must show. Deers have narrow faces and even though they are graceful and swift, the Lion is KING of the forest.

   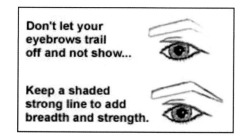

Men with sparse or balding eyebrows can darken their brows by lightly brushing with a dark eyebrow wand, or better still, using a hard brown or charcoal pencil. Carefully done, the pencil effect is natural (certainly more natural than no eyebrows!) The added shaded color makes a man look younger because it brings features back into focus, fills in the original brow hair-color and keeps him from looking washed out. After men try it and see the difference a full eyebrow can make, they are convinced—eyebrows are as important for men as they are for women. Distracting bushy eyebrows can be trimmed.

Best Tip For Balding Eyebrows:

These balding eyebrows can be darkened by using a hard Stanford *Design* Ebony art pencil #14420. Even though the pencil says "Jet Black Extra Smooth," it is actually a non-lead pencil that is just hard enough to draw lightly on the skin and looks natural when used to pencil-in the brow area that has become sparse. If there is any Winter in the coloring (dark color in hair, darker hair roots or even dark eyes) this will always work and look natural. For lighter coloring experiment with a brown or taupe pencil.

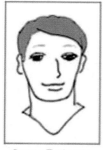

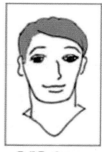
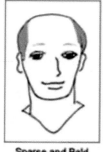
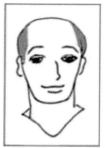

Sparse Eyebrows   Full Eyebrows   Sparse and Bald   Bald but with Brows

"A MAN IN A SUIT IS TRANSFORMED"

All men look wonderful in classic suits! Women fall in love with men in suits—they can't help it. Suits are derivatives of the military uniform which technically is the apex of all attire being decorous, functional, dignified and perfectly cut as well as comfortable. Men, regardless of body type, can wear Oval classic lines in suits because these suits have set-in sleeves and this is the most flattering look for every man.

HOW TO WEAR COLOR COMBINATIONS

Suits are basic for men. Everyone can wear <u>black, charcoal and navy</u> colored suits. However, it is important to wear the right accessories and accent colors which will connect a man to his outfit. Keeping accessory colors within the Homebase colors will serve efficiently and distinctively without having to guess and make mistakes.

The Law of Attraction will assist in connecting a man to his suit if the hair and eye colors are repeated in accessories. In the examples below, the 3 classic suit colors can be adapted for each Homebase merely by wearing shirts and ties chosen from the personal Season and Inter-season colors.

Black Suits – Charcoal Suits – Navy Blue Suits

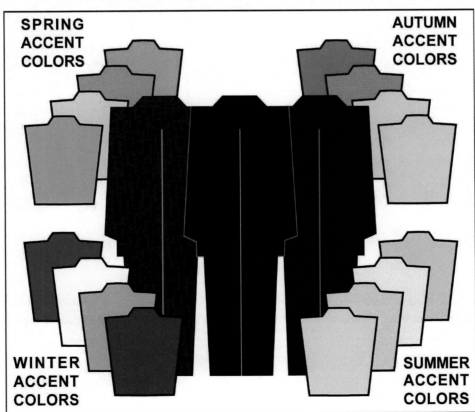

WINTER HOMEBASE

Notice the striking statement of "poise" these Winter colors make as The Law of Attraction connection draws forth and brings out cool color changes and adds contrast.

AUTUMN HOMEBASE

Notice the casual statement of "strength" these Autumn colors make as *The Law of Attraction* connection draws forth and brings out warmer color changes and adds medium value contrast.

SUMMER HOMEBASE

Notice the subtle statement of "genteel" gentleman these Summer colors make as The Law of Attraction connection draws forth and brings out cooler changes and adds light value contrast.

SPRING HOMEBASE

Notice the colorful statement of "life" these Spring colors make as *The Law of Attraction* connection draws forth and brings out warm color changes and adds bright value contrast.

GOOD COLOR COMBINATIONS FOR DARK HAIR

There are more black-haired people in the world than the other categories so the following descriptions are detailed examples to show how to combine colors with black.

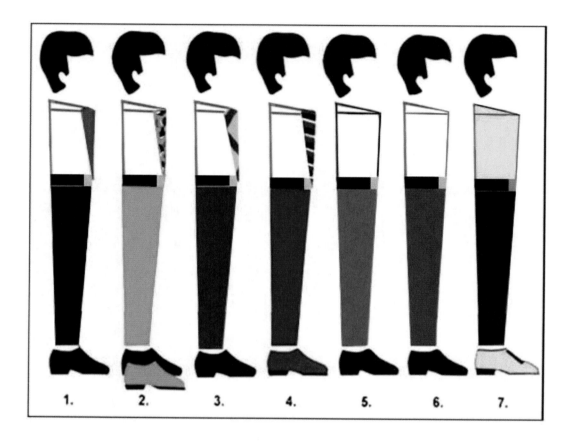

1. The classic white shirt, black pants, bluish-red tie, black shoes, silver belt buckle and watch.

2. When wearing an outside color (camel,) combine it with black, white and silver. Make sure a matching (camel) shoe has a dark sole and heel.

3. Navy blue pants will substitute for a dark hair color match.

4. Cordovan shoes if soles are black, with white shirt, silver buckle and watch.

5. Medium value taupe pants should be worn with stark white, black and silver.

6. Ash-olive slacks are excellent if worn with stark white, black and silver.

7. Outside colors such as tan, sand or oatmeal are excellent if combined with black. A bronze buckle is also good—and notice the soles of the light shoes are black.

MEN WEAR "MAKEUP" COLORS IN THEIR TIES

Women wear flattering pinks and reds in their makeup—men wear pleasing pink and red accent colors in their ties and shirts. This adds healthy color to skintones. Be aware of correct Homebase pink and red colors and repeat them often in color schemes.

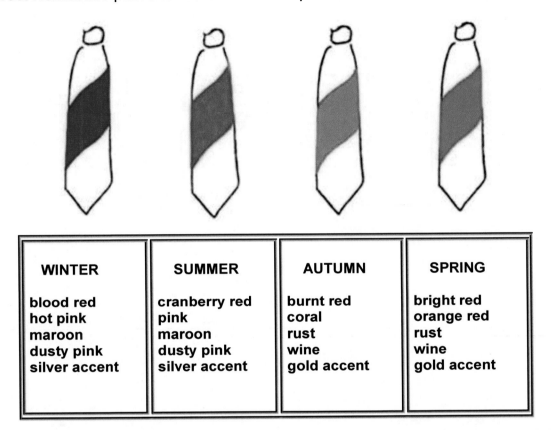

WINTER	SUMMER	AUTUMN	SPRING
blood red	cranberry red	burnt red	bright red
hot pink	pink	coral	orange red
maroon	maroon	rust	rust
dusty pink	dusty pink	wine	wine
silver accent	silver accent	gold accent	gold accent

DRESS HANDKERCHIEFS AND ACCENT COLORS

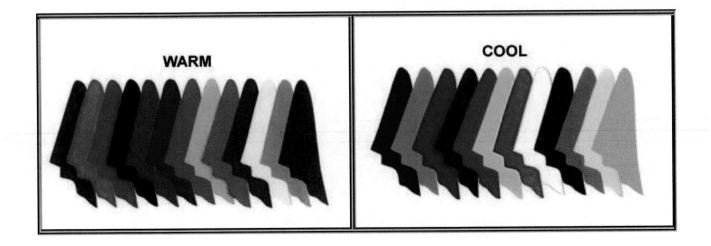

WARM　　　　COOL

SHOE COLORS FOR MEN

All men can wear black shoes because the strong image of a man calls forth a sturdy, dark foundation represented by a dark shoe color. Even though it is balanced to have the top and bottom of the person's "frame" match, a light haired man still wears dark colored shoes as well as light shoes. Dark haired men are more limited in shoe colors, but if they do wear a light colored shoe it will be better when balanced with a black sole which will connect to the dark hair (see example above.) Men with white hair can obviously wear white shoes with a dark sole; cream colored white hair is best with cream or tan shoes with a darker sole.

On the subject of shoes…a suggestion...

It has been put forward that men's feet are not their most attractive point. Richard Torregrossa, the man Fortune 500 companies named as a menswear and style consultant, states that nothing emasculates a man like sandals or flip-flops. Loafers, driving shoes and moccasins are smart alternatives; however there are marvelous sandals for men which are made with woven leather covering the toe area with a strap around the heel—comfortable and casual with nice style.

BELT COLORS FOR MEN

Notice that Spring and Autumn belts (the top half of the oval diagram) are warm leather colors with gold or bronze buckles; Winter and Summer belts (on the bottom half) are cool leather colors with silver buckles. The balanced belt colors on the sides of the oval diagram can have either gold or silver buckles depending on one's Homebase.

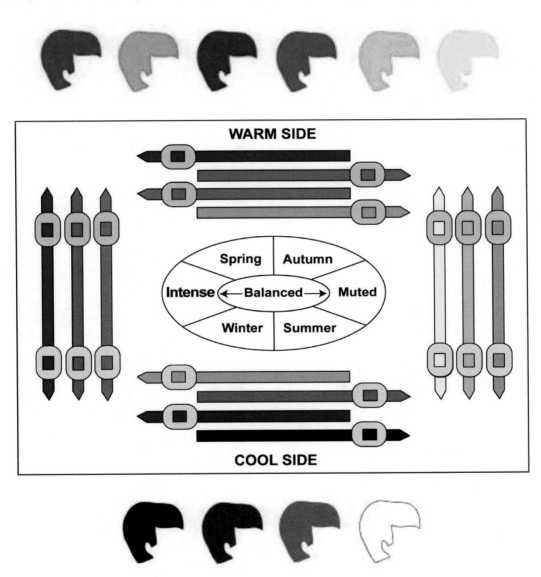

Business Accessories:

Invest in the best quality possible. Have briefcases in Homebase hair-color and a compatible color in a pen. When business accessories become worn and leather-bare around the corners and edges, replace them just as one would worn-out shoes.

MEN'S WARDROBE COMBINATION GUIDELINES

The following four basic wardrobe plans will help coordinate an easy-to-put-together wardrobe. Locate the Homebase category.   *Accent colors for ties and accessories..

O **FOR WINTER MEN**

SUIT JACKET	SLACKS	SHIRT	TIE COLOR COMBINATION	SOCKS/ SHOES & BELT
black suit pinstripe suit		white, light pink or any icy pastel	black/white/blood red black/gray/white/*accent	black/black
navy suit		white or lt. gray icy blue	navy/white/cranberry/silver navy/gray/light blue/silver	navy/black
charcoal suit (pinstripe is great option)		white light gray icy lavender icy pink	black/gray/silver/blood red black/gray blend/yellow black/silver/lavender black/pink/silver/gray	charcoal/black
charcoal brown suit		stark white icy pink	brown/taupe/white/silver brown/ pink/silver	brown/dk brown
taupe suit		stark white	black/white/silver/taupe	taupe/ black
light gray jacket (micro suede is good option)	black burgundy navy hunter charcoal charcoal	white light pink navy turtleneck hunter " charcoal " white on white	black/white/silver/*accent black/pink/burgundy/gray black/white/silver/*accent	black/black burgundy/black navy/black hunter/black dk charcoal/black dk charcoal/black

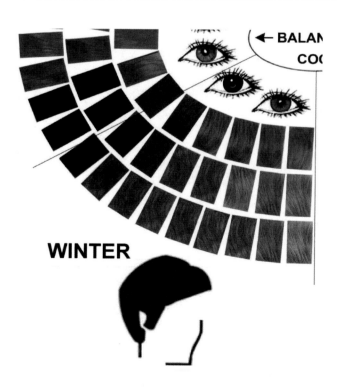

WINTER

282

FOR SUMMER MEN

SUIT/JACKET	SLACKS	SHIRT	TIE COLOR COMBINATION	SOCKS/ SHOES & BELT
navy suit		white or bone pinky-beige powder blue	navy/silver/cranberry navy/blue/pinky beige navy/white/blue/yellow	navy/soft black navy/brown navy/soft black
taupe suit		white-on-white	taupe/white/black/+*accent	taupe/black
soft brown suit (milk chocolate)		white Icy pink powder blue	gray/brown/ white/rose brown/silver/pink/ maroon dark blue/silver/taupe	brown/brown brown/brown brown/brown
dusty teal suit		Icy-aquamarine white	hunter/bone/icy-aqua hunter/teal/silver/white	teal/soft black teal/soft black
gray suit		white	gray/silver/ cranberry	gray/soft black
navy jacket	taupe	white	navy/taupe/white/yellow	taupe/black
light gray jacket (micro suede)	charcoal wine navy	white wine turtleneck navy turtleneck	charcoal/silver/**accent	charcoal/black wine/cordovan navy/soft black

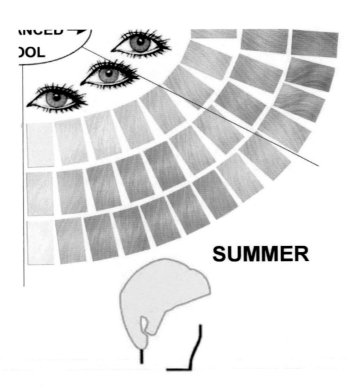

SUMMER

☐ **FOR AUTUMN MEN**

SUIT/JACKET	SLACKS	SHIRT	TIE COLOR COMBINATION	SOCKS/ SHOES & BELT
brown suit		white aquamarine	brown/off-white/coral brown/teal/aquamarine	brown/brown brown/brown
ash-olive suit		white	dark olive/light olive/ white/ touch of black	ash-olive/ soft black
navy suit		cream	navy/cream/brown/gold	navy/brown
wine suit		light sand	wine/sand/gold	wine/brown
teal blue suit		ecru or wheat	teal/ecru/aquamarine	teal/brown
camel suit		white	camel/off-white/red	camel/brown
beige or tan suit		white	beige/white/brown/gold	beige/brown
rust suit		off-white	rust/off-white/gold	rust/cordovan
camel jacket (optional ultra suede)	charcoal navy charcoal black	cream navy turtleneck charcoal " black "	charcoal/camel/gold	camel/dark brown charcoal/ black black/black black/black
brown tweed jacket	brown	off-white	any *accent colors in jacket	brown/ brown

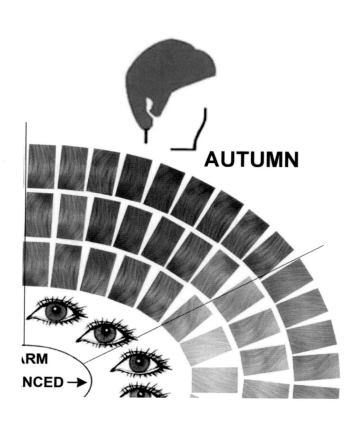

AUTUMN

RM

NCED →

284

 **FOR SPRING MEN**

SUIT/JACKET	SLACKS	SHIRT	TIE COLOR COMBINATION	SOCKS/ SHOES & BELT
camel suit		white	camel/gold/bone/red	camel/brown
black suit		beige, ecru or cream	black/cream/beige/gold/ red or *accent color	black/black
beige or tan suit		white	tan/beige/dkbrown/*accent	beige/brown
ash-olive suit		white	ash olive/white/black/gold	olive/ black
reddish- brown suit		off-white	brown blend/**accent colors	cordovan/ cordovan
navy suit		ecru	navy/gold /brown-blend	navy/brown
wine suit		cream	wine/cream/black accent	wine/black
reddish-camel jacket	charcoal black	off-white black turtleneck	camel/gray/charcoal/gold	charcoal/black black/black
gold jacket	black	black turtleneck		black/black
navy jacket	camel camel	cream shirt camel turtleneck	navy/cream/gold/brown	camel/brown camel/brown
dark red-rust jacket	black charcoal	black turtleneck charcoal turtleneck		black/black charcoal/black
tweed jacket	brown	cream, beige, sand, wheat or ecru	brown, cream, *accent colors in jacket	brown/brown

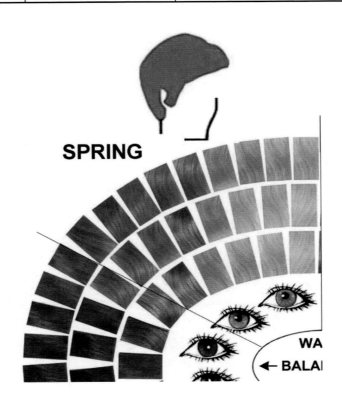

SPRING

WA

← BALA|

COMBINATIONS FOR DARKER WARM/COOL BALANCED COLORING

○ □ **Winter Homebase with Autumn Influence**

□ ○ **Autumn Homebase with Winter Influence**

△ ○ **Spring Homebase with Winter Influence**

SUIT/JACKET	SLACKS	SHIRT	TIE COLOR COMBINATION	SOCKS/ HOES & BELT
charcoal suit		white for Winter cream for Sp/Aut	charcoal/cream/gold/ Homebase *accent color	charcoal/brown
navy suit		warm beige	navy/beige/camel/blue	navy/dark brown
dark brown suit		pinky beige	dark-brown/beige/and burgundy	dark brown /dark brown
beige, tan or ecru suit		stark white	black/white/beige/tan Homebase *accent color	beige/black
camel jacket	burgundy black navy	burgundy shirt or turtleneck turtleneck black navy shirt or turtleneck		burgundy/cordovan or black for Winter back/black navy/brown or black for Winter
black jacket	camel	camel shirt or turtleneck	black/camel/red/gold	camel/black

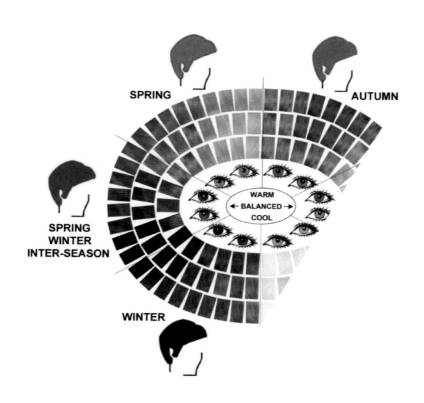

COMBINATIONS FOR LIGHTER WARM/COOL BALANCED COLORING

○ □   **Summer Homebase with Autumn Influence**

□ ○   **Autumn Homebase with Summer Influence**

△ ○   **Spring Homebase with Summer Influence**

SUIT/JACKET	SLACK	SHIRT	TIE COLOR COMBINATION	SOCKS/ SHOES & BELT
navy blue suit		ecru or beige	navy/ecru/blue/gold/brown	navy/brown
medium brown		white-on white	brown/taupe/wine or peach *accent for Sp/Aut	brown/dark brown
medium brown		icy aquamarine	brown/taupe/teal/aqua	brown/dark brown
tan		white-on-white	tan/brown/white/red/gold	tan/dark brown
dusty teal suit		icy aquamarine	hunter green/aqua blend	hunter green/black
light dusty teal suit		hunter green turtleneck		hunter/soft black or brown
charcoal suit		beige or cream	gray blend/red/gold/silver	charcoal/brown or soft black
charcoal suit		cornsilk yellow	gray blend/yellow	charcoal/brown/black
ash olive suit		white	ash-olive/red/black/gray	ash olive/black
burgundy or wine jacket	camel	cream shirt	wine, cream/camel/gold	camel/brown or cordovan
navy jacket	camel	cream shirt	navy/lt. blue/cream/gold	navy/brown or black
ligtht gray jacket	brown	brown turtleneck		brown/brown
light brown tweed jacket	brown	cream or pastel warm icy colors	brown blend, cream Homebase *accent colors	brown/brown

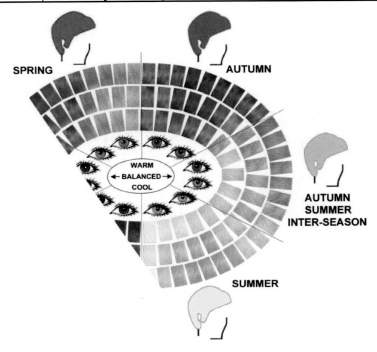

287

WARDROBE TIPS FOR MEN

• Go into the closet and look at your shoes. If you are not regularly using shoe trees to re-shape your shoes, the toes of your shoes are all tipping up. Using shoe trees will keep your shoes looking like new for a long, long time. The key is the habit of inserting shoe trees right away while the shoes and boots are still warm from wearing.

• Stiff shirts are not classy. The higher thread density give fabric a softer more luxurious feel. Look for quality finishing; no puckering or loose threads in stitching.

• Over dry-cleaning suits give them a cheap shine. If soiled have them spot-cleaned, or if wrinkled have them pressed.

• Be sure shoes are not scuffed and unpolished. Otherwise, keep them polished and maintained. Check all shoes to make sure the heels are not run down. Ankle boots are attractive and women love them on men.

• Shoes and belt colors should be a close match. Polish and renew belts just like you would shoes. Be sure there are no strings hanging out the sides of belts.

• Cary Grant advised not to wear suit sleeves too long. He insisted his shirt sleeves extend a quarter of an inch beyond his suit jackets—but oh, that sliver of white cuff was elegant.

• Look for buttons made from shell or high-quality material as opposed to plastic. Buttons can be easily changed to connect with your Homebase—the wrong metal color disconnects, thus adding clutter to your dress. Autumn men, take care to look for cream colored or wooden buttons; no white buttons.cuff This awareness can make all the difference.

• Remember to choose ties, sweaters, shirts, robes, and even swimwear in colors that match the your eye colors or in shades of hair and Homebase colors.

• Buy good quality shoes because even when they are old they will always be seen as good shoes.

• If custom or top designer's suits are not available, just be sure suits fit properly.

• Men of power and status wear dark suits. To avoid a staid look, add an individual touch of a flower, handkercheif or put a gem stud in the lapel of the suit jacket. A man does not have to "dress to kill" but he very much needs to dress to live. Dress up. Dress for your success and dress for your loved ones.

• French cuffs are distinctive and the mark of classic dress. Start with a simple but elegant black onyx or Mother-of-Pearl cuff links set in the Homebase metal.

• Limit tennis shoes for sports and recreaton; wear nice casual shoes for dates, and dress shoes for special events.

THE SCIENCE OF DRESS — WHAT WISE MEN KNOW

Over the years, men's styles do not change drastically like in women's clothing. The main changes in men clothing styles go from wide lines to narrow lines in suits, pants, jackets, shirts and ties. Based on the universal language of color and line, the body shapes and color information presented in this work are classic because they never change—these are the basic tools used by nature. Knowing how, why and what gives one an intuitive edge. And most of all, good taste can be learned...absolutely!

Tom Wolfe, an author well known for his elegant dress explains attention to this subject in his lofty essay *The Secret Vice*. He writes about custom tailoring and the mania for the marginal differences that go into it. "Once you know about it, you start seeing it all the time! There are two classes of men in the world; men who know and men who do not. And it is a secret vice that is rarely talked about. It is a taboo subject. They don't want it known that they even care about it.*"*

Cary Grant said he discovered that "developing a personal style is worth a grown man's time.*"*

Thomas Dunn English "The sense of being well dressed gives a feeling of inward tranquility which religion is powerless to bestow."

Giorgio Armani "In my designs, elegance is the most important quality as it gives the wearer confidence and the look of someone not trying too hard."

Kilgore Bandelli "Effortlessness is not effortless; anything but. If you are naturally interested in how you live in all areas of your life and care fundamentally, you're going to apply that to every part of your life; your wardrobe, what you say, where you live and the work you do."

Lou Junod, in his day, internationally known for his fine dress and high profile, was quoted in the *Gentelmen's Quarterly* as saying, "The better you look, the more money you make." He believed that:

- Clothes had to be worn with intention
- Fashion begins with an impeccably clean body
- A turtleneck is the most flattering thing a man can wear
- Jacket sleeves should not be too long
- Socks should go up over the calf
- Bikini underwear worn for a smooth line
- White should be worn next to the face whenever possible
- Show plenty of French cuff – at least an inch
- A handkechief should just show a graceful puff in the pocket
- That a man's clothes both determine and mark his place in the world.

QUESTIONNAIRE — COLOR AND BODY ANALYSIS FOR MEN AND BOYS

There are 21 question areas to help establish your Homebase color category and Inter-season influences, including your body shape. This analysis will lead to common sense information and directions for an efficient wardrobe—saving time and money. No more guessing.

FIRST YOUR COLORS...THEN YOUR LINES

QUESTION 1, 2, 3 — HAIR COLOR Will establish your Homebase Season.

QUESTION 4, 5, 6 — EYE COLOR Establishes your Inter-season colors.

QUESTION 7 — SKIN characteristics will fine-tune Homebase/Inter-season colors.

QUESTION 8 — HAIR characteristics will further establish your Inter-seasons

QUESTION 9 — EYEBROWS and LASHES finish the fine-tuning color process.

QUESTION 10 thru 21 — BODY SHAPE ANALYSIS will set the stage for your personal style.

HOMEBASE COLORS:	HOMEBASE BODY SHAPE:
Spring Points _____	**Oval Body Points** _____
Summer Points _____	**Circle Body Points** _____
Autumn Points _____	**Square Body Points** _____
Winter Points _____	**Rectangle Points** _____
Balanced-Soft Points _____	**Triangle Body Points** _____
Balanced-Intense Points _____	**Triangle Type 2** _____

QUESTION 1. HAIR COLOR CATEGORY

Everyone has one Homebase, either a SPRING, SUMMER, AUTUMN OR WINTER. If you had to choose one of the following Homebases, which one would come closest to the color of your natural hair color in your prime or teenage years— otherwise, not gray or artificially colored.   Add a point.

Important: Judge by roots of hair, not by sun-bleached ends

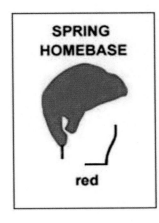
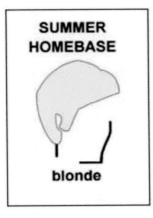
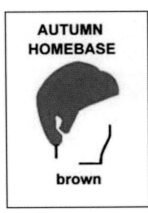

SPRING HOMEBASE — red

SUMMER HOMEBASE — blonde

AUTUMN HOMEBASE — brown

WINTER HOMEBASE — black

QUESTION 2. HAIR COLOR IN HARMONIC SEQUENCE

Into which section does your hair color fall? Count as another point.

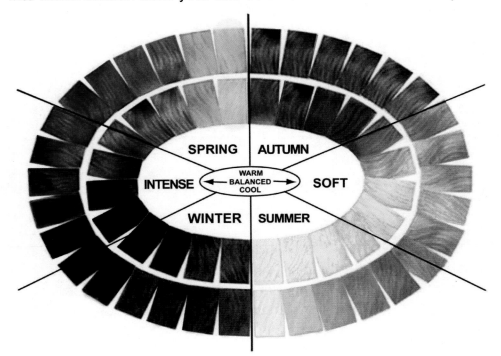

QUESTION 3. HAIR COLOR NAMES

There are 6 general categories of information; the white check-boxes represent traits in each section. Check the box (add a point) for <u>each item</u> that describes the color of your hair; if undecided mark both. Go by the hair color near the roots, not the sun-bleached ends.

1 BRIGHT SPRING	2 MUTED AUTUMN	3 LIGHT SUMMER	4 DARK WINTER	5 SOFT BALANCE	6 INTENSE BALANCE
☐ red hair ☐ strawberry blonde ☐ bright-gold blonde hair ☐ auburn hair ☐ reddish hair as a baby	☐ light brown hair ☐ warm-medium brown hair ☐ warm-dark brown hair ☐ golden-chestnut brown hair	☐ blonde hair ☐ taupe or "mousy" colored hair ☐ medium ash-brown hair ☐ towhead as a child *	☐ black hair ☐ soft-black or off-black hair ☐ very dark brown hair ☐ dark-ash brown hair	☐ honey-blonde hair ☐ sand-colored hair ☐ champagne colored hair	☐ very black-black hair ☐ dark auburn hair

*If a person was a "towhead" as a child (white-blonde) it always substantiates a Summer Homebase.

Trivia: Why are people with white-blond hair called "towheads?" In early times, flax fibers were combed through a bed of nails to separate the long thin fibers from the shorter coarser ones. This process was called towing, and the shorter fibers which were extricated were "tow." This led to the term "towheads" to describe people, particularly children, whose hair resembled the light flaxen strands.

QUESTION 4. EYE COLOR CATEGORY

Choose the colored eye section closest to your eye color. Add a point.

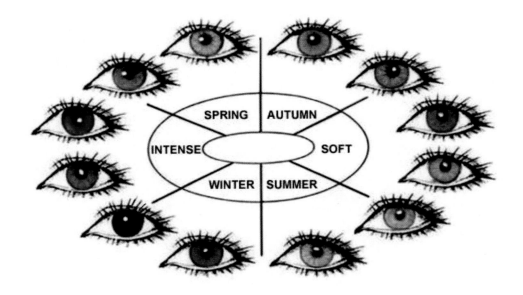

QUESTION 5. EYE COLOR IN HARMONIC SEQUENCE

In this eye-color display, choose the section in which your eye colors are most represented. Add another point.

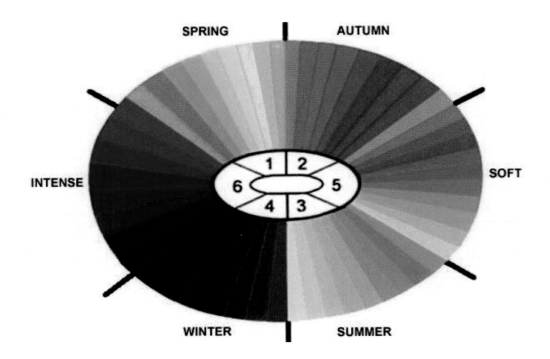

QUESTION 6. EYE COLOR NAMES

Fine-tune by adding one point for every trait that describes your eyes, regardless of season category.

1 BRIGHT SPRING	2 MUTED AUTUMN	3 LIGHT SUMMER	4 DARK WINTER	5 SOFT BALANCED	6 INTENSE BALANCED
☐ green eyes ☐ golden-colored eyes ☐ amber-colored eyes ☐ translucent "pool-like" window into the eye	☐ light brown eyes ☐ medium brown eyes ☐ golden-brown eyes ☐ muted-rust eyes ☐ dusty olive or khaki colored eyes ☐ hazel or autumn colors in eyes (no blue)	☐ blue eyes ☐ gray eyes ☐ very light colored eyes	☐ black eyes ☐ brown eyes ☐ dark brown eyes ☐ dark "appearing" eyes	☐ dusty teal-blue eyes ☐ bluish-green eyes ☐ greenish-blue eyes ☐ soft gray-green eyes ☐ matte-like appearing eye (more like an opaque "door" than a window)	☐ jet-black eyes ☐ dark amber-cast to eye color ☐ violet-cast to eye color

QUESTION 7. SKIN CHARACTERISTICS

Add a point for every trait that describes your skin characteristics regardless of season category.

1 BRIGHT SPRING	2 MUTED AUTUMN	3 LIGHT SUMMER	4 DARK WINTER	5 SOFT BALANCE	6 INTENSE BALANCE
☐ thin skin ☐ "peaches and cream" glowing skin ☐ blushes or flushes easily (shows red on neck and upper chest area when rubbed) ☐ freckles ☐ sunburns easily	☐ pale skin ☐ lacks red in skin	☐ light skin ☐ porcelain-like skin ☐ olive skin (lacks red)	☐ fair skin ☐ fair skin with sallow cast ☐ fair skin with olive cast ☐ black skin ☐ thick skin ☐ tans easily	☐ extremely freckled skin on face and arms ☐ skin, hair and eyes near the same color (less contrast) ☐ brown skin	☐ very black-black skin ☐ "Irish" rosy cheeks with light-skin ☐ Ethnic very warm skin ☐ "orangey" warm skin

NOTE: Certain characteristics are distinctive to each category. These traits and characteristics provide short-cut information without having to peer into layers of skin trying to determine the Homebase. The type of skin: thin, thick, oil content, blood circulation near the surface and even freckles are consistent and every little aspect indicates something.

QUESTION 8. HAIR CHARACTERISTICS

Add a point for each characteristic of your hair.

1 BRIGHT SPRING	2 MUTED AUTUMN	3 LIGHT SUMMER	4 DARK WINTER	5 SOFT BALANCE	6 INTENSE BALANCE
☐ coarse-textured hair ☐ extremely defined widow's peak	☐ straight hair ☐ thick hair ☐ off-centered widow's peak	☐ fine hair ☐ curly hair ☐ wavy hair	☐ centered widow's peak ☐ slight widow's peak ☐ medium texture hair	☐ extremely fine-curly hair	☐ very coarse kinky-curly hair

QUESTION 9. EYEBROWS & LASHES

Add a point for each characteristic that applies to you.

1 BRIGHT SPRING	2 MUTED AUTUMN	3 LIGHT SUMMER	4 DARK WINTER	5 SOFT BALANCE	6 INTENSE BALANCE
☐ thick eyebrows ☐ bushy eyebrows	☐ medium eyebrows ☐ straight eyelashes	☐ light-color eyebrows ☐ blonde eyelashes ☐ curly eyelashes	☐ dark eyebrows ☐ dark appearing eyebrows and lashes	☐ sparse eyebrows (reduces contrast)	☐ extremely black eyebrows ☐ "wild" hairs in eyebrows

Instructions for continuing BODY SHAPE Questionnaire

Your body type is the same if you weigh 100 pounds or 250 pounds—your actual body frame is what dictates your body shape. If necessary, think of your body shape as it was when you were thinner. Men have the same general characteristics as women's body shapes. The shoulder lines, either straight or sloping are the same, the top hipbone has the same comparison, and men first put on weight in the same areas as their women counterparts. The Square has straight lines and the Rectangle has longer straight lines. The Triangle has in-and-out angles; the Inverted Triangle has broad shoulders and angles down to trim thighs.

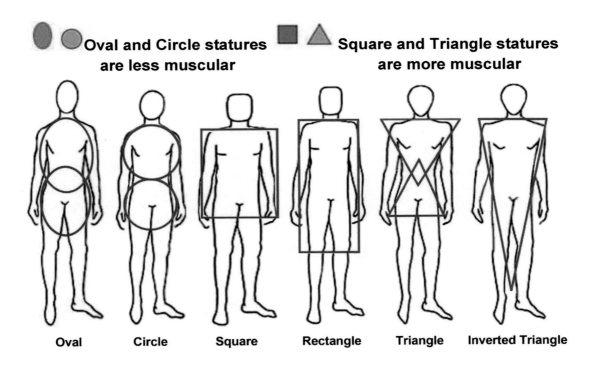

Oval and Circle statures are less muscular

Square and Triangle statures are more muscular

| Oval | Circle | Square | Rectangle | Triangle | Inverted Triangle |

MEASURING SUGGESTIONS

Shoulders: In front of a mirror, raise shoulders until they look straight across. Now relax them. An Oval is going to drop more than a Circle. As people grow older their shoulders may not be as straight across as when younger.

Rib Cage: You can see the shape of the ribcage better from the back.

Hipbone: Hips are the biggest clue and set the stage for a clothes that ride easy on the body. Triangle and Square bodies have high-set hipbones that sit right at the waist; the Oval and Circle bodies always have lower-set hipbones.

QUESTION 10. HEAD

On the following 12-part Questionnaire, symbols are used to indicate categories:

 Oval/Winter    Circle/Summer    Square/Autumn    Triangle/Spring

Oval head — is shaped more like an egg; oval on top. Neck — the oval neck is medium in length.	Round head — is shaped more like a ball. Neck — the circle neck is shorter than the oval neck.	Square head — is shaped more like a box; flatter planes; shorter neck. Rectangle head and neck is less wide and longer.	Triangle head — can be wide at top and narrow at jaw or vice-versa. Neck — the triangle neck is longer, or appears longer if jaw line is angled down to V.

QUESTION 11. SHOULDERS

  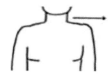 

Shoulders — sloped with smooth angle at base of neck and at shoulder points.	Shoulders — extra muscle at base of neck and rounder shoulder points.	Shoulders — more square and straight across, square angle at neck and shoulder points.	Shoulders — straighter across and broad in proportion to small waist; Type 2 appears very broad.

QUESTION 12. CHEST & RIB CAGE

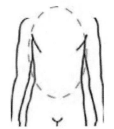 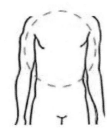 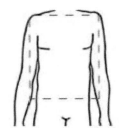 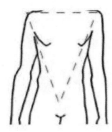

⬤ Ribcage — Oval chest fuller, breast muscles tend to have ovular shape. Collarbone area is moderately smooth. Ribcage more ovular than boxy.	⬤ Rib Cage — Circle chest fuller and breast muscles more circular. Collarbone area is smoother because more flesh hides boniness. Ribcage is rounder and somewhat thicker.	⬛ Rib Cage — Square chest area more flat, breast muscles not as prominent. Ribcage thicker; more straight up and down. ⬛ Rectangle is longer and less thick. Collarbone more prominent than shorter square type.	▲ Rib Cage — Triangle chest area straighter across, breast muscles more triangular. Ribcage V-shaped. Collarbone more prominent. ▼ Type 2 angles down into inverted triangle so waist is not small.

QUESTION 13. WAIST

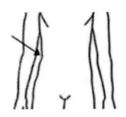 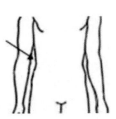 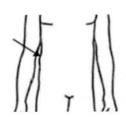 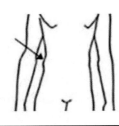

⬤ Waist — medium, smooth flowing oval curve.	⬤ Waist — smaller but tends to disappear with weight gain.	⬛ Waist — has less indention, "short waisted." ⬛ Rectangle is longer waisted.	▲ Waist — small in proportion to hip and shoulder ▼ Inverted triangle lines.

299

QUESTION 14. HIPBONES

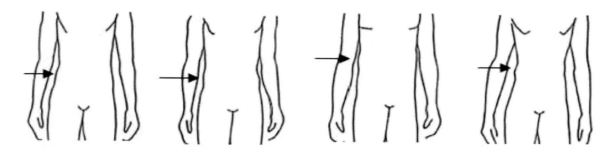

● Hipbone — top of hip is 2" lower than actual waistline.	● Hipbone — top of hip is 1½-2" lower than actual waistline.	■ Hipbone — set high right at waistline.	▲ Hipbone — set high right at the waistline.

QUESTION 15. THIGHS

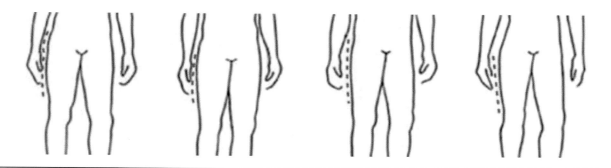

● Thighs — have oval curve, have definite dip at side halfway between hipbone and thigh.	● Thighs — slight dip with rounded curve.	■ Thighs — flat back and sides; no curves or dips.	▲ Type 1 — angles out to fuller thigh area. ▽ Type 2 — "The Lion" broad fuller chest and back which angle down to narrow tapered hips.

300

QUESTION 16. BACK

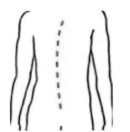 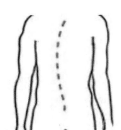  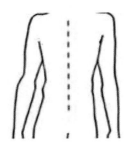

⬤ Back — back slightly cylindrical from the side view.	⬤ Back — fuller, bit more rounded, not as straight.	◼ Back — back is flat and straight.	▲ Back — back is straight.

QUESTION 17. DERRIERE

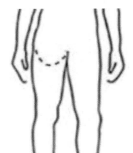 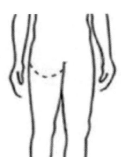 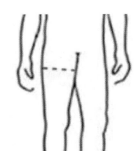 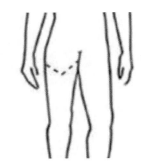

⬤ Derriere — Overall oval shape.	⬤ Derriere — fuller, bit more full and rounded shape.	◼ Derriere — flatter, more straight down.	▲ Derriere — Angles in from sides forming fuller derriere at center back. ▼ Type 2 has a flatter derriere as part of the inverted triangle shape from hip downward.

QUESTION 18. ARMS

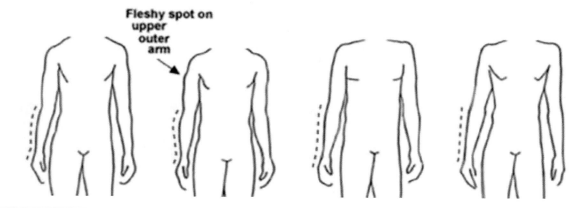

Fleshy spot on upper outer arm

⬭ **Arms —** arms have gradual smooth oval line.	◯ **Arms — arms** are curved, a bit fuller and round, not as straight; distinctive round fleshy spot on upper outer arm.	▪ **Arms — arm** lines are less curved and are more straight and trim.	▲ **Arms — arms** have straight taper to elbow and wrist.

QUESTION 19. LEGS

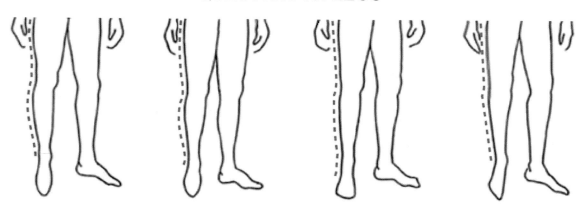

⬭ **Legs —** gradually shaped oval line to ankle.	◯ **Legs — some** curve to legs; round line can add fullness to calves.	▪ **Legs — slim** hips make nice leg line; Square body type legs are more stocky.	▲ **Legs —** straighter angled leg line; not curvy.

QUESTION 20. ANKLES

 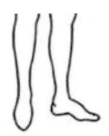 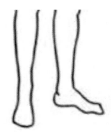 

● **Ankles —** medium but because of oval curve, appear slim.	● **Ankles —** leg curves down accentuating slim ankle.	■ **Ankles —** stocky type medium in size. ▮ **Rectangle has** slimmer ankles.	▲ **Ankles —** full lower leg and ankle; no curve. ▼ **Both types, no** curve.

QUESTION 21. HANDS & FEET

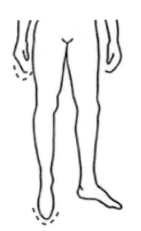  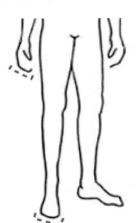 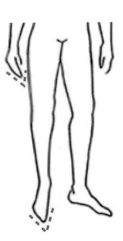

● **Hands & Feet** — fingers and toes longer and more oval shaped; longer vamp on foot, oval shape fingernails.	● **Hands & Feet** — ends of fingers and toes are rounder, rounder palms and ball of foot; shorter vamp, fingernails are more rounded.	■ **Hands & Feet** — palms and balls of feet more square-shaped. ▮ **Rectangle tall** type more long and rectangular.	▲ **Hands & Feet** — ends of fingers and toes more tapered; palm of hand not as flat; unique feature is a high instep of foot.

THE END

303

A DESCRIPTION OF HOW MANY WOMEN FEEL ABOUT SHOPPING

This little dialogue from Joan Fabrique, businesswoman *extraordinaire*, is just one well-said example of what colorists have been hearing from clients for thirty years—especially from the women who have Oval and Circle bodies. Joan was a Circle.

"I would go out looking for anything to look good in. I'd pay any price to find something that would make me look and feel good, because I knew that it affected my whole day. I am a busy woman, yet constantly needing to check out stores, hoping to find something. It was frustrating because it took time going from store to store. I felt so lucky if I found something—it was like finding a needle in a haystack. Then for a while I would have something new to wear, but then found myself wearing the same thing day after day, which women do not like to do. I wanted to increase my wardrobe so that I could feel that special way more, but I had shopped the stores out, at least for a while. I tried to find things that would change the look of a suit and bought things to make it look different, but often made bad purchases. As I compromised, I would start feeling less attractive and even "heavy".

"Then I would cycle into trying not to think about clothes. But, after a while I got sick of what I was wearing and, dreading it, would start the shopping cycle again. It used to exhaust me. I even tried an in-store personal shopper. I felt things were made for young slim people—I was out of the loop. What really made me resentful was that I had more money than they did, yet I felt designers were designing for the youth and didn't care. Why wouldn't all women want to look wonderful?

"I was determined to find someone who would design for the mature figure and even considered having my clothes custom made by a dressmaker. I was willing to buy the best fabric at Britex, but guessing what would work was such a gamble. How do I find a dressmaker that is a designer? I don't have time to sew because I am a business woman. If I go to a meeting and I don't feel good about the way I look, it holds a part of my attention. *When I look good I am totally present with what I am doing.*

"Getting up in the morning and searching through my closet for something to wear is not the way I want to start the day. My son-in-law has suits with dress shirts and ties that match.....hanging in his closet. He is a successful businessman and doesn't want to bother with clothes anymore that I do. In fact, my daughter actually goes shopping with him and picks his suits and colors. She has the knowledge, he doesn't. Where do woman get this service? During a business meeting, woman often are thinking, "Where did she get that suit?" instead of what is going on in the meeting. That's how desperate we women are.

"With women, it's not about doubling their income. They want to know more about themselves and express themselves fully. When you look and feel great you feel a part of everything. When you don't, you feel on the outside. And I am not an outsider. The adage, *a new hat makes a woman feel better,* is true. This is what it is for women. Men make money and women spend it—and often make purchases they are dissatisfied with. I made my own money so that I wouldn't feel guilty. What a waste of energy. I could have built a bridge with the energy I expended looking for something to look and feel good in. I did get my colors done, and I know some colors are better than others. But overall, I still pulled and tugged at my clothing, always a bit dissatisfied with my body and how I looked in most clothing. The store personal-shopper didn't know quite what to do—she just needed to sell and it was even hard for her to come up with something. This was a never ending dilemma.

"Then I met Irenee. I was open to finding a solution for this never ending problem. I assumed there was something wrong with my body. In talking with her I found out that there was nothing wrong with me, I just had a circle body type and didn't understand it. I didn't have to be younger or slimmer—I just had to wear lines that naturally fit my body shape. She taught me two concepts which made all the difference: 1. First, as far as color, it is vital that I repeat the color(s) of my hair or eyes somewhere in the color scheme of my outfit or accessories. This repeated color-tie-in automatically customizes the outfit for me, beautifully. 2. Then, I learned how to adjust my clothing lines so that garments are flattering to my figure. I was amazed to find that I could look good if the clothes simply fit me properly. It is in the fitting.

"Simply repeating my body's natural lines and colors was the key. I realized there was a *formula* for my clothing. In observing Irenee, one would think she could wear anything and look good. Then she began to demonstrate different lines of clothing on her own body, and before my eyes, certain lines actually made her look dumpy and awkward—I was dumbfounded.

"If lines made that much difference, I was determined to find clothes that fit me. Irenee marked and pinned a suit I was considering. So what I did was go back to Bloomingdales and insist they alter my suit properly before I kept it. The saleswoman argued with me saying, 'We can't do that.' I said, 'Look, you do this for men all the time, I want to see the store manager.' Bloomingdale's store manager came down, looked and asked what I wanted done. I said, 'This suit doesn't fit my shoulders.' I told him this is a service offered to men at minimal charge, why not women? He eventually agreed to have my suit altered to fit perfectly."

— Joan Fabrique

SURROUND YOURSELF IN YOUR OWN BASIC COLORS

On the following illustrated chart, each section area represents color suggestions that can be used to repeat your coloring in suits, pants, jackets, sweaters, shoes, ties, and leather goods.

Find the Homebase colors that match your coloring and then you will have the basics covered leaving room to add other creative touches. It is just common sense, now that you know your natural coloring is designed with purpose and balance, to follow through and take advantage of the simplicity of this great money and time saving maneuver.

This gives a solid basic foundation of neutral colors upon which to build a smart, connected, economically practical and striking wardrobe.

NEUTRAL COLORS FOR PLANNING BASIC WARDROBE

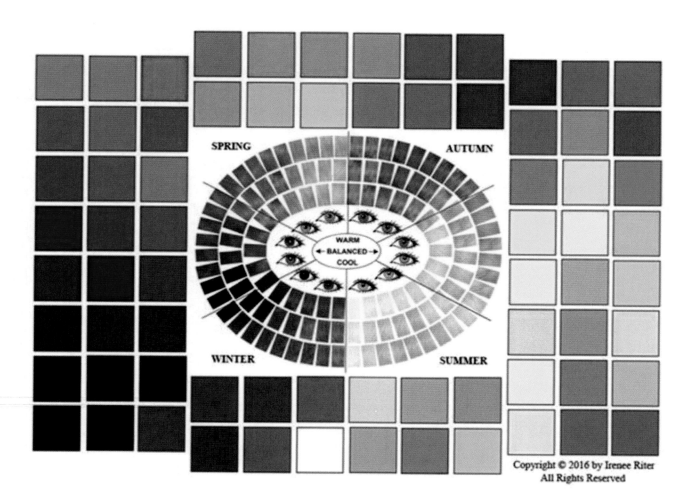

The True Purpose of this Book is Beauty

Love is the heart of Truth and Beauty and we all want it. The importance of Beauty is that it is at the heart of all creation, and the fact that our spirits can respond to the truth in beauty is what elevates us. To begin with:

1. **Beauty seems to incite duplication and makes you want to copy it**—draw it, photograph it, describe it, write poems and music about it.

2. **Beauty makes us want to locate what is true and to be near it**—to the scientist, truth is pure beauty; if we will submit our minds to the search for truth, beauty will ultimately emerge from the core of all education.

3. **Beauty always takes in the particular**—if you don't pay attention to details, the chances of seeing beauty will diminish; man's urge for beauty, possessions or mimicking the rich is only a limited effort to be beautiful.

4. **Beauty forever affirms life energy**—if you are careless in your approach and are cut off from it you will feel a retraction of life energy; anything around you that you judge as not beautiful saps your energy.

5. **Beauty causes us to gape and suspend all thought**—stunned by beauty we stare at it and a whole new perimeter for what we thought was beautiful has graduated to a new level; it lifts out of a neutral background and stands out singularly to say "hello" as if seen for the very first time.

This book has been designed to assist in the search for beauty in all its aspects beginning with one's own body and expression of dress. It is the culmination of many years research and experience to present a new language and tools that can be used consciously to adjust lines and colors for creative expression when applied to one's sense of design and artistry.

SACRED GEOMETRY

The belief that the universe was created according to a geometric plan and has its roots in the study of nature. These and other connections are sometimes interpreted in terms of sacred geometry and considered to be further proof of the natural significance of geometric form. Plato said, "God geometrizes continually." Otherwise—mathematics.

COMMENT ON DRESS FORMULAS

Women now have a formula for ease in dress. These principles usher in a new paradigm of color and body analysis that provide the short-cut to individual style which every woman seeks.

Just as men have a *masculine* clothing formula (suits, shirts, ties and belts which are easily replaced), women can have a *feminine* clothing formula. They need basic classic clothing that can easily be altered to flatter their bodies. We can encourage marketers to provide Homebase neutral basic colors in classic suits, slacks, skirts, leotards, camisoles, opaque hose, accessories, shoes and boots. This means basic styles that are classics—that fit the same four body types every time with planned allowances for adjustments or alteration (sleeve lengths, skirt and slacks all need to be customized.) Shoulders and waistbands can be altered to fit just the same as is provided for men.

Women need easy, comfortable, refined, attractive, practical basic clothing upon which to build. From there they can add their individual element of beauty in lovely blouses, sweaters, jewelry, accessories and accouterments which is paramount for feeling good. Purposeful beauty that never goes out of style, merely changing to express individual taste and fashionable creative enhancements. However, the dream is to offer simple *Armani* style and Audrey Hepburn class for everyone.

MOST IMPORTANT – CONCEPTS APPLIED TO SHOPPING

These concepts save time and money. I know that sounds cliché, time and money. But it truly does in this case. If properly analyzed, right hairstyles and hair-coloring problems have been solved once and for all. So, in shopping, first, simply knowing the range of one's best colors makes going through racks of clothing very efficient (in the manner of a fast drive through.) You walk in and start looking for color.

Next, you start looking for styles that could possibly work, quickly eliminating lines you already know without even trying on simply won't work. You already know your outside lines, and for sure the waistlines that do or don't fit your body shape.

Then, if something you like doesn't fit all the criteria—you now know *why* and hopefully can begin to improvise looking for color repeats somewhere in texture, buttons or possible accessories that could make a connection. Maybe alterations. Makeup is also a factor and can be adjusted to bring about balance. And the most important advantage of all, is that you may already have things in your wardrobe that make it easier to coordinate, and you surprisingly find things complementing other items you didn't even see before. You avoid wasting time, avoid mistakes and save money. And that is huge.

ALL BOOKS AVAILABLE IN eBOOK FORMAT AT ADDRESS BELOW

The Universal Language of Face Analysis – How One's Face Structure Impacts the Art of Personal Dress

New Aspect of color and line archetypes based on how the body is structured and automatically reacts to stimuli. These inherent traits are so valid that reference to them is used in our everyday language; such as "a nose for news" "high-brow," "thin-skinned," "level-headed" and an "ear for music" are actual traits that can be easily observed on people. Background of structure-analysis is reviewed and covers the history all the way from Hippocrates to longitudinal progressive studies that are used in research today. 90 traits are Illustrated with full descriptions and the positioning of each trait shown on the body. Free Face Analysis classes at www.scienceofdress.com

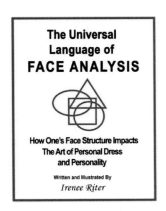

Impeccably Sharp—What Wise Men Know…Young Men Can Learn

This is Irenee's favorite book. Gives minute details on how to become a master of attraction, charm and standout elegance. A synopsis of the wisdom of true gentlemen who discovered that developing a personal style is worth a grown man's time. Covers the protocol of social exchange, manners, table etiquette, charming conversation, a formula of dress for each body type and coloring, what women remember, and based on an extensive survey — studied details of what women really prefer. Also important for young girls to help set the tone of expectation for a man of strength and character grounded in love.

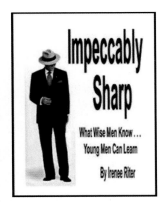

The Science of Personal Dress for Men and Boys

This 104 page book is a synopsis of the classic work, *The Science of Personal Dress Complete Study*, adapted specifically for the selection of attractive clothing for men and boys. Sound universal principles of color and line applied to the shape and coloring unique to each man will save hours of guessing and costly mistakes. Fully illustrated and presented in practical, common sense formula, these concepts reveal the scientific mathematical basis of fine dress. Once realized, men take a closer look and discover that the 4 aspects of attractive dress are easy to understood and apply. They become their own expert.

<u>NEW</u>   The Science Beneath The Dress — The Designers Handbook Based on Body Structure, Coloring and Face Features What designers need to know. Especially valuable for clothing manufactures, architects, wardrobe sales consultants, beauticians, tailors, film, interior design, writers, artists, jewelers and creative design of every venue who personally value beauty in all its aspects. This 144 page book is the condensed version of "The Science of Personal Dress Complete Study." It has been written and turned around in reverse engineer fashion to provide the quickest way to learn the universal language of fine dress. In a step-by-step tutorial, it includes 547 basic clothing illustrations aligned with each body shape and details connecting relevant data from the body up through every aspect of dress and style. Everyone who embraces this teaching "gets it," bringing to conscious awareness what elite designers have intuitively known. This is now made available for all levels of interest to assist informed creative self-artistry. Best book to have in hand in print form.

The Science of Personal Dress For Women and Girls This 166 page book is a fully illustrated synopsis of the classic work, *The Science of Personal Dress Complete Study*, and has been adapted specifically for the selection of beautiful clothing for women and girls. The study is based on universal laws of order and harmony which extend to a woman's body shape, features, coloring and clothing. All salient information for the female body is covered in a medium larger font for easy reading. Because of this simple colorful presentation with the included detailed Questionnaire, lovely dress becomes an exacting science by simple formula and assures good taste can absolutely be learned at any age!

The Vivid Beauty Manners, Charm and Etiquette Handbook for Women and Girls — By Irenee Riter who is a Certified Graduate of The American School of Protocol in Atlanta, Georgia "Etiquette" is a French word meaning "a ticket" and will gain entrance into a special world. This timely and relevant book is presented to give young women and girls something true and powerful to be in alignment with to inspire qualities of kindness and charm. Charm cannot exist without good manners. Confidence in social skills, knowing what to expect and what is expected removes anxiety and gives one the freedom to focus on the matter at hand. It means educating oneself in society's cultural customs and acquiring that exterior polish which comes from understanding the rules of exchange for the common good. This book is 8.5 X 11".

Timeless Manners, Charm and Etiquette – **For Ages 3 To 100**. The best book of its kind for everyone, especially in print for parents and grandparents as a guide to play with and enthrall young people with facts and points of interesting etiquette and manners—which charm the heart and ennoble the Soul. A complete checklist brings to conscious awareness attributes of character, poise and beauty to benefit a rich full life of relationships and social exchange. Based on teachings of The American School of Protocol, along with a comprehensive study of traditional rules of convention which address the mind, body and spirit. Makes a strong case for the advantage of at least knowing the difference, and how culture and polish adds to enrich all our relationships.

Color Analysis Pure and Simple ~ Holistic Color & Body Analysis This special 133 page condensed version is the same as *The Science Beneath The Dress* minus the summary technical lists of tools. This is to make available a concise holistic teaching of the art of dress to support those "just wanting to know more about myself" and becoming intrigued with the knowledge that there are universal principles that are consistent, orderly and thrilling to recognize. This work summarizes with illustrated easy to see connections which colors and lines make with everyday objects and associations illustrated by students of the Academy of Art in San Francisco. It is a solid first step, guaranteed to expand awareness and provide an understanding of one's best colors and clothing lines. Perfect for astute creative teenagers.

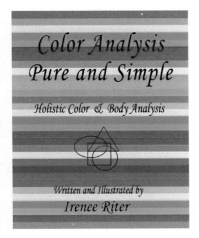

The Personal Color Tester This new 8½x11"color tester analysis method proves what your Homebase is and your specific individual range of colors. The colors are exaggerated so that you can test yourself, your family and friends, and even the reluctant become interested and want to see the color changes. The 80 durable ink-dyed easy flip-down color tester pages give the chance to compare differences through quick comparisons. Then the 20 split-page testers show how to combine colors for balancing outside colors and skintone variances. Invaluable to determine hair-coloring and makeup. Includes complete detailed instructions.

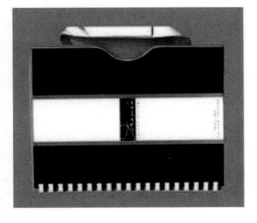

All books also available in print at Amazon.com under author ~ Irenee Riter. To order Personal Color Tester call Irenee at 925-462-6255. For questions and all eBooks see www.thescienceofpersonaldress.com or www.scienceofdress.com

Made in the USA
Middletown, DE
31 July 2020